The Thistle and the Rose

LINDA PORTER was born in Exeter, grew up in Kent, and has a doctorate in History from the University of York. A regular contributor to history magazines and broadcasts, and the author of several books including biographies of Mary Tudor and Katherine Parr, she won the 2004 Biographers' Club *Daily Mail* Prize. She lives in Kent.

ALSO BY LINDA PORTER

Mary Tudor: The First Queen
Katherine the Queen: The Remarkable Life
of Katherine Parr
Crown of Thistles: The Fatal Inheritance
of Mary Queen of Scots
Royal Renegades: The Children of Charles I
and the English Civil Wars
Mistresses: Sex and Scandal at the Court
of Charles II

LINDA PORTER

The Thistle and the Rose

The Extraordinary Life of Margaret Tudor

HEAD ZEUS

An Apollo Book

First published in the UK in 2024 by Head of Zeus,
part of Bloomsbury Publishing Plc.

9 7 5 3 1 2 4 6 8

A catalogue record for this book is available from the British Library.

ISBN (HB): 9781801105781
ISBN (E): 9781801105767

Typeset by Siliconchips Services Ltd UK

Printed and bound in Great Britain by
CPI Group (UK) Ltd, Croydon CRO 4YY

Head of Zeus Ltd
First Floor East
5–8 Hardwick Street
London ECIR 4RG

WWW.HEADOFZEUS.COM

For my nephew, Matthew Ford, and his wife,
Dr Hannah Warrington Ford

'The fair lady Margaret, our illustrious
King's firstborn daughter'.
Bernard André, *The Life of Henry VII*

Contents

Abbreviations, monetary conversions and a note on spelling xi

Family Trees xii

Prologue 1

PART I ❋ The First Tudor Princess, 1489–1503

  1. A Pleasant Childhood 7

  2. Arthur and Katherine 23

  3. Betrothal 31

  4. Loss 48

  5. A Royal Progress 60

PART II ❋ The Queen of Scots, 1503–13

  6. The King Comes Calling 77

  7. 'Welcome of Scotland to Be Queen' 92

  8. The Court of Queen Margaret 106

  9. Wife and Mother 120

  10. A Festering Rivalry 133

  11. Flodden 148

PART III ❋ The Struggle for Power, 1513–24

  12. Aftermath 169

  13. The Second Husband 180

  14. The Queen at Bay 190

15. Confrontation at Stirling   199
16. Flight   209
17. A Year in London   223
18. A Change of Heart   241

PART IV ✢ A Divided Family, 1521–28

19. A New Direction   257
20. Margaret and Her Family   275

PART V ✢ Twilight, 1528–41

21. The Queen Mother   297
22. Methven Castle   324

Epilogue   334
Notes   340
Bibliography   358
Image Credits   363
Author Note   364
Index   367

Abbreviations, monetary conversions and a note on spelling

BL: British Library
NLS: National Library of Scotland
NRS: National Records of Scotland
TNA: The National Archives, Kew

I have used the TNA currency convertor to give modern equivalents of monetary values.

Spelling has been modernised but quotations have not been rendered into modern English because I have always believed that we should let people in the past speak for themselves.

The Douglases of Angus

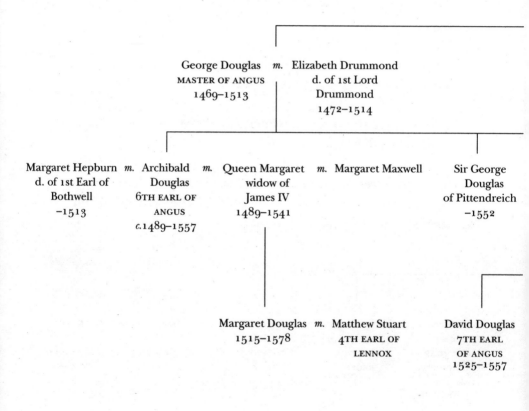

George Douglas *m.* Elizabeth Drummond
MASTER OF ANGUS   d. of 1st Lord
1469–1513   Drummond
1472–1514

Margaret Hepburn *m.* Archibald *m.* Queen Margaret *m.* Margaret Maxwell   Sir George
d. of 1st Earl of   Douglas   widow of   Douglas
Bothwell   6TH EARL OF   James IV   of Pittendreich
–1513   ANGUS   1489–1541   –1552
*c.*1489–1557

Margaret Douglas *m.* Matthew Stuart   David Douglas
1515–1578   4TH EARL OF   7TH EARL
LENNOX   OF ANGUS
1525–1557

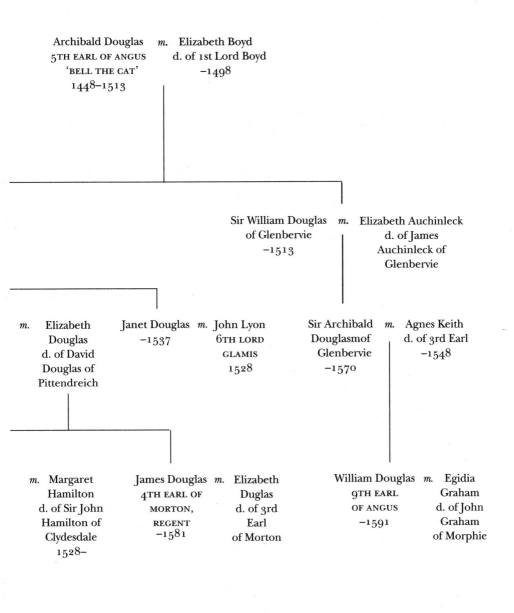

Archibald Douglas   *m.*   Elizabeth Boyd
5TH EARL OF ANGUS   d. of 1st Lord Boyd
'BELL THE CAT'   −1498
1448−1513

Sir William Douglas   *m.*   Elizabeth Auchinleck
of Glenbervie   d. of James
−1513   Auchinleck of
                                          Glenbervie

m.   Elizabeth   Janet Douglas   *m.*   John Lyon   Sir Archibald   *m.*   Agnes Keith
Douglas   −1537   6TH LORD   Douglasmof   d. of 3rd Earl
d. of David   GLAMIS   Glenbervie   −1548
Douglas of   1528   −1570
Pittendreich

m.   Margaret   James Douglas   *m.*   Elizabeth   William Douglas   *m.*   Egidia
Hamilton   4TH EARL OF   Duglas   9TH EARL   Graham
d. of Sir John   MORTON,   d. of 3rd   OF ANGUS   d. of John
Hamilton of   REGENT   Earl   −1591   Graham
Clydesdale   −1581   of Morton   of Morphie
1528−

The Stewarts

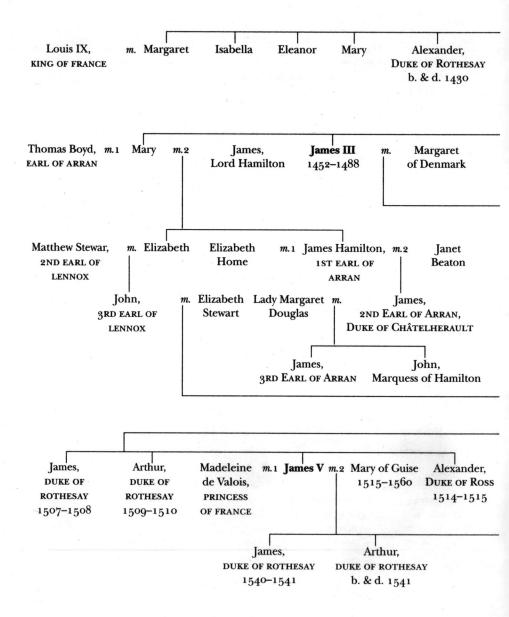

Louis IX, KING OF FRANCE *m.* Margaret   Isabella   Eleanor   Mary   Alexander, DUKE OF ROTHESAY b. & d. 1430

Thomas Boyd, EARL OF ARRAN *m.*1 Mary *m.*2 James, Lord Hamilton **James III** 1452–1488 *m.* Margaret of Denmark

Matthew Stewar, 2ND EARL OF LENNOX *m.* Elizabeth   Elizabeth Home *m.*1 James Hamilton, 1ST EARL OF ARRAN *m.*2 Janet Beaton

John, 3RD EARL OF LENNOX *m.* Elizabeth Stewart   Lady Margaret Douglas *m.* James, 2ND EARL OF ARRAN, DUKE OF CHÂTELHERAULT

James, 3RD EARL OF ARRAN   John, Marquess of Hamilton

James, DUKE OF ROTHESAY 1507–1508   Arthur, DUKE OF ROTHESAY 1509–1510   Madeleine de Valois, PRINCESS OF FRANCE *m.*1 **James V** *m.*2 Mary of Guise 1515–1560   Alexander, DUKE OF ROSS 1514–1515

James, DUKE OF ROTHESAY 1540–1541   Arthur, DUKE OF ROTHESAY b. & d. 1541

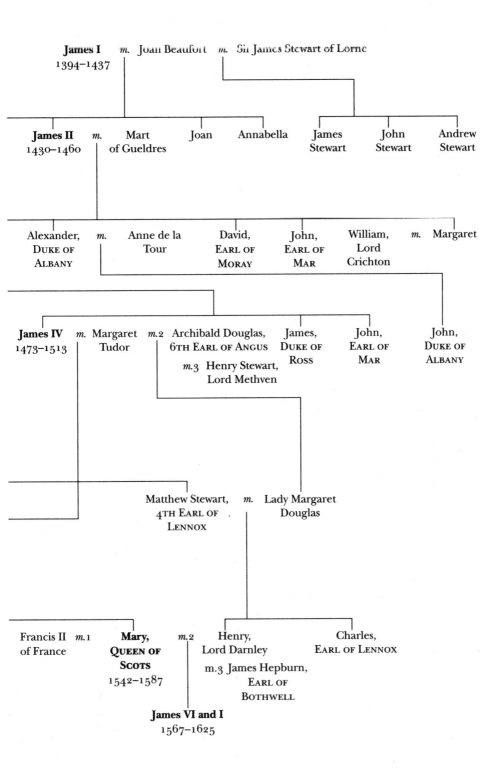

James I
1394–1437
m. Joan Beaufort   *m.* Sir James Stewart of Lorne

James II
1430–1460
m. Mart of Gueldres   Joan   Annabella   James Stewart   John Stewart   Andrew Stewart

Alexander, **DUKE OF ALBANY**   *m.* Anne de la Tour   David, **EARL OF MORAY**   John, **EARL OF MAR**   William, Lord Crichton   *m.* Margaret

James IV
1473–1513
m. Margaret Tudor   *m.2* Archibald Douglas, **6TH EARL OF ANGUS**
  m.3 Henry Stewart, Lord Methven   James, **DUKE OF ROSS**   John, **EARL OF MAR**   John, **DUKE OF ALBANY**

Matthew Stewart, **4TH EARL OF LENNOX** .   *m.* Lady Margaret Douglas

Francis II of France   *m.1*   **Mary, QUEEN OF SCOTS**
1542–1587   *m.2* Henry, Lord Darnley
  m.3 James Hepburn, **EARL OF BOTHWELL**   Charles, **EARL OF LENNOX**

James VI and I
1567–1625

The Tudors and Lancastrians

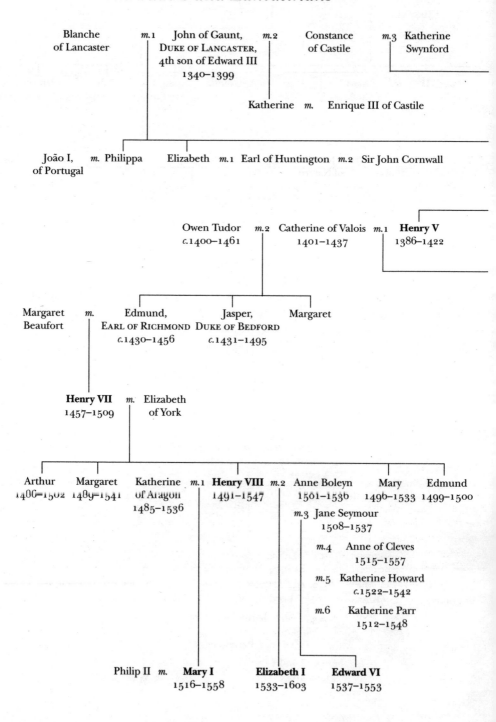

Blanche of Lancaster   *m.*1   John of Gaunt, DUKE OF LANCASTER, 4th son of Edward III 1340–1399   *m.*2   Constance of Castile   *m.*3   Katherine Swynford

Katherine   *m.*   Enrique III of Castile

João I, of Portugal   *m.* Philippa   Elizabeth   *m.*1   Earl of Huntington   *m.*2   Sir John Cornwall

Owen Tudor c.1400–1461   *m.*2   Catherine of Valois 1401–1437   *m.*1   **Henry V** 1386–1422

Margaret Beaufort   *m.*   Edmund, EARL OF RICHMOND c.1430–1456   Jasper, DUKE OF BEDFORD c.1431–1495   Margaret

Henry VII 1457–1509   *m.*   Elizabeth of York

Arthur 1486–1502   Margaret 1489–1541   Katherine of Aragon 1485–1536   *m.*1   **Henry VIII** 1491–1547   *m.*2   Anne Boleyn 1501–1536   Mary 1496–1533   Edmund 1499–1500

*m.*3   Jane Seymour 1508–1537

*m.*4   Anne of Cleves 1515–1557

*m.*5   Katherine Howard c.1522–1542

*m.*6   Katherine Parr 1512–1548

Philip II   *m.*   **Mary I** 1516–1558   **Elizabeth I** 1533–1603   **Edward VI** 1537–1553

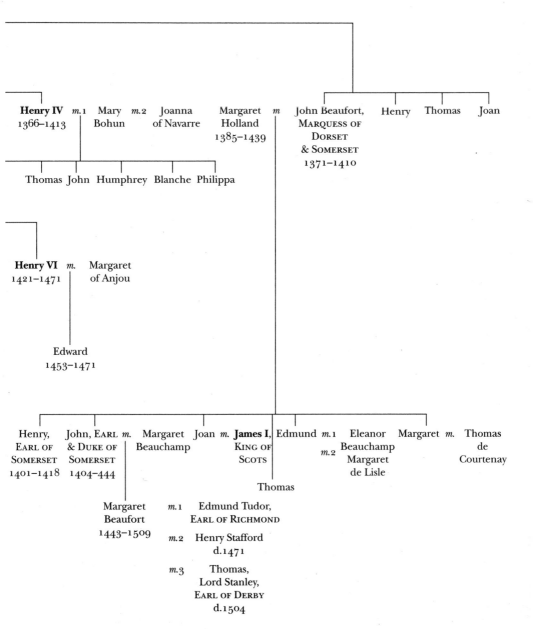

Henry IV *m.*1 Mary *m.*2 Joanna   Margaret *m* John Beaufort,   Henry   Thomas   Joan
1366–1413   Bohun   of Navarre   Holland   MARQUESS OF
1385–1439   DORSET
& SOMERSET
1371–1410

Thomas John Humphrey Blanche Philippa

Henry VI *m.* Margaret
1421–1471   of Anjou

Edward
1453–1471

Henry,   John, EARL *m.* Margaret   Joan *m.* **James I,** Edmund *m.*1 Eleanor   Margaret *m.* Thomas
EARL OF   & DUKE OF   Beauchamp   KING OF   *m.*2 Beauchamp   de
SOMERSET   SOMERSET   SCOTS   Margaret   Courtenay
1401–1418   1404–444   de Lisle

Thomas

Margaret   *m.*1   Edmund Tudor,
Beauchamp   EARL OF RICHMOND
1443–1509
*m.*2   Henry Stafford
d.1471

*m.*3   Thomas,
Lord Stanley,
EARL OF DERBY
d.1504

Prologue

Greenwich, 23 November 1487

Queen Elizabeth left Greenwich Palace and boarded a barge to take her downriver to the Tower of London on a day in late autumn, more than two years after her husband, Henry VII, the first monarch of the new Tudor dynasty, had won the throne at the Battle of Bosworth. Though the River Thames was the major artery for travel in London, used every day by all classes of people to get around the capital and its environs, this was no ordinary journey. The river was crowded with boats and the royal barge in which the queen and her mother-in-law, Margaret Beaufort, sat was especially decorated and gilded to mark the occasion. Elizabeth of York herself was 'richly apparelled', as well she might be, since this was the first of several elaborate celebrations that would culminate in her coronation two days later.

Accompanying the queen's craft as it floated down towards the Tower of London was a colourful flotilla bearing the dignitaries of London, the mayor, sheriffs and aldermen and 'divers and many worshipful commoners chosen out of every craft, in their liveries, in barges freshly furnished with banners and streamers of silk, richly beseen with the arms and badges of their crafts'. One of these barges contained 'a great red dragon spouting flames of fire into [the] Thames', a reminder of the king's Welsh heritage, though Elizabeth

1

also claimed a more distant descent from the Welsh hero Cadwallader. Many noble lords and ladies, in their best finery, were also on the water, anxious not to be left out of the magnificent display. Music was an essential part of Elizabeth's journey, as 'trumpets, clarions and other minstrelsy' serenaded her progress.[1]

The king was waiting to welcome her when she landed at Tower Wharf. The report of his reception of his wife emphasized their closeness and its effect on those watching. It 'was to all the estates, being present, a very goodly sight and right joyous and comfortable to behold.'[2] Henry VII had created fourteen new knights of the Bath in honour of Elizabeth's coronation and the queen joined him in the royal apartments at the Tower to acknowledge their elevation.

The next day, she made her official entry into London before her coronation. She left after dinner, a meal normally taken in the mid- to late morning in Tudor times, and was carried in a litter in which she was easily visible to crowds of Londoners eager to see the procession. It wended its way past St Paul's Cathedral to the Palace of Westminster, where the queen spent the night before the coronation ceremony itself. Contemporary descriptions dwell on the richness of the clothes and jewels that she wore, the kirtle of white cloth-of-gold damask, a mantle furred with ermine to keep out the autumn chill, 'fastened with a great lace curiously wrought of gold and silk and rich knots of gold at the end, tasselled'. Her fair hair (described as yellow) hung down her back, caught in a coif criss-crossed with gold bands, a fashionable style in France and Italy. On her head she wore a circlet of gold, 'richly garnished with precious stones'.[3] Her sister, Princess Cecily of York, carried her train.

Superb as all this was – and undoubtedly enjoyed by the populace of London, suitably impressed by the display of the king's majesty, the loyalty of his nobility and the strength of his union with the daughter of the House of York – the coronation itself was always intended to be the climax of these November festivities. It took place on Sunday, 25 November in Westminster Abbey. Dressed in purple velvet furred with ermine to highlight her regal status, she entered by the west door of the Abbey, her train again borne by Cecily. The ceremony was carried out by John Morton, the Archbishop of Canterbury, who anointed her on the forehead and breast and crowned her. In what was by then a rare moment of self-effacement, Henry VII stayed out of sight. His presence might have distracted from the sacredness of the moment and its significance for his wife. Instead, he was seated behind a lattice, accompanied by his mother and Lady Margaret Pole, Elizabeth's cousin, on a specially constructed platform between the altar and the pulpit.

Elizabeth of York was, at last, acknowledged as a crowned consort. Her husband had been in no hurry to accord her this honour, determined as he was to ensure that the survival and legitimacy of the new Tudor dynasty was centred on him. Theirs was, however, a partnership that worked well and appears to have been founded on genuine affection. If Elizabeth had sacrificed her claim to the throne, she had done so for a security that would still ensure her rare privileges and make her the first lady in the land. There had never been a queen regnant in England and her claim would always have been clouded by the uncertainty over the fate of her two brothers, Edward V and Richard, duke of York, the missing Princes in the Tower of London. While pretenders to Henry VII's throne continued to emerge, Elizabeth's own status would remain under threat. She was now a wife and queen with a vested interest in the new order. And she was also the mother of a son, Prince Arthur, born the year before, in September 1486. Two years after her coronation, she would bear another child. This time, it would be a girl.

Part I

The First Tudor Princess,
1489–1503

1

A Pleasant Childhood

'On the morn of St Andrew's day the newborn Princess
was christened. The rich font of Canterbury and
Westminster Church were prepared as of old times
accustomed for King's children.'

The antiquary John Leland, in his *Antiquarii de Rebus*
Britannicis Collectanea (1770)

Henry VII was presiding over the ancient ceremony of purification by bathing that saw his three-year-old son, Prince Arthur, dubbed a knight of the Bath when news was brought to him that his wife had gone into labour.[1] This would have seemed a happy coincidence, but it was also a source of anxiety. Death in childbirth was no respecter of persons and Elizabeth's regal status offered little protection against the very real possibility that either she or the child, or even both of them, might not survive. She had been very unwell for some time after Arthur's birth, which may partly explain the otherwise surprising gap between her first and second child. There is no record of the queen suffering stillbirths or miscarriages in this period, though this is not conclusive proof that she did not become pregnant between the births of Arthur and Margaret.

7

Still, for a king so uncertainly on the throne as Henry VII, facing the ever-present threat of revolt and pretenders hoping to overthrow him, having just one child, albeit a son, presented an additional insecurity. His mother-in-law, Elizabeth Woodville, had conceived regularly during her marriage to Edward IV but the early years of her daughter's marriage were not so productive. So Henry was delighted to learn of his wife's pregnancy and its uneventful progression. He showered her with gifts that would ease her confinement: bolts of black velvet, russet cloth, cannaber (a soft linen), white blankets and squirrel fur, as well as a fine carpet and featherbeds filled with down and expensive sheets.[2] Elizabeth could expect every creature comfort as the time for the birth approached.

The queen took to her chamber in Westminster Palace on All Hallows' Eve, 31 October 1489. The procession that accompanied this occasion was led by the earl of Oxford, who had played a vital part in the Battle of Bosworth, and by her stepfather-in-law, the earl of Derby. She heard mass in St Stephen's Chapel and then spent some time among the lords and ladies assembled in her outer chamber, who partook of sweet wines. Prayers were then said for a safe delivery and Elizabeth entered her richly furnished bedchamber. In the doorway she paused, 'recommended herself to the good praises of the lords' and disappeared behind the curtain into the inner chamber.

Strictly speaking, she was now in an entirely female environment, under the supervision of Margaret Beaufort and Elizabeth Woodville. The precise nature of the relations between these two great ladies is hard to determine but they seem to have tolerated each other and were certainly united in their concern for the queen's wellbeing. Nor were men entirely excluded. The new French ambassador was the sieur de Luxembourg, a cousin of Elizabeth Woodville, and his request to meet the queen was granted. He was given a private interview to which the queen's chamberlain and the Garter Principal King of Arms were also admitted. The dictates of diplomacy and good relations with France clearly overrode the niceties of protocol surrounding royal births. This meeting, soon after Elizabeth's withdrawal from public life, was the only intrusion into her isolation from the outside world and, as such, a welcome distraction from contemplation of the rigours that lay ahead.

She gave birth at nine o'clock on the evening of 29 November. Her midwife, Alice Massey, who would attend the queen in all her subsequent deliveries, was paid £5, the equivalent of £10,000 today. If Henry VII was disappointed that his second child was a daughter, he did not show it. Princesses, like male heirs, had a crucial part to play in royal life. They were dynastic fodder, the hopes of many an alliance with other noble houses, their marriageability an asset to be carefully fostered and used to maximum effect in diplomacy. Henry, a shrewd and intelligent monarch, was no doubt thinking of prospective suitors for his daughter's hand very soon after he was informed of her safe arrival. And because he was also an affectionate parent and genuinely fond of his wife, he was relieved that Elizabeth and the baby appeared to be thriving. She was named Margaret, after her paternal grandmother, and christened the day after her birth.

A detailed description survives of Margaret's christening in St Stephen's Chapel on St Andrew's Day. The marchioness of Berkeley, Anne Fiennes, took the baby girl from the queen's chamber and carried her to the porch of Westminster Abbey, which was decorated with 'a rich ceiling of brodery work'. The marchioness was supported by the earls of Arundel and Shrewsbury and received by the bishop of Ely, John Alcock, who christened the princess. The silver font of Canterbury Cathedral had been specially brought to London and Margaret's forehead was anointed with its holy water as her godparents stood by. These were her grandmother, Margaret Beaufort; the earl of Shrewsbury, John Talbot, representing one of England's oldest families; the duchess of Norfolk; and the Archbishop of Canterbury, John Morton. Each one gave the baby impressive gifts and their bounty – of cups, flagons and, in her grandmother's case, a silver-gilt chest full of gold – preceded the princess as she returned, in torch-light procession, to her parents. Though the exact timing of the ceremony is not recorded, the torches would suggest that it was in the late afternoon, as dusk was falling. Wrapped against the cold and decked with a crimson velvet train edged with ermine, Margaret was the centre of attention. It was a position she would grow to expect and which she would learn to fill with grace.

Many of the leading members of the English aristoc-racy were already gathered in London for a ceremony that marked Prince Arthur's investiture as Prince of Wales. The coincidental arrival of his daughter allowed the king to impress his most powerful subjects with a double spectacle. Henry VII was never one to miss an opportunity for display. He and Queen Elizabeth received their daughter when she returned to the Palace of Westminster and, as was custom-ary, gave her their blessing. Then Margaret was removed to the care of her nurse and the women known as rockers, who tended her oaken cradle.

Though Elizabeth was a frequent visitor to her children, they saw their father more rarely. Nor did they share accom-modation with the king and queen, whose duties meant that there were many calls on their time. Royal children through-out Europe were brought up in their own households, courts being considered unsuitable places for infants. Just how dangerous the court might have been for a newborn was underlined soon after Margaret's birth, when a measles epi-demic broke out at Westminster. Several ladies of the court died and Henry decided to remove to Greenwich for the Christmas season to escape the contagion. Elizabeth's purification ceremony, or churching, an important ritual after childbirth, did not take place till 27 December, and then the ceremony was private. It did, though, permit her to return to her public duties as Henry VII's wife.

After this glittering debut, Margaret passed quietly from public view into her own secluded and privileged world. For a year and a half, she was the sole focus of attention. Arthur already had an establishment of his own, at Farnham in Surrey, and this became more formalized around the time of his sister's birth. The elder children of Henry VII and Elizabeth of York saw each other only rarely during their childhood. Margaret grew up in palaces to the south of London, at the manor of Sheen on the banks of the River Thames and in Eltham, another, larger, medieval palace that had been extensively improved by her grandfather, Edward IV. Offering an abundance of fresh air and landscaped with walks, gardens and orchards, these were pleasant places for a child. They offered peace and the prospect of a healthy environment impossible in the bustle and ever-present threat of deadly epidemics in London. There were occasional visits in the late 1490s to Hatfield Palace and the Tower of London, but these were not common.

Margaret was not alone at Sheen for long. In June 1491 she was joined by a younger brother, named Henry after his father. The royal nursery grew regularly, if not speedily. Another daughter, Elizabeth, was born in 1492. Said to have been a beautiful child, she died at the age of three. The precariousness of life, especially for young children, was brought home early to Margaret. Two more siblings would follow before the dawn of the new century: Mary, born in 1496, and Edmund, born in 1499. Despite Princess Elizabeth's death, the royal nursery seems to have been a happy place. The children clearly adored their mother, who supervised their upbringing with love and care, and it is clear from Margaret's later references to her father that, although they saw him less frequently, Henry VII was not just respected but also viewed with deep affection.

Their daily lives would have begun with prayers and probably some lessons before breakfast. The Tudors ate the main meal of the day in the late morning and the children would have resumed studying with their tutors in the afternoon, followed by further religious observance, depending on the ecclesiastical calendar, a light supper and then bedtime. Exercise was believed beneficial both for health and mental welfare and was an integral part of the day unless the weather was severe. The stables also provided a recreation that helped develop grace and dignity. Being able to sit a horse impressively and hunt was a vital part of the image of royalty. Those who lacked it could not expect to command respect.[3] The royal children would have been put on a pony almost as soon as they could walk. But the life of the mind was equally important.

There is little specific information on Margaret's education; we only know for certain the name of one of her tutors, Giles Duwes, who taught her French. At a time when English was an unfamiliar tongue in Europe, linguistic proficiency was vital, taken for granted as part of the education of the sons – and daughters – of kings. There is plenty of information about Prince Arthur's education, which would have been viewed as being at once more specialized and more comprehensive than that of his siblings, as he was being prepared for kingship. Yet Henry VII well knew that his younger children needed sufficient training for the significant roles that awaited them once their nursery days were over. From what we know of those who instructed Arthur and Henry, the king entrusted the education of his children to a group of men who have been described as 'unprecedentedly professional and scholarly'. Men such as John Rede, John Holt and William Hone, as well as literary figures like Bernard André and John Skelton, exemplified the new ideas in scholarship and education that were grounded in the developing influence of humanism, known as the New Learning, at the turn of the fifteenth and sixteenth centuries.

What we know of the early education of Henry VIII is suggestive of that which Margaret must also have experienced, though perhaps with a different emphasis. If, as seems likely, he shared some of his lessons with his elder sister, then she would have been educated to roughly the same standard until the death of Prince Arthur in 1502 thrust Henry into the role of heir to the throne, necessitating a crash-course in the rigours of government. But by that time Margaret was already prepared for a future as queen consort and her education was largely complete. Did the fact that his sister had learned alongside him rankle with Henry, especially when their sibling rivalry became more apparent? While there is no clear information on the extent to which Henry may have been educated separately from his sisters, Erasmus of Rotterdam, visiting England in 1499, reported that he had been taken to Eltham by Thomas More, 'for there all of the royal children were being educated, except for Arthur, who was, at that time, the firstborn.'[4]

There is no evidence that Margaret was less studious than her siblings, though criticisms later levelled at her would make much of this assertion. Ladies of her rank learned Latin and arithmetic, were at least introduced to the works of classical scholars and the history of ancient civilizations and sometimes possessed copies of medieval romances. The wider accomplishments of a princess were Margaret's particular strength. She learned dancing, archery and embroidery and became, like all the Tudors, an able musician, especially proficient on the lute and clavichord. These skills were prerequisites for finding a suitable husband and they needed to be displayed with confidence on the occasions when the children were at court. And there was one further area that formed a key part of Margaret's education: that of letter-writing.

Until recently, little attention has been paid to Margaret's letters, despite the fact that she was a prolific correspondent and that more of her letters survive than those by the rest of the Tudor monarchs put together.[5] This indicates that she had received excellent training in the art of written communication, perhaps initially coached by her mother, Elizabeth of York. Claims that Margaret was barely literate, based on her appalling handwriting, are entirely untrue. Her hand is not the clear italic of her niece, Elizabeth I, being more open and discursive, but it is legible with some familiarity. There is no evidence that contemporaries found it impossible to read. Margaret knew well the forms of correspondence available to her: dictation to a secretary (itself a skill if it is to be done effectively); personal missives, often to underline a request; postscripts in her own hand to make official documents more immediate; and the use of the memorial, in which a trusted messenger essentially learns the letter by heart and 'performs' it in front of the person to whom it is addressed, adapting its contents by gauging the body language and response of the hearer. In demonstrating her subsequent mastery of these techniques, Margaret tells us much about the schooling she received and its inestimable value to her.

There is, of course, more to education than that which can be imparted in the school-room, even by the best of tutors. The main influences on Margaret were her mother and grandmother, two very different women whose personalities shaped her devotion to family, her personal determination to deal with adversity and her keen awareness of her status. Queen Elizabeth's life, as Margaret would have come to know and understand it, provided an example of how one could move from security and privilege to uncertainty and loss in a short space of time, but also emerge strongly to fulfil a role that required mental adjustment and coming to terms with the past. Often represented as being under the thumb of an ambitious and overbearing mother-in-law, Elizabeth of York was no cipher.[6] She worked effectively as a queen consort beside a man whom she had never met before he overthrew her uncle, Richard III, in 1485, and whose claim to the throne in strict terms of lineage was inferior to hers. Elizabeth performed her role with intelligence and tact, realizing from the outset that Henry VII's mother was not going to fade into the background and that the best way forward was to work with her rather than against her.

Combining the potentially contradictory demands of supporting her Yorkist connections with the need to ensure the security of the dynasty that she was establishing with Henry VII was a challenge that Elizabeth handled to great effect. Here she co-operated with her mother-in-law to demonstrate the advantages of what has been described as a blended household. On both the male and female side, the distinctions of Yorkist versus Lancastrian that had blighted much of the second half of the fifteenth century were expunged through a series of marriages that would, it was hoped, give the descendants of both houses a stake in the new Tudor dynasty. Elizabeth was particularly active in arranging marriages for her sisters as they came of age. These matches with Henry VII's wider family and loyal Tudor supporters did not fulfil Edward IV's grand vision of each of his daughters sitting on a European throne, but they ended a prolonged period of uncertainty for the young women. Margaret's aunts became great ladies of the first Tudor court, present at state occasions, in frequent contact with their elder sister and participating fully in court life. This picture of family unity did not, sadly, survive her childhood, becoming inevitably compromised by the different paths that she and her siblings would take.

Margaret also had the opportunity, as she grew up, to observe her mother on public occasions and to appreciate the importance of spectacle and pageantry. She saw her mother magnificently dressed, at ease with foreign dignitaries, on display to the populace, gracious and refined. From Elizabeth of York, Margaret learned the most important lesson of all – something that no amount of formal instruction could impart – how to be a queen.

The influence of her grandmother, Margaret Beaufort, was also considerable. She was especially important in preparing the princess for the life that lay ahead of her. 'My Lady, the king's mother' was an example of how to survive separation, loss of position and the dangers of factional fighting. Her life had been remarkable. Married at twelve years old to a half-brother of Henry VI, Edmund Tudor, earl of Richmond, she had found herself a widow at the age of thirteen, when the husband she barely knew died of plague. Alone in rural Wales and seven months pregnant, she was fortunate to find a protector in her brother-in-law, Jasper Tudor, who was then living at Pembroke Castle, a large fortress not known for its creature comforts. It was there, on 28 January 1457, that Margaret gave birth to the future Henry VII. Only thirteen years old, she was apparently very small for her age and the birth was so traumatic that, for a while, Margaret's life and that of her baby son hung in the balance. Margaret's experience was unusual even for an age when women could marry at twelve.[7] Normally an interval of several years was observed before full sexual relations were started but Edmund Tudor, eager to claim his wife's lands through the children of his marriage, had not shown the consideration that was generally offered to very young brides. His own death was more than a little ironic.

Once the initial danger was past and Margaret had had time to recover from a difficult birth, she took her future in her own hands, admittedly with Jasper Tudor's help. In early 1458 she was married again, to Henry Stafford, second son of the powerful duke of Buckingham. The young widow herself took an active part in the marriage negotiations. Stafford was more than twice her age, but these new connections offered the wider protection that Margaret sought for the son she always adored. The duke of Buckingham was a power broker in the struggle developing for direction of government, and ultimately the crown itself, which history knows as the Wars of the Roses. Eventually, at the age of fourteen, young Henry Tudor found that he and his uncle Jasper were on the losing side. Compelled to flee England, he would not see his mother again until he was twenty-eight, but she never entirely lost touch with him, or her faith that he might one day achieve greatness. Theirs is a remarkable story of maternal love and filial respect played out against the sporadic but vicious disputes and unpredictable changes of fortune that characterized the Wars of the Roses.

Margaret Tudor could not have failed to observe this bond between her father and grandmother. It was immutable, despite the long gaps in their physical contact.[8] Margaret Beaufort showed her granddaughter that indirect power could be a highly effective weapon if deployed at the right time. Of all the examples her grandmother offered, it was perhaps the one that the princess might have better taken to heart. Often presented in historical fiction and its screen counterparts as a vicious schemer, complicit in the murder of the Princes in the Tower, Margaret Beaufort was a well-educated, almost ostentatiously pious woman, who liked to stay close to the centre of power once the son from whom she had been separated for half his life won the throne. In her own right, she was a patron of the arts and learning, a friend of leading thinkers of the day and a capable manager of her extensive estates. All these aspects of the life of a great lady would figure in Margaret Tudor's later life. Though devoid of the high drama that both of these close female relatives had lived through, her own childhood, though largely tranquil, was not without incident.

In 1497 the unpredictability and occasional danger that any life, however uneventful, can sometimes face was brought home to Margaret. Her father still sat uneasily on his throne, despite the passage of more than a decade since the Battle of Bosworth. Yorkist conspirators would not fade away and their cause had, for some time, been taken up by the imposter who claimed to be Richard, duke of York, the younger son of Edward IV. Perkin Warbeck was, in fact, a Fleming who had been carefully trained by unscrupulous supporters of the Yorkist cause to play his role convincingly. Among his backers was the embittered sister of Edward IV, Margaret of Burgundy, willing to lend credence to the pretender's claim by embracing him as her nephew. If she really believed this, then she was a much more gullible woman than what we know of her character suggests. But Margaret was a true Yorkist and she hated Henry Tudor. Anything that she could do to thwart him, to bring about his fall, gave her satisfaction, even if it would mean installing an imposter in England and disadvantaging her own niece, Henry VII's wife.

To the chagrin of Henry and the amazement of other European monarchs, notably Ferdinand and Isabella of Spain, Warbeck's challenge proved difficult to break con-clusively. In the mid-1490s it received a further boost from an uncomfortably close quarter. James IV of Scotland saw in Warbeck a means of adding further pressure on England by enthusiastically espousing the pretender's cause. Warbeck was welcomed to court in Edinburgh, rode out with the Scottish king on raids in the violent and disputed area of the Scottish Borders and even married a distant Stuart relative, Lady Katherine Gordon. This was likely a cynical move. James was canny as well as restless and while he may have enjoyed the prospect of a good fight, he was more concerned with the damage he could do to his Tudor rival by heightening uncertainty and tension. There were ominous signs that this might lead to popular unrest, particularly in the west of England.

So, in 1497 Henry faced the daunting prospect of a northern war and a rising in Cornwall. The main source of discontent here was the cost of supporting his campaign against James IV, in terms of both men and money. Initially the Cornishmen were organized by Michael Joseph, a local blacksmith, but as they strong-armed their way into Exeter and moved further east across the border to Somerset, they found that their protest had set off a widespread revolt. Men of influence like Lord Audley, a Yorkist sympathiser who felt victimized by Henry VII, joined the rebels and organized a more focused rebellion. Their aim, ambitious but not wholly unrealistic, was to march on London. By mid-June, bolstered by hesitation among aristocrats in the Thames Valley whose loyalty to Henry was still far from certain, the rebels reached the outskirts of London. Most of them were camped on Blackheath on 16 June, where they were surprised by a force led by Giles Daubeney, the king's chamberlain, early the next morning. More than a little conflicted himself – he owned substantial lands in Somerset – Daubeney nevertheless fought in the vanguard of the king's army with what has been described as reckless courage, until the main force, commanded by the ever-faithful earl of Oxford, arrived and led a pitiless assault on the West Country rebels. Audley and his immediate supporters were executed ten days later.

The Battle of Blackheath might have begun in local grievances far to the west but it had developed into a direct assault on Henry VII and the fledgling Tudor dynasty. It certainly had an impact on the royal children themselves. Margaret, Henry and Mary were moved with their mother to the safety of the Tower of London. No doubt Elizabeth of York would have hidden the anxiety she must have felt from them, and as they were accustomed to a change of residence perhaps the reassurance of the queen's presence seemed like nothing more than a pleasant opportunity to enjoy her company. Children are shrewd at sensing tension, however, and this unanticipated break in their normally quiet daily lives could not have gone entirely unnoticed. Arthur was miles away, in Ludlow on the Welsh Borders, and therefore safe from the immediate peril that threatened his siblings.

Warbeck was not involved in the Western Uprising, remaining with his Yorkist backers in Ireland. But the menace he represented was not quite over. In September 1497, he again set foot on English soil, coming ashore with three ships near Land's End. It would turn out to be his last attempt at removing Henry VII from the throne of England. This time Exeter held out against the rebels and they were soon divided and surrounded. Warbeck was eventually captured in the New Forest, where he had taken refuge in Beaulieu Abbey. The king finally came face-to-face with this troublesome imposter, who had threatened his rule for six years, on 5 October 1497 in Taunton. On the promise that his own life would be spared, though many had died in supporting his false claim, Warbeck gave a full account of who he was and those who had tutored him throughout this long charade. The king made all of this public without loss of time, though he waited until the dust had settled before summoning his wife and three younger children back from East Anglia, where Margaret had been with the queen on a progress, well away from the continuing upheaval posed by Perkin Warbeck. Foreign ambassadors reported that ships were ready to take them out of England altogether if the insurrection could not be contained.

After an uneasy year, with more disruption than she had ever encountered before, Margaret was back at Sheen for Christmas. It was intended as a family celebration, as Henry, Margaret and Mary welcomed their parents. But the year 1497 still had one more trick to play on them, as *The Great Chronicle of London* recounted.

> While the king was holding his Christmas this year at the manor of Sheen, on the night after St Thomas the Martyr's Day [21 December], about 9 o'clock, a huge fire began suddenly in the king's lodging, and continued until midnight. It was so violent that a very large part of the old building of that place was burned, and much more harm done to wall hangings and bed curtains of cloth of gold and silk, and many more valuable furnishings, with plate and other multifarious rich things belonging to such a noble court.

But though the damage was extensive, those inside escaped.

> Nevertheless, God be praised, no Christian person died there, which was to the king's great relief, considering the notableness of the court there during the holding of that important feast; at which his grace was then accompanied by the queen, my lady the king's mother, my lord of York [Prince Henry], my lady Margaret and many other people of standing in the realm.[9]

Sheen was rebuilt over the next five years and became

known as Richmond Palace, both because of its location and the connection of the title of the earls of Richmond with Henry VII's family. Its design echoed that of earlier medieval and Burgundian styles, but although it was less frequently used by the court after the 1530s, it is worth remembering that Elizabeth I died there. The younger royal children now spent most of their time after the fire at Eltham Palace, with visits to Hatfield in Hertfordshire and other residences in the Home Counties of southern England. There was excitement when Queen Elizabeth gave birth to a third son, Prince Edmund, in 1499. An additional male heir was always welcome and all the more so for a fledgling dynasty. But the little prince lived only fifteen months, dying in the summer of 1500. His parents were out of the country on a visit to Calais at the time.

The dawn of a new century promised more stability. Henry VII had finally rid himself of the two greatest threats to his throne, the imposter Perkin Warbeck and the hapless young earl of Warwick. Imprisoned for much of his life, Warwick was the son of George, duke of Clarence, the volatile brother of Edward IV, and therefore a claimant to the throne himself. Accused of further plotting to overthrow Henry, Warbeck and Warwick were executed in 1499. The Yorkist threat had not quite died out – it would be resurrected, again without success, by Edmund de la Pole in 1501 – but it was muted now. There were other preoccupations for the king, made the more urgent by the realization that his health was beginning to fail. Margaret's childhood was coming to an end. But before her future could be assured, her elder brother, Arthur, must make the splendid marriage that his parents had long intended for him. In the ceremony surrounding this 'wedding of the century', Margaret would play her part and also learn much about the challenges facing a young bride in a new country as she got to know her sister-in-law, the Spanish princess, Katherine of Aragon.

2

Arthur and Katherine

*'I am told that the King has ordered great preparations
to be made, and that much money will be spent
on her reception and wedding.'*

Queen Isabella of Spain on the forthcoming wedding
of her youngest daughter, Katherine, to Arthur,
Prince of Wales, autumn 1501

Shortly before her twelfth birthday, Princess Margaret stood with her sister, Mary, her mother and grandmother at a high window in a house on Cornhill, in the City of London, watching with great interest a splendid procession pass by below. Though scarcely visible to the crowds of celebrating Londoners who lined the streets, Margaret was dressed for the occasion. She wore cloth of gold. Beside her, Mary was cosily but royally dressed in crimson velvet. But both girls knew that they would not be the centre of attention on this occasion. They were, though, curious to see the Spanish *infanta* who was about to join their family and take precedence over them as the second lady of the land.

Katherine was a short, slim girl with auburn hair and an attractive face. She would remain petite in figure until frequent pregnancies added to her girth and emphasized her lack of height. But for now she was something of a conundrum to her prospective sisters-in-law, at once a slightly exotic foreigner and the living symbol of their father's success as a ruler. In a day or two she would be Princess of Wales, a small, wet country that Margaret had never seen. Prince Arthur was in a different room in the same building, observing how his Spanish bride conducted herself in the arena of public display. He must have been gratified with what he saw, as, indeed, he had been when the couple first met. Impatient to see the young woman who had been the object of prolonged diplomacy, sometimes on a knife-edge during the escapades of Perkin Warbeck, Henry VII had taken Arthur to see his bride once she had recovered from the rigours of a difficult sea-journey.

The unexpected arrival of the king and prince at Dogmersfield in Hampshire, where the Spanish party was staying en route from Plymouth, where it had unexpectedly landed, to London, scandalized some of Katherine's servants. This was not how things were done in Spain. Henry, however, was determined to reassure both himself and his son that the girl was presentable and that the Spanish had not duped him by palming him off with someone who had mental or physical disabilities. Perhaps his attitude seems distasteful nowadays, but he had invested too much in Arthur's education and preparation for kingship to accept someone who could not, one day, fill the role of queen consort with aplomb. Elizabeth of York had set a high standard in this respect and her husband's concerns were real. Fortunately, Katherine, raised with both grace and steel by her mother, was instantly able to allay any worries. Dr de Puebla, the ambassador of the Spanish monarchs, translated the greetings and responses and some mutual discourse took place in Latin, the common language of diplomacy at the time. Arthur was definitely smitten and the match seemed propitious for both partners.

As Katherine neared London, she was greeted by the duke of Buckingham, the greatest peer of the realm, and by Margaret's younger brother, Henry. The ten-year-old duke of York had been given a major role in the wedding arrangements, something which he seems to have relished despite his young age. Katherine entered the City of London on 12 November, having stayed several nights at Lambeth Palace. The preparations for her entry, a great festival of pageants and public display, were now complete. The citizens, both great and small, were agog. The atmosphere is superbly caught in a contemporary source, *The Receyt of the Ladie Kateryne*. The identity of the author is unknown, but he was probably a courtier and not a herald, since his interest is not primarily in heraldic matters. Instead, he conveys with a fine eye for detail the excitement – the thrill, even – of this masterpiece of Tudor spectacle.

> In the mean season, the steadfast, sure and secret chamber of England, the opulent rehearsed City of London, was then full excellently accompanied with the most great multitude of people – what for the citizen inhabitants of the same, what for the estates of every county, shire and party with their servants awaiting, what with other of honest commons of every town, hold and border of the realm of England ... every lord both spiritual and temporal was keeping their open household with right great ryaltie of fare and victual.

Most important of all, as the writer of the *Receyt* notes, was the king himself, who 'had to his noble person most great and diligent waitings and attendances'. Supporting Henry VII were not just the nobility but the spiritual heads of the realm, the Archbishops of Canterbury and York, with a crowd of other bishops, abbots and priors. One of the most splendid sights in all this was the assembled ranks of the yeomen of the waiting King's Guard, 'in clothing of large jackets of damask, white and green goodly embroidered both on their breasts before and also on their backs behind, with round garlands of vine branches beset before richly with spangles of silver and gilt and in the middle a red rose, beaten with goldsmith's work'.[1]

The City itself was fully represented, for no one in the mayoral administration or the guilds and liveries wanted to miss out on the opportunity to show their loyalty. Crowd control was not overlooked, as barriers were erected along the route from Gracechurch Street to St Paul's Churchyard. The roads were gravelled and sanded and the participants in the six pageants that would greet Katherine as she passed along were all in place on the morning of 12 November, as Margaret watched from her discrete viewpoint. Katherine herself, a diminutive figure sitting on 'a great mule, richly trapped after the manner of Spain', was herself magnificently attired in the Spanish fashion, 'and upon her head a little hat fashioned like a cardinal's hat of a pretty braid, with a lace of gold ... her hair hanging down about her shoulders, which is fair auburn and in manner of a coif between her head and her hat of a carnation colour'.[2] This had been fastened so as to show her face to the crowd, in contrast to the veil she had been wearing when she first met Henry VII and Prince Arthur. Behind her rode eight ladies, four Spanish and four English, wearing cloth of gold. The Spanish princess's party stopped at each of the pageants, where actors presented tableaux of her namesake, St Catherine and St Ursula, of Virtue and Honour, as well as of King Arthur and the signs of the zodiac. In one of the pageants, Henry VII was represented as God the Father and Prince Arthur as God the Son. What Katherine might have made of this allegory, intended to show the power of the Tudor dynasty, even if it did border on the sacrilegious, is impossible to say. She was far too well rehearsed to show any signs of surprise.

But the timetable for the day was tight, and Katherine had to move on as swiftly as politeness allowed, sometimes before the speeches were entirely finished. Given their verbosity (they are all fully printed in the *Receyt* and in *The Great Chronicle of London*), this may have been something of a relief. She ended her day at St Paul's Churchyard, where the mayor of London presented her with gifts of gold and silver plate and coin. Escorted by the Archbishop of Canterbury, Katherine then entered the cathedral, prayed and made an offering at the shrine of St Erkenwald, a bishop of London in the seventh century credited with upholding Christianity in difficult times.[3]

The next day, Saturday, 13 November, Margaret met her sister-in-law for the first time. This introduction to Elizabeth of York and her daughters had been planned for a more informal setting – or as informal as protocol allowed. At four in the afternoon Katherine received an invitation to attend the queen at Baynard's Castle, where a reception was planned with dancing and general merriment. Henry VII was also there, presiding over the entertainments and graciously receiving the large delegation of Spanish diplomats, prelates, lords and ladies who had accompanied Katherine from her native land. But this was the opportunity that Queen Elizabeth and the princesses had been eagerly awaiting – to talk to the new member of their family, make her feel welcome and form an initial impression, in a private setting.

This would seem to have been favourable on both sides. It has been said that the conversations took place in Latin but they are more likely to have been in French. Elizabeth of York had suggested to Queen Isabella that it would be a good idea for her daughter to acquire some French before she left Spain, so as to facilitate communication in the months before she became more familiar with English. Elizabeth and Margaret spoke good French and even six-year-old Princess Mary would have been able to participate in conversation when called upon to do so. This breaking of the ice demonstrates the queen's concern for her daughter-in-law and her good sense. If nearby courtiers did eavesdrop on the pleasantries that were no doubt passing between Katherine and the royal ladies, they knew better than to gossip about them. But we do know that at the reception itself Katherine danced, both a stately, slow Spanish dance and a much more lively one. Then she retired to the nearby bishop's palace to prepare for the wedding ceremony the next day.

The king and queen watched the ceremony in St Paul's from a specially constructed closet with lattice windows. They naturally wished to have a good view of the ceremony without becoming the centre of attention themselves. That role was to be filled by Katherine and, to a lesser extent, her young husband. In the event, it seems to have been Prince Henry, who entered the cathedral with the bride-to-be on his arm, who attracted almost as much comment as his quieter, less demonstrative brother. The prince clearly revelled in his role and carried it off with great aplomb. Little did he know that he would marry the Spanish princess himself eight years later. It is not clear where Margaret and Mary were during the ceremony. Their parents would surely have wished them to attend but, as all the focus was on Arthur and Katherine, the presence of the princesses evidently passed unnoticed. Instead, concentration was centred on the bride and groom, whose matching outfits of white satin glittered with precious stones and luminous pearls. Katherine's dress and those of her ladies were expanded by great hoops on the outside, the first time the English had seen a farthingale. Given that she was slight, this must have almost enveloped the princess.

The entire ceremony probably took about two hours – a

long time to be on display in clothing that was more magnificent than comfortable. The couple left the cathedral to great shouts from waiting crowds, whose enthusiasm was no doubt increased by the plentiful supply of wine from a fountain, concocted in the shape of a mountain, a pun on Henry's newly rebuilt palace at Richmond (rich mount). It did its job in keeping Londoners happy but distant from the royal party and all the dignitaries surrounding them. While the citizens returned again and again with their cups to this source of enjoyment, the guests and the newlyweds partook of a splendid wedding breakfast, intended to underline the sophistication of England and the wealth of its royal family. Preparations for the bedding of the newlyweds began as early as late afternoon but Katherine had to wait in the royal bed until her husband emerged from carousing with his friends and gentlemen (as was expected of him) to join her much later. What happened that night, described as one of the most famous wedding nights in history, has remained a subject of speculation ever since, though discussion of it did not come out into the open until 1529, when Henry VIII was seeking to annul his marriage to Katherine of Aragon.

Margaret was present at the jousts and disguisings that took place over ten days after the wedding. One of the greatest of these was held at Westminster Hall and was followed by feasting and dancing. Here she would play an unexpectedly public role, thanks to the exuberance of her younger brother. 'Henry, duke of York, having with him his sister, Lady Margaret, in his hand, came down and danced two dances and then went up to the Queen.' Their prowess led to a huge round of applause and, thus encouraged, they danced together again. Henry was so delighted by the reaction of the onlookers that he 'threw off his robe and danced in his jacket with the Lady Margaret in so goodly and pleasant a manner that it was to the King and Queen a great and singular pleasure.'[4] No doubt Margaret was pleased to have participated in this public display of her dancing skills. And she had a particular reason to appreciate the opportunity it gave her. On 14 November commissioners had arrived from Scotland to finalize the diplomacy that would facilitate her own wedding. Attention would shortly shift from the Prince and Princess of Wales to Princess Margaret herself, in preparation for the day that she would become Queen of Scots.

3

Betrothal

'On St Paul's Day in January in the year of our
Lord God 1502, in the King's Royal Manor of Richmond
were the Fyancells of the right Highe and Mighty and right
Excellent Prince and Princesse, James, King of Scots,
and Margaret, eldest daughter of our Soveraigne
Lord Henry the Seventh.'

John Young, Somerset Herald, begins his account
of Margaret's betrothal and marriage

E nglish historians, with their exaggerated reverence for
the Tudors, have sometimes taken the view that Margaret
Tudor's marriage to James IV of Scotland conferred a
great favour on the Scots. It is unlikely that contemporaries
would have seen it that way. True, the marriage of Arthur
and Katherine of Aragon was a considerable achievement for
Henry VII but the Catholic Kings, her parents, had taken some
persuading. There was uncertainty still about the longevity of
the new dynasty and its right to the throne. In Scotland, the
Stewarts had ruled since 1371, when they had inherited the
throne by rightful descent from the line of Robert the Bruce.
Despite a succession of minorities, a manipulative nobility and
the untimely deaths of the first three Stewart kings, no one

had challenged their legitimacy. James IV's father and grand-father had both made advantageous marriages to wives from prominent European royal houses. The Scots did not lack confidence in their international standing and this had reached ambitious new heights under the vigorous James IV.

It was an impressive trio of Scottish negotiators who had come to London shortly before Christmas to work with their English counterparts on the finishing touches of the treaty that would include the provisions for Margaret's marriage. The delegation was led by Andrew Forman, an experienced diplomat who had spent time in Europe as James IV's representative to the pope. Like most diplomats in the early sixteenth century, he also had a parallel religious career. It was a favoured path for intelligent and able men with an ability to represent their country and strike deals that would support the interests of their sovereign.

Forman's commitment to the peace process between England and Scotland had seen him play a prominent role in the discussions that resulted in a truce between the two countries in 1497. By that time, James IV had abandoned Perkin Warbeck, which probably came as a relief to Forman, who had been required by the king to act as the pretender's minder. His role in bringing about an end to hostilities earned Forman the approval of Henry VII, who granted him the Yorkshire rectory of Cottingham. Shortly before coming south, he had also been awarded the bishopric of Moray by his own grateful monarch.

Accompanying Forman were Patrick Hepburn, earl of Bothwell, who was to act as proxy for James IV in the betrothal ceremony, and Robert Blackadder, Archbishop of Glasgow, who would represent the Scottish church in proceedings. Bothwell's base was in south-east Scotland and he was connected by marriage with the powerful Homes, the other major family of the region. James IV trusted him implicitly – indeed,

Bothwell had helped to put the king on the throne in 1488 – and his loyalty and effectiveness in the Borders brought him the rewards of extensive royal patronage and a position on the royal council. A seasoned survivor in the maelstrom of Scottish politics, Bothwell had succeeded in maintaining royal support while accruing influence and wealth. Very few other magnates had managed this balancing act nearly so effectively.

Aged nearly sixty, Blackadder was the oldest of the three. His name may bring a smile to the face of readers of a certain age, but he was from a well-established family and was educated at the universities of St Andrews and Paris. Much-travelled, he was a frequent visitor to Rome, where he pursued a joint agenda of representing his king and trying to further his own interests. In this he was not entirely successful. Though he apparently knew his way around the papal see, he had to live with the fact that the Archbishop of St Andrews, William Elphinstone, had the status of a primate, which he lacked. But in terms of his presence in London as the year 1501 drew to a close, Blackadder had already been involved in the search for a bride for James IV, one of the most eligible bachelor kings in Europe. Before the English marriage was actively pursued, Blackadder had visited Spain to see if Ferdinand and Isabella could be persuaded to marry Katherine of Aragon to James and not to Prince Arthur. His overtures were met with polite obfuscation from the Catholic Kings at a time when they were still considering their options. This current mission would prove more satisfactory.[1]

On the English side, the signatories to the marriage treaty were led by the recently appointed Archbishop of Canterbury, Henry Deane, who had officiated at the marriage of Prince Arthur and Katherine of Aragon. Born in about 1440, Deane's background was in monastic orders (he had been prior of a religious community near Gloucester), an unusual background for an archbishop at the time. He was an experienced and able administrator, something that was becoming equally uncommon as the smaller religious houses of England fell increasingly into poor management and financial difficulties. Deane had also, for reasons that are not entirely clear, earned the confidence of Henry VII, perhaps through the support of the brother of his predecessor at Canterbury, John Morton. Henry VII would have viewed him as eminently sensible and reliable.

Deane did not, though, have the familiarity with Anglo–Scottish politics of his colleague Richard Fox, bishop of Winchester, nor as colourful a background. Fox, who would go on to found Corpus Christi College at Oxford University, was born in Lincolnshire and had a background in canon law. By early 1485 he had fallen foul of Richard III, who deprived him of the lucrative living of vicar of Stepney in London because of his suspected association with Henry Tudor. In fact, Fox had never set foot in Stepney and was already in France. He may well have acted as secretary to Henry at this crucial phase of his plans for invading England. After Bosworth, Fox's career advanced swiftly. Offices and appointments came his way and he was made keeper of the Privy Seal in early 1487. By then, and having been ordained a year earlier, he was established on the twin paths of politics and religion so characteristic of success at the time. He and Archbishop Morton were close advisers to Henry VII, who began to use Fox extensively in diplomatic missions. One of the earliest of these took him to Scotland in 1487, to pursue the possibility of a marriage alliance involving one of Elizabeth of York's sisters. The overthrow of James III of Scotland and the succession of his teenage son scuppered those particular plans, but Fox had been heavily involved in the Truce of Ayton and was sole commissioner in 1499, when serious negotiations for Margaret Tudor's marriage began. It is unclear whether he expected to be made Archbishop of Canterbury when Morton died in 1501, but his appointment to Winchester the same year made Fox bishop of the richest see in England. Perhaps he felt it sufficient recompense for the loss of Canterbury and the chancellorship, both of which went to other men. But he remained very close to Henry VII, 'the king who was my maker'. Now, with years of diplomatic experience and a wiliness to match his surname, Fox would help put the finishing touches on the arrangements that would define Margaret Tudor's future as Queen of Scots.

The third representative of Henry VII round the table at Richmond Palace on those short winter days was Thomas Howard, earl of Surrey. A Yorkist who had risen through his support for Edward IV, he fought for Richard III and was wounded at Bosworth. Surrey, like others, soon decided to make his peace with the new Tudor king. He was by nature and upbringing primarily a soldier, cast in the mould of late-medieval chivalry, but also a pragmatist. Surrey made two advantageous marriages and took part in local politics in his native Norfolk. He was a man who could adapt when he sensed which way the wind was setting. Also a seasoned diplomat, he fought against the Scots in the 1490s but was equally willing to get along with them as circumstances changed. Then nearly sixty years old, bluff and hearty to the point of being overbearing, he would be the man chosen to escort Margaret to Scotland. She came to greatly resent his manner.

Thus it was a group of impressive, sophisticated men, all with the complete confidence of their masters, who met to hammer out the details of this alliance between the new Tudor dynasty and the much longer-established Stewarts over Christmas 1501. Three weeks into the New Year, they had achieved their aim. It had been a long time reaching fruition. The possibility of a marriage between Margaret and James IV had been mooted as early as 1496 by Henry VII, who hoped the prospect might encourage the King of Scots to drop his irritating support for Perkin Warbeck. James did not respond at this point, but two years later, when relations were improving and Border warfare had come to a halt following the Truce of Ayton, James's priorities were changing. There were clearly advantages to marriage with an English princess, not least of which was the possibility it offered, however remote at that point, of uniting the two crowns. Late-medieval monarchs knew well the frailty of life and the marriage would certainly enhance James's standing, both within the British Isles and beyond. But at this point, Henry VII became more coy. He was not going to send his eight-year-old daughter to Scotland yet. He was also considering a match for Margaret with Prince Christian, the twelve-year-old son of King Hans of Denmark. The age gap (James was seventeen years Margaret's senior) was slight and a Scandinavian alliance would be a riposte to the King of Scots, who was half-Danish himself. The possibility that Margaret's descendants, rather than those of his two sons, might eventually rule England as well as Scotland had not escaped the English king. He did not necessarily view this as a calamitous outcome, reportedly saying to his council, 'in that case England would not accress unto Scotland but Scotland would accress unto England, as the most noble head of the whole isle'.[2]

This was not just a bargaining chip. Elizabeth of York and Margaret Beaufort voiced their concerns about Margaret still being very much a child. Henry explained to Pedro de Ayala, the Spanish ambassador to Scotland, who was visiting England, that his wife and mother were set against concluding the marriage at the moment, no matter how desirable it might be in the longer run. They were, he said, 'very much against this marriage'. If Margaret were to be sent to Scotland now, 'they fear the king of Scots would not wait [to consummate the union], but injure her and endanger her health'. Margaret Beaufort had been compelled to have sex at the age of twelve and the thought of her granddaughter, who 'has not yet completed the ninth year of her age', several years later enduring what she had encountered was too much. The English king went on to say that Margaret 'is so delicate and weak that she must be married much later than other young ladies'.[3] He went on to state that James would have to wait another nine years.

It is unlikely that James would have agreed to such a long delay, almost a lifetime in diplomacy. He was already in his mid-twenties and though he had a succession of mistresses and a growing brood of illegitimate children, his priority was to find an appropriate queen consort. Besides, Henry VII had rather overstated his case. There is no evidence that Margaret was weak or unhealthy, though the drawing of her in the *Receuil d'Arrras*, made at about the time of her marriage, suggests that she was thin in her early teens. In the end, a compromise was reached which suited both parties. The betrothal would take place when Margaret had completed her twelfth year, by which time she would be deemed competent both mentally and physically to undertake marriage. For her father, the timing was perfect. Now that Arthur was married and the splendid nuptials were finished, he could reinforce his dynastic standing – and ensure peace with a troublesome neighbour – through his daughter's wedding.

We do not know how much of the final wording of the marriage treaty was communicated to Margaret. It would probably have been felt that burdening a girl of twelve with the detail was inappropriate. Later, there would be time to familiarize herself with its clauses and how they affected her standing as Queen of Scots. The key areas were financial and dealt with Margaret's dower and the financial support she would get from James IV once she became his wife. The princess's dower was to be £10,000, the equivalent of over £6.5 million nowadays. If this does not necessarily sound a huge amount for a princess to bring with her, it is worth remembering that the Scottish king was not well off and the injection of cash was welcome in a small country. James had far-reaching, ambitious aims to become a European power and his marriage to Margaret would help finance them. Care was also taken to safeguard the princess's interests and ensure that she could keep up the lifestyle to which she had become accustomed. James was to endow her for life with lands and other income intended to yield £2,000 a year, or £1 million today. In addition, she was to have £300 per year at her own disposal (roughly £174,000) and twenty-four English attendants, to help ease her transition between the two courts. The sums seem surprisingly modest for a queen consort when one considers the pay of many senior executives in business nowadays, but they were considered reasonable at the time. Whether they would be honoured was another matter.

There were also two other treaties finalized at the same time: one specified how relations between the two countries were to be conducted, under the terms of a Perpetual Peace, and the other, more specific but no less important, clarified contentious issues in the Borders, where distinct legislation in the resolving of disputes made the area's governance of special importance. The Treaty of Perpetual Peace also had a European significance, since it was supported by the monarchs of France and Spain and the Habsburg emperor, who all had an interest in the wider repercussions of relations between England and Scotland. The significance of all of this would come into play once Margaret became a queen. For the present, it was her betrothal that took centre stage.

The princess would have been well prepared for the ceremony that took place at Richmond Palace, in the Queen's Great

Chamber, on 25 January 1502. It was a fitting place for Margaret to become a queen, in the apartments of her mother, recently refurbished to an appropriate degree of magnificence following the disastrous fire of 1497. The choice of venue was both comforting and symbolic, for it was Elizabeth of York who would guide Margaret through the transition from childhood to womanhood, teaching her the responsibilities of queenship by example and experience. Whether or not there was an actual rehearsal beforehand, Margaret had clearly been briefed as to the form of the betrothal ceremony and what was expected of her. She probably learned the responses by heart. Although the occasion did not involve the general public – they would get to see the young queen at a later stage – it was still a significant display of early Tudor prestige, conducted in front of an impressive audience of churchmen and diplomats. In attendance were the Spanish ambassador to Scotland, Pedro de Ayala (whose presence in London and ill-defined role caused a great deal of friction with the resident ambassador to England, Dr de Puebla), and his Venetian counterpart, Francisco Capello, as well as diplomats from France and the papacy and, of course, the Scottish delegation who had negotiated the treaties. Three archbishops, Deane of Canterbury, Savage of York and Blackadder of Glasgow, were also present, as were the bishops of Chester, Norwich, Rochester and Winchester.

Not to be outdone by this impressive list of foreign and clerical witnesses, the English nobility were well represented. Prince Arthur was resident at Ludlow for barely a month, and there was no question of his returning, but Prince Henry, duke of York, was the senior member of the royal family present after the king himself. The English aristocrats were led by the duke of Buckingham, accompanied by nineteen earls and lords, including the earl of Derby, the king's step-father, and a further twenty-eight knights, many of whom had led their own troops in battle under their personal banners. This impressive roll-call, designed to demonstrate Tudor success both at home and abroad, was balanced by the presence of a similar number of important ladies. Six-year-old Princess Mary watched as her sister plighted herself to James IV, and Elizabeth of York's sister Katherine, as well as the duchess of Norfolk, looked on. One can only speculate on the thoughts of Lady Katherine Gordon, the Scottish noblewoman once the wife and now the widow of Perkin Warbeck, who had been taken into the English royal household, where she would remain in the service of several queens consort until her death in the 1530s. A notable absentee from Margaret's betrothal was her grandmother, Margaret Beaufort, who may either have been ill or detained elsewhere by bad weather. Winter roads in England were notoriously difficult for travellers.

The day had started with the royal family hearing High Mass in the chapel at Richmond, which was across the court-yard from the Great Hall. There followed a 'notable sermon' from the bishop of Winchester, Richard Fox, a man who had a great deal of experience in Anglo–Scottish affairs and for whom this betrothal marked, in many respects, the apogee of his diplomatic career. Moving back to the queen's chamber, the ceremony itself commenced with a formal dec-laration of papal dispensation (Margaret and James IV were distantly related, as were many members of the ruling dynas-ties of Europe at the time) and a statement that there was no impediment on either side. And now the princess, who had celebrated her twelfth birthday just two months earlier, took centre stage.

She was asked by the Archbishop of Glasgow the key ques-tion that marked her passage from childhood to womanhood: was she content to undertake this marriage without compul-sion and of her own free will? Margaret answered, in words that she had no doubt practised beforehand: 'If it please my Lord and Father the King and my Lady my Mother the Queen.' After Henry VII indicated that his daughter had both their blessings, the earl of Bothwell stepped forward to play his part as his monarch's representative. He was resplendent in cloth of gold, as perhaps was Margaret, though there is no surviving record of what she actually wore. As there was a fashion for matching outfits at wedding ceremonies at the time, it is probable that Margaret's dress echoed that of the Scottish earl. The disparity in their ages must have made them an incongruous pair as they stood together. Bothwell undertook marriage with Margaret on behalf of his sovereign, 'James, by the grace of God, king of Scotland'. Margaret replied as follows.

> I, Margaret, the first begotten daughter of the right excellent, right high and mighty prince and princess, Henry, by the grace of God, King of England and Elizabeth, Queen of the same, wittingly and of deliberate mind, having twelve years complete in age in the month of November last be past, contract matrimony with the right excellent, right high and right mighty prince, James, King of Scotland, the person of whom, Patrick, earl of Bothwell, is procurator and take the said James, King of Scotland, unto and for my husband and spouse and all other for him forsake, during his and mine lives natural; and thereto I plight and give to him, in your person as procurator aforesaid, my faith and truth.[4]

So Margaret left childhood behind, consigning to memory the quiet days at Sheen, the expanding royal nursery, the occasional sense of loss of younger siblings, the excitement and joy of her mother's visits and the warmth of her father's approval. She knew that she still had their love and pride in the way she had conducted herself in this, her first great test. There would be more to come, and eventually a parting, but she was not to leave for Scotland before the month of May 1503, by which time she would be thirteen and much better prepared for what lay ahead. For now, she was already Queen of Scots, at least technically, and entitled to be treated as such. This meant that she took precedence over her brother Henry. There were rumours that the active and high-spirited boy, whose exuberance at the wedding of Arthur and Katherine had made him, rather than his sister, the centre of attention, did not take well to Margaret's more exalted status. It is possible that the seeds of a sibling rivalry that would manifest itself more openly in years to come were sown in Richmond that day when his sister became a queen.

The conclusion of the betrothal ceremony was met by trumpet fanfares in the palace and peals of bells in London. Street bonfires were lit and drink was supplied – 'and at each one of the twelve of the chief fires was set out a hogshead of Gascony wine for whoever wished to drink it'.[5] This added to the air of festivity, though celebrations were not on the scale of the huge public spectacle of Prince Arthur's wedding. However, any excuse for celebration in the depths of winter was no doubt welcome to the citizens of the capital. And there were other entertainments for the aristocratic visitors. On the afternoon of 25 January, after the betrothal ceremony was concluded, the duke of Buckingham and other courtiers participated in a joust. Margaret, in her first official act as a queen, gave out the prizes.

The tournament was followed by pageants, dancing and disguisings over several days and finally an elaborate exchange of costly gifts. The Scottish delegation went home with an impressive haul of gold and silver plate for the chief negotiators and velvet gowns for their retainers. While undoubtedly designed to impress on the Scots the power and wealth of their new queen's dynasty, such largesse was an integral part of successful diplomacy in the sixteenth century. Leading politicians representing their country were not sent home empty-handed. As a method of buying permanent support from key players it was unlikely to succeed. The English aristocracy were regarded as notoriously venal and unreliable, willing to take pensions from anyone for short-term benefit. But in 1502, the gift-giving added to an undoubted air of goodwill. Bothwell and his clerical colleagues went home well-satisfied, able to demonstrate to James IV just how well they had succeeded. They did not, however, bring the new Queen of Scots back with them. Under the terms of the marriage treaty, Margaret was to remain in England until the spring of 1503, allowing more time for her to reach physical maturity. Wholly unforeseen events would mean that she did not, in fact, arrive in her new realm until late summer of that year.

In the interim, Margaret spent much more time with her mother, learning from Elizabeth of York what it meant to be a queen consort. The importance of this period of training has not always been adequately appreciated by historians, but the role Elizabeth played in preparing her daughter for what lay ahead has recently been emphasized in a reappraisal of queenship in early-modern Britain and in modern biographies of the first Tudor queen.[6] Elizabeth used to be written off as a pliable, pretty but increasingly plump childbearer, completely overshadowed by her mother-in-law. She was very much more than that and her contribution to the successful establishment of the Tudor dynasty is now acknowledged. The marriage of Henry VII and Elizabeth of York was a successful partnership and this the queen demonstrated by example as she and Margaret spent much time in each other's company over the next twelve months. Their closeness and what it signified was apparent immediately after the betrothal ceremony, when 'the queen took her daughter, the Queen of Scots, by the hand and dined both at one mess covered.' The gesture of hand-holding is touching, showing maternal affection and pride. But as Henry VII dined with his male nobility and the Scottish delegation separately, Elizabeth and the great ladies of her own court welcomed Margaret as one of their number. This was a female world to which Margaret had gained admission, but its existence depended on a positive interaction with the male universe of the king – and, in crucial respects, an understanding of the parts they both played in royal life.

The partnership was not, however, an equal one, not merely in the British Isles but throughout Europe, and would remain like this for centuries to come. Neither Henry nor Elizabeth would have understood such a concept. Woman was the inferior of man in every respect, physically, intellectually and, above all, morally. She was a prey to her emotions and her body, racked by whims and desires that were only checked by a firmly patriarchal society. Not all women accepted this characterization of the weaknesses of their sex and a number found ways to deal with it so that they were not permanently disadvantaged, though true independence in female lives was a rarity. Inevitably, being a queen offered advantages of wealth, privilege, influence and even power, in some circumstances, but there were boundaries, both practical and societal. Treading the difficult path between the expectations of a queen and the reality that could intrude so unpredictably would occupy much of Margaret Tudor's future. But, for the present, she was fortunate to have her mother's example to learn from and to attempt to emulate.

One of the most important aspects of queenship was the functioning of the consort's household. This had ramifications for all the other key aspects of the queenly role:

diplomacy, pageantry, patronage, piety and public image. Margaret would soon be in charge of her own household, though she would be, like her mother, dependent on her husband to meet its expenses. Before 1502, she had her own small staff of domestic servants, under the overall direction of Elizabeth Denton, who was lady mistress of the royal nursery. Their duties were to see to her material needs and help raise her as a princess, but in this environment Margaret was still very much a child under direction. The world she was moving into would put her in the centre of the frame and its significance, not just in England but throughout Europe, is now widely acknowledged. 'A court without women is like a body without a nervous system', as one historian has aptly described it. The queen's ladies were her companions and confidantes, expected to reflect her magnificence in their own wardrobes and manners. On journeys long and short they were by her side, quietly attending to her daily needs through instructing lower servants, anticipating her desires, careful of her comfort and emotional requirements. Most came from good families, some from among the leaders of the aristocracy. They formed a phalanx of support on public occasions, resplendent in outfits only slightly less stunning than those of the queen herself. They were present at the beginning and end of every day, helping to dress the queen and put her to bed. One, or perhaps more, of them would have slept in her chamber. But though they must have discussed the intimacies of life, including the expectations of the marital bed and the frustrations of menstruation, if the queen felt it necessary to share her thoughts and fears with them, it was not their part to initiate such conversations, at least, not without approaching such subjects with extreme tact.[7] Queens lived their lives surrounded by other women but always supremely conscious of the necessary separation between their royal status and those who served them. The queen's household was her own realm but the women in it, no matter how nobly born, were not in any way her equals. Affectionate and social as Elizabeth of York seems to have been, Margaret would have observed that her mother knew the distance between herself and her ladies.

It was an invisible line that neither side could cross. The one area in which this distinction was probably more blurred was in Elizabeth of York's relations with her family. The queen's achievement in safeguarding the interests of the female members of her large family was considerable, and apparently done with less aggravation to other members of the nobility than had been the case with her own mother, Elizabeth Woodville. It was understood as an inevitable perk of queenship but needed to be handled with care. We know nothing of Margaret Tudor's relationship with her Woodville aunts and cousins but, once in Scotland, they would not form part of her network of ladies. Indeed, the absence of an importunate wider group of relatives would largely be a blessing for Margaret as queen, even if it did deprive her of the company of her closest kin.

A queen was also expected to be on the move, never staying in one house for more than several months at a time. This was partly because of the need to be visible to her husband's subjects at occasions of state, to make visits to religious shrines (such piety was required from all queens consort, as was the giving of alms to the poor) and to allow for a complete, regular cleansing of the sanitary provisions, such as they were, of royal residences. A palace could literally become little better than a sewer if inhabited for too long. The peripatetic royal household was something that Margaret grew up to expect. Financial security was less certain. Elizabeth of York signed off her accounts monthly but she had a tendency to spend beyond her means. Undeterred, she purchased part of what was probably intended to be Margaret's trousseau, including a gown of crimson velvet with fur cuffs, ideal for the harsher winters of Scotland. So were perhaps intended the pair of bellows and a fire-pan. There were also new strings for Margaret's lute, an instrument dear to the princess, on which she was able to display her talent as a musician. The lute was also a favoured instrument of James IV, something which might well have been reported by the Scottish delegation who had negotiated the terms of Margaret's marriage. A shared interest in music would form a good base for a developing relationship as Margaret got to know her husband. James was also able to look upon the face of his young bride before he met her in person. When the Scots returned, they took with them gifts for their monarch from Henry VII. He had commissioned portraits of himself, his wife and his two elder children from the court painter, the Fleming Meynnart Wewyck. Sadly, this portrait of Margaret has been lost. The line drawing said to be of her at about the same age is in the *Receuil d'Arras* but the Daniel Mytens portrait of Margaret as Queen of Scots, holding a marmoset monkey, dates from the seventeenth century, though it is based on an earlier one, also lost.

Elizabeth of York had clearly given thought as to how to prepare Margaret for the great step which she must take the following year. As Easter approached and the rule of Henry VII seemed finally to have weathered all the long years of uncertainty, neither the queen nor her elder daughter had any idea of the great and calamitous changes which would take place before Margaret was expected to set out for Scotland.

4

Loss

'God is where He was and we are both young enough.'

Elizabeth of York's words of comfort to her husband
on the death of Prince Arthur

Easter fell very early in 1502, at the start of what was to be a cold, wet spring in the west of England. On Maundy Thursday, 24 March, Prince Arthur officiated at local ceremonies in Ludlow to mark the beginning of the most holy rite in the Christian calendar. Nine days later, he was dead.

The cause of this shockingly swift demise is still disputed by historians, in part because the sources, which give only brief descriptions of his illness, are subject to varying interpretations and have given rise to dramatic diagnoses, which, over so much distance in time, cannot be justified with any certainty. Arthur's most recent biographer suggests that the evidence supports a very sudden decline, perhaps the result of a highly infectious epidemic such as the sweating sickness. Local records in Worcester, in whose cathedral Arthur was buried, say that his funeral was attended by all those that could go but add the interesting qualification, 'saving those of the city because of the sickness that then reigned amongst them'.[1]

Certainly the year 1502 had the third-highest mortality of the sixteenth century and was particularly grim in the Welsh Marches. There is also an indication that Katherine of Aragon was herself unwell at the time. She and Arthur had arrived in Ludlow in the depths of winter, with a substantial number of Spanish attendants who were not acclimatized to the weather and had even less resistance to local disease. All of this points to an outbreak of deadly infection as the cause of Arthur's death, rather than testicular cancer or tuberculosis, even though the Tudors seem to have been subject to the latter disease. There is no contemporary comment on any visible ill health in Arthur before this time and certainly not at his wedding only four months earlier. One might possibly detect in surviving portraits of Arthur a boy who lacked the robust frame of his brother, Henry, but it would be unwise to draw any firm conclusions from this.

The king and queen had spent Easter at Greenwich Palace. Given her status as Queen of Scots it is likely that Margaret was with them, and perhaps Prince Henry and Princess Mary as well, since Henry VII seems to have liked having his family around him for the major religious feasts. Arthur, being prepared for kingship separately, had not been one of this intimate circle and now he never would be. Yet although we know nothing of their reaction to this distant older brother's disappearance from their lives, we know a great deal about the grief of the king and queen.

The Prince of Wales's chamberlain immediately wrote to the king and royal councillors in London. The messenger who carried the awful tidings of the death of the heir to the throne made the journey to London in just two days. His missive was read first, as was the custom, by the council, who summoned Henry VII's confessor and asked him to break the news to the king. The name of the man who performed this unenviable task is not recorded but we know he was an observant friar, perhaps from one of the houses that the king had founded recently at Greenwich itself. Henry was woken earlier than usual on Tuesday, 5 April and prepared for what he was about to hear by a phrase in Latin which translates as 'If we have received good things by the hand of God, why should we not receive evil?'[2] Judging by the king's reaction, he was still stunned by the revelation that Arthur was dead, as indeed one might have expected him to be. He sent at once for his wife, 'so that they could take the painful sorrows together'.[3]

The intimate details of the anguish of the couple are unique in English history. Traditionally royal grief was (and still is) something to be processed privately, without public observation or comment. But the writer of the *Receyt of the Ladie Kateryne* was either present himself at the time or knew someone who was, because his account is full of moving insights as to just how overwhelmed Henry and Elizabeth were by this bitter blow to their hopes. Coming so unexpectedly, and just after a period of unalloyed joy, it seemed as if all that they had been through as Henry struggled to keep his crown had crumbled into dust with the already decaying body of their firstborn. And it was Elizabeth who sought to reassure and comfort her devastated husband, to try and make him see a wider perspective and bring home to him that all was not suddenly lost.

She reminded Henry VII that he needed above all to consider his own wellbeing because on it depended that of the entire country and, indeed, herself. He could take strength from the remembrance that he was his mother's only child and yet God had preserved him and brought him to his current great estate.

Over that, God had lent them yet a fair, goodly and toward young Prince and two fair Princesses, God is where He was and we [are] both young enough, and that the prudence and wisdom of His Grace sprung over all

Christendom, so that this should please him to take this according thereunto.[4]

The possibility of having more children was a brave suggestion since Elizabeth's most recent pregnancy had apparently been difficult, and perhaps even a bold one, coming from the queen to her husband and made in front of witnesses.

Henry clearly took strength from his wife's attempts to calm him. But when she returned to her own apartments the full extent of her own emotional toll became quickly apparent.

[N]atural and motherly remembrance of that great loss smote her so sorrowful to the heart that those who were about her were fayn to send for the King to comfort her. And then his Grace of true, gentle and faithful love in good haste came and relieved her and showed her how wise counsel she had given him before, and he for his part would thank God for his sons, and would she do in likewise.[5]

It is remarkable that this moving account of the royal couple's desperation and dependence on one another survives. Writing more than a century later, Francis Bacon asserted that Henry VII was far from being a doting husband: 'Towards his queen he was nothing uxorious, nor scarce indulgent, but companionable and respective and without jealousy.' This does not entirely justify the interpretation by some historians that Bacon said Henry was a cold and unfeeling spouse, but his need of his wife and his concern for her breakdown in the face of Prince Arthur's loss are surely indications that the relationship was genuinely loving and more than just 'companionable'. Any of his son Henry VIII's six wives would surely have settled for a marriage like that of Henry VII and Elizabeth of York.

Bacon went on to characterize the first Tudor king's attitude towards his children in a more positive light: '[H]e was
full of paternal affection, careful of their education, aspiring
to their high advancement, regular to see that they should not
want of any due honour and respect, but not greatly willing
to cast any popular lustre upon them.' If it means that Henry
did not facilitate his children becoming celebrities in their
own right it is undoubtedly correct, but this would not make
him different from most monarchs of the period. In terms of
how he saw their roles in reflecting and enhancing the new
Tudor dynasty, it is entirely wrong. As we shall see, Margaret
would have a greater role than either of her brothers in realizing this aim.

But for the present she must observe mourning for the
elder brother who had never been much more than a name
to her, a brief, glittering presence at the heart of the nuptials
with Katherine of Aragon, the sister-in-law now left stranded in
Ludlow. Meanwhile, the preparations for Margaret's departure for Scotland continued. She expected to have another
year under her mother's direction before she was required
to fulfil her destiny. Sadly, they were to be separated sooner
than she had expected as a second – and, for Margaret and
her siblings, greater – loss sent the Tudor royal family reeling
again within the year.

Margaret had expected to pass the majority of the remaining
time before her departure for Scotland with her mother,
the queen's duties and health permitting. Elizabeth of York
seems to have been unwell for much of the time after Prince
Arthur's death. Though grief for Prince Arthur may well
have been a factor, there were further troubles on her own
side of the family when Cecily of York, the sister nearest to

her in age, made an unsuitable and secret remarriage in the spring of 1502. Cecily's third husband was Thomas Kyme, an obscure, untitled gentleman whose origins remain unclear. This was not a union undertaken in haste – Welles had died in 1499 – but it was a *mesalliance* socially and the furtive wedding infuriated Henry VII, whose permission had not been sought. The sister who had carried Elizabeth's train at her coronation was banished from court and the lands Welles had bequeathed Cecily were confiscated by the crown.

There is no record of Elizabeth's reaction but, as a loving sister who had devoted a great deal of energy over the years to promoting the interests of her siblings, the inappropriateness of Cecily's behaviour combined with the king's unyielding displeasure must have come as a further blow to the queen's equilibrium. Even the understanding displayed by Margaret Beaufort, a long-time supporter of Cecily, did not soften Henry's response. He could not afford a show of family clemency while putting effort into the final crushing of the threat posed by the family of Edmund de la Pole, earl of Suffolk, the most persistent of his Yorkist adversaries. The repercussions of this onslaught on the man who called himself the 'White Rose' and was now in exile in Europe, under the protection of Emperor Maximilian, also encompassed another of Elizabeth's sisters, Katherine, married to William Courtenay. Katherine's husband was suspected of conspiring with the de la Poles, arrested and his lands confiscated. Elizabeth had been compelled to take Katherine into her household and make provision for Katherine's children. On top of this, Sir James Tyrell, long under suspicion, confessed to the murder of Elizabeth's brothers, Edward V and Richard, duke of York, in the Tower of London in 1483.

So it was a troubled queen who, true to her emotional assurances to her husband, became pregnant again in the early summer of 1502. Whether she knew this when she set

53

out on what was to become a long progress west of London, all the way to Wales, is uncertain. Yet even if she did discover it en route, she did not consider turning back. There has been considerable speculation about her motivation in travelling at such a difficult time, including the possibility of a rift in the royal marriage, but she could not just have taken off without her husband's knowledge and assent. Summer progresses were common and it may have been felt that she would be safer outside the London area, with its ever-present danger of summer epidemics. The journey, which took Elizabeth all the way to Raglan Castle, where Henry VII had passed the formative years of his childhood, was done in easy stages but must still have been demanding for someone in the early stages of pregnancy at the age of thirty-six. Payments to apothecaries in the queen's privy purse expenses indicate that she was not well for part of the time, while an unusually high consumption of venison suggests that she particularly craved a meat that is lean but rich to fortify her as she wended her way through Oxfordshire and Gloucestershire, into the Forest of Dean and on to Monmouth, arriving at Raglan on 19 August.[6] The king joined her on the return journey late in September and thereafter she spent her time in London, moving between Richmond, Baynard's Castle, Westminster and Greenwich. Anyone who assumes that early-modern monarchs had static lifestyles would surely be amazed by the sheer amount of upheaval involved in being a queen consort. Margaret could have had no illusions about this before she left England.

It was at Richmond that Margaret spent her last Christmas with her mother. Margaret's minstrels entertained the queen in the days after Christmas and were duly rewarded. Now in the final stages of pregnancy and increasingly unwell, perhaps because of the anaemia from which many women suffered after multiple pregnancies in those days, Elizabeth was nevertheless able to accompany her husband to the Tower of London for Candlemas, on 2 February 1503. That she had not yet taken to her chamber for the seclusion that was customary for queens before their delivery indicates that the birth was not believed to be imminent. Indeed, Elizabeth had planned to give birth at Richmond. Yet it was at the Tower that she went into premature labour, on the evening of Candlemas itself. After an especially difficult time, she gave birth not to the longed-for prince, but to another daughter, named Katherine. The child was christened the next day, in the chapel of St Peter ad Vincula, in the Tower of London. This was not necessarily because she was weak, though she evidently was frail, but was common for royal christenings. Margaret had herself been christened the day after her birth. But that was thirteen years ago, when both mother and child were stronger. Now, neither her mother nor her sister would survive.

A week after the birth, the queen's health deteriorated sharply. The labour was apparently very difficult – Thomas More later referred to her as being 'doubled with pain'[7] – while this and anaemia may have contributed to her increasing weakness. Equally plausible as an explanation is puerperal fever, a bacterial complication of childbirth common until well into the nineteenth century, though now largely confined to the developing world. It was no respecter of rank and would kill Henry VIII's last wife, Katherine Parr, in 1548. Concerned that his wife was sinking, the king sent for a physician from as far away as Plymouth. But it was to no avail. Elizabeth could not be saved. She died on 11 February, her thirty-seventh birthday. Princess Katherine, for whom her father had already ordered the full paraphernalia of rockers, laundresses and a great wooden cradle, died a week later.

Elizabeth's death, coming within a year of Prince Arthur's, shook the royal family to its core. Although no record survives of the reactions of Margaret or Mary, Henry VIII later described the loss of his beloved mother, the major figure of his childhood, as a bitter blow. For a prince not yet twelve years old, already having to cope with the great changes to his life now he was the heir to the throne of England, the impact was overwhelming. He spent the rest of his life looking for a woman who could replace her, finding elements of Elizabeth in several of his wives, but no one who could truly match her memory.

Henry VII's suffering was overwhelming. He had married Elizabeth out of dynastic necessity, but she had committed to their union wholeheartedly, supporting him through all the crises posed by successive attempts to unseat him, offering the kind of companionship that he never knew during the long years of exile. The king shut himself away, refusing to eat or drink for several days and then falling victim to a severe throat infection which lasted for weeks. He did not return to a semblance of normal life until the end of March 1503. The tragedies of the preceding twelve months took a permanent toll on his already dubious health and his appearance. His interesting, enigmatic face became haggard and pale, the fair, curly hair that crowned it thin and grey. Yet he would live for another six years, driven by the determination to ensure that his surviving son inherited a stable country with efficient government and adequate financial resources.

The king's priority in the spring and early summer of 1503 was, however, his elder daughter. Margaret's time in England was drawing to a close. As Queen of Scots, it was time for her to embrace a new role and new kingdom in person. The final arrangements for her departure were supervised by Margaret Beaufort, her grandmother, and by the king himself. There was no question that she would leave England in a rush, inadequately supplied for her new role. Henry VII was proud that his daughter was a queen and spent lavishly on furnishings and clothing, and a huge sum on jewels. Even

Margaret's horses looked splendid. Their collars, bridles, stirrups of copper and gilt and harnesses of black and crimson velvet were all duly recorded. Henry lost no opportunity to use Margaret's possessions as symbols that would proclaim her importance and the prestige of his dynasty. Most magnificent of all was Margaret's bed 'of cloth of gold estate', its valance lined with yellow damask, a silk-and-gold fringe, crimson sarcenet curtains and a counterpane made of fifteen yards of green velvet. Cocooned in this luxury, the queen would be able to keep out the chill of Scottish winter nights.

The royal bed was one of two outstanding pieces in Margaret's inventory. Equally grand was the litter in which she would travel for most of her journey north, with its cloth-of-gold covering. The royal accounts also reveal her father's meticulous attention to detail.

No item was too small to be overlooked, including pins, needles and threads. There were warrants for hose, shoes, sheets and bedclothes, for dresses, hoods, riding boots and slippers as well as altar cloths and a needlework crucifix. Margaret's staff were to be appropriately arrayed, her ladies in gowns of damask and velvet while her two footmen were supplied with doublets of black velvet and green damask, with 'the portcullis crowned' (Henry VII's badge), jackets of green and white cloth of gold, crimson hose, two hats and two bonnets and a generous twelve pairs of shoes.[8]

Everywhere, the red rose of Lancaster (largely an invention of the king himself, to balance the white rose of York) was prominently featured. There was nothing drab in this parade of material wealth. It was all glitter and gold, the sheen of velvet and silk, the rich colours of crimson and green and yellow.

But which of the ladies of the court would travel with Margaret to support her as Queen of Scots? This was a question of immediate significance following the death of Elizabeth of York and further complicated by the uncertain position of Katherine of Aragon now that she was a childless widow. It seems likely that the late queen and her mother-in-law had collaborated on the staffing of Margaret's household but that there were considerable changes when Elizabeth died. There was an obligation to find roles for great ladies suddenly left without their mistress and their experience was, in itself, important. Margaret was only thirteen and would benefit from their guidance and the comforting continuity they represented. Lady Eleanor Verney, chief lady-in-waiting to Elizabeth of York, was the wife of Margaret's recently appointed Lord Chamberlain, Sir Ralph Verney. She was accustomed to travelling with Elizabeth and would now serve her daughter in Scotland. Verney himself knew something of the Scottish court and the more detailed aspects of the marriage settlement between James IV and Margaret, as he had participated in some of the negotiations. At least two other ladies, Eleanor Jones and Elizabeth Denton, who had been lady mistress of the royal nursery, accompanied Margaret on her journey.

A similar continuity of personnel was evident on the male side of Margaret's household. Wardrobe staff, who had the responsibility of managing all aspects of the sourcing and care of the queen's clothing, were picked from among those who had served her mother. Then there were chaplains and yeomen who had served in Elizabeth of York's chamber and who would have been known, at least by sight, to Margaret herself.[9] Despite the popular conception of an untried young girl, scarcely out of childhood, being sacrificed on the altar of dynastic ambition, Margaret certainly did not go to Scotland without the comforting presence of a number of ladies and

gentlemen that she had known since her earliest childhood.
Margaret was well prepared and well supported during her
journey and after her arrival. This did not, as we shall see,
mean that things always went smoothly.

By 27 June 1503, all was ready for Margaret's departure.
Henry VII and his daughter left Richmond for her grandmother's estate, Collyweston in Northamptonshire. The first
stage of her journey had begun. The Queen of Scots would
not see the south of England again for thirteen years. In fact,
she may well have believed that she would never return.

5

A Royal Progress

'Then came the Queen richly arrayed in a gown of cloth of gold, a rich collar of precious stones and a girdle wrought of gold hanging down to the earth. The countess of Surrey bore her train, a gentleman usher helping her.'

Margaret attends mass in York Minster
on Sunday, 16 July 1503

Margaret Beaufort's impressive home, the favourite of many estates she had been granted by her son, lay a few miles south of the market town of Stamford, on the Great North Road in the county of Northamptonshire. It was originally a pleasant manor house, built by Sir William Porter in the early fifteenth century, a typical if unpretentious country seat. During the Wars of the Roses the house was acquired first by the Kingmaker, the earl of Warwick, and then passed to his son-in-law, Edward IV's younger brother, George, duke of Clarence. But after Clarence's arrest for treason and his mysterious death in the Tower of London in 1478, the house became crown property. From 1499 onwards it was Margaret Beaufort's main residence and she effected a transformation from country house to a veritable palace, fit for a queen – which Margaret was, in all but name. In the words of Margaret's most recent biographer, Nicola Tallis, 'she spent staggering sums on the property, in so doing ensuring that the magnificence of Collyweston ... inspired awe in those who visited'.[1] From the moment they saw its two imposing clockhouses as they neared the main entrance, visitors would have known that this was hardly the quiet rural home of an elderly noblewoman. From its lavishly furnished interior to its gorgeous gardens, everything about Collyweston shouted money and power, though not in a vulgar way. Margaret Beaufort was a woman of taste and discernment, her experience sharpened by years of political and personal uncertainty. Small wonder, then, that she now found an outlet for all the anxiety of past times in creating a home that reflected her personal tastes and the security she felt, at last, in her son's hold on England. It was in the sumptuous surroundings of Collyweston's Presence Chamber, well-stocked library and luxurious private apartments that the final preparations were made for Margaret Tudor's journey to Scotland. The Queen of Scots would also have heard mass in her grandmother's chapel, where a feast of colourful altar cloths and gleaming, bejewelled religious plate reminded worshippers of God's splendour and Margaret's wealth.

The king's mother had already played a significant part in the lives of her grandchildren because of her frequent presence at court on family occasions. They seem to have held her in great affection, despite her ascetic appearance. Her long face, its narrowness accentuated by old age, and her desire to demonstrate her religious faith has given us an image of a woman who looked more like a nun than a queen. Her clothes are sombre widow's weeds, her hands held together in prayer. The face is contemplative but with a hint of hardness behind the eyes and around the mouth. This would not have been the rosy-cheeked granny of later fairy tales, bouncing children on her knee. If she did tell Margaret and her siblings stories, they would have been based on the Bible rather than folklore. Nevertheless, she seems to have been loved as well as respected. And her granddaughter could be confident that Margaret Beaufort would have left nothing to chance in supervising all the last-minute details of the most momentous journey she would ever undertake.

So it was from Collyweston, in the heart of England, that Margaret Tudor set off on 8 July 1503. She bade a dignified and poignant farewell to her father and grandmother that day. Displays of public emotion would have been unseemly, so if any tears were shed they were in private. Margaret knew better than to show any girlish weakness while being publicly scrutinized. Her father had given her a beautiful prayer book, inscribed from 'your kind and loving father'. He asked her to pray for him and reminded her that, 'at all times', she carried with her God's blessing and his own. Henry VII was an affectionate father but he knew what he was asking of his elder daughter. At thirteen years old, she was about to undergo a huge change in her life, having passed, as did other aristocratic women, from childhood to womanhood at the age of twelve. Her marriage to James IV of Scotland would cement relations between two neighbours always on the brink of war and bring, at least for a while, the promise of peace. Margaret had been prepared for this moment all her childhood. But both she and Henry VII knew, as she rode away on her palfrey and disappeared from his sight, that it was unlikely they would ever see each other again.

For the next three weeks of a carefully planned itinerary, Margaret would be relentlessly on public view. She was the living image of Henry VII's success, carrying, on her slim shoulders, the responsibility of showing the towns and boroughs of the Midlands and north of England, whose loyalty to the crown might still be suspect, that the Tudor dynasty was powerful and here to stay. Margaret's journey is often passed over in a few sentences in general histories of the Tudors but it was the most magnificent royal progress of the sixteenth century, far surpassing in significance and symbolism the later, better-known summer progresses of Henry VIII and Elizabeth I. Here was a deftly produced piece of theatre, a moving pageant with a young girl as its star. The responsibility laid upon her and the awareness of the reaction she aroused stayed with Margaret for the rest of her life. In adversity – and she would face plenty of that – she clung to the memory of the summer of 1503. No one could outshine Margaret, the celebrity of her day. She was feted at every town she entered, surrounded by the great men and ladies of the English shires, who vied with each other to look the most stunningly arrayed in their silks and velvets, their bejewelled badges of office glittering in the sun. Margaret's entourage made sure that she looked her best, whether mounted or sitting in her litter, covered with cloth of gold. Makeup and wardrobe were changed before each official entry as Margaret, dripping with precious stones, carried herself like the queen she now was.

Yet the intention was not just entertainment. Politics and drama were intertwined in both her old and new countries. Once she crossed the border, the Scottish aristocracy assumed the roles of their English counterparts. We are fortunate to have a full description of all of this from John Young, the Somerset herald who accompanied the royal party.[2] Little is known personally of this diligent observer, who was at pains to do justice to the impressiveness of the spectacle he witnessed without favouring the efforts of one country over the other, but he was able to convey brilliance and colour effectively. He was no political commentator. That was not his purpose. But he did emphasize the imagery which was intended to demonstrate the unity that the marriage would bring about.

While providing detailed lists of all the dignitaries who came out to greet Margaret, Young also gives descriptions that are sensory and immediate, full of sights and sounds. Musicians and actors accompanied Margaret, going before her as she entered and left the different towns on her route. Henry Glasebury, marshal of the minstrels, and John English, leader of a company of players, were responsible for the music and performance aspects of each stage. Their efforts, according to the Somerset herald, were 'a joy for to see and hear'.[3]

The young queen was accompanied by various dignitaries on all the stages of her journey, mostly local magnates who joined for the space of a few days as the route passed through towns closest to their estates. There was a core of ladies and gentlemen who were with her for the entire three weeks before she crossed the border into Scotland. Among them was Andrew Forman, bishop of Murray, senior representative from her new country and one of the chief architects of the treaties that underpinned her marriage. The overall responsibility for delivering Margaret safely to her husband, for ensuring that everything went smoothly and met the aims of Henry VII from both a personal and political perspective, fell to Thomas Howard, earl of Surrey, a man who would figure large in Margaret's life, both in the joyful summer of 1503 and ten years later, in wholly different circumstances.

Surrey was sixty years old, a veteran soldier and diplomat. But given his chequered past he was by no means an obvious choice to take charge of the first Tudor princess on such an important occasion. He was the son of John Howard, first duke of Norfolk, who came from the junior branch of the Mowbray family, who had long held the title. Given their prominence and overweening pride in themselves during the sixteenth century, it is easy to forget that the Howards were something of an upstart family who had risen comparatively recently, at the expense of the Pastons, in Norfolk. During the Wars of the Roses the Howards had been squarely on the Yorkist side and were especially loyal supporters of Richard III. It has even been suggested that Surrey and his father might have been implicated in the murders of Edward V and his younger brother, as they stood to benefit from the convenient disappearance of Richard, duke of York, who had married Anne Mowbray, thus snuffing out the Howards' last chance of gaining their kinswoman's lands.[4] Certainly, they were mocked for their unwavering support for Richard III in the famous couplet circulating before the Battle of Bosworth attacking John Howard: 'Jockey of Norfolk be not so bold, for Dickon thy master is bought and sold.'

John Howard was killed at Bosworth, the battle's highest-born casualty after the king himself. Thomas, his son, was wounded and taken prisoner. Attainted in Henry VII's first Parliament and stripped of all his lands and titles, he languished for three years in the Tower of London. This period of imprisonment brought about a reflection on where his best interest actually lay. Though there might be no great certainty for the longer term, Surrey decided not to risk an extended incarceration, or perhaps worse, when he declined to participate in the earl of Lincoln's rebellion against Henry VII in 1487. Sufficiently convinced by this change of heart and ever mindful of the continuing need to mend fences with erstwhile Yorkist supporters, the king seems to have accepted that Surrey could become a valuable supporter of the new dynasty, if properly managed. He restored the earl to his title in May 1489 but withheld most of the Howard lands. Instead, Surrey would have to prove himself in the field and at the negotiating table.

It was a shrewd compromise, typical of Henry VII's approach to government. Surrey spent ten years in the north of England, putting down rebellions in Yorkshire and effectively governing the region from his residence in

Sheriff Hutton Castle. He was instrumental in bringing the border warfare of 1497 to a stalemate that resulted in James IV's abandonment of Perkin Warbeck. His Yorkist past was now fully forgiven, if not entirely forgotten, and Henry VII recalled him to court in 1499. The king seems to have viewed Surrey's main contribution to government as likely to be in the diplomatic sphere. He accompanied Henry on a visit to France and was also involved in the negotiations for the marriage of Prince Arthur to Katherine of Aragon. Steadily, his lands in Norfolk were restored to him, as Henry VII recognized his continuing loyalty and service. By the time he left Collyweston with Margaret Tudor in July 1503, Surrey was a wealthy man. He was also the father of eleven surviving children from two marriages. His second wife, Agnes Tilney, and one of their daughters accompanied him on the road to Scotland. Agnes would go on to acquire unwonted notoriety nearly forty years later as the step-grandmother of Henry VIII's fifth wife, Katherine Howard, when the goings-on among the girls nominally in her care at her Sussex home were exposed in all their prurient detail. Yet in 1503, as the countess of Surrey, she seemed a very proper lady to be given oversight of Margaret and her train.

Her husband was no doubt aware of the honour – as well as the duties – of his position as Margaret's protector but there are indications that he found certain aspects of it irksome. Surrey had little empathy for a thirteen-year-old girl, even if she was a queen. He belonged to the male world of the later Middle Ages, with its emphasis on chivalric values and manly pursuits. Of course, pageantry and display were very much a part of this world and fair ladies were to play their part, but only as a supporting act. It might have been different if the earl were escorting a prince in the same circumstances. He would have got along famously with the duke of York, Margaret's younger brother. It is not clear when tension between Surrey and Margaret first surfaced, but once she got to Edinburgh she had endured quite enough of Surrey's high-handedness and disregard for her commands. Unaccustomed to being ignored, Margaret's resentment against Surrey reached its peak when she finally left England behind. It may well have begun as soon as the huge train of ladies and gentlemen, religious advisers, entertainers and servants left Collyweston, the procession's carts full of furniture, clothing and all the paraphernalia of a queen, under Surrey's peremptory orders. He knew what Henry VII required of him and if this meant irritating a slip of a girl, he did not much care.

Grantham in Lincolnshire was the first stop on Margaret's journey. She left there on 10 July and then traversed Nottinghamshire, stopping at Newark, Tuxford and Scrooby before entering Yorkshire, where she stayed overnight in Doncaster and Pontefract. After dining at Tadcaster, she entered York on the evening of 15 July. It was the most important city in the north of England, proud of its past, but its older citizens, who had supported Richard III and the Yorkists, might well have had reservations about the daughter of a new dynasty, even one that had striven mightily to unify the kingdom and move on from the deep divisions of the fifteenth century. Margaret's time in York had therefore a significance beyond outward display and was superbly stage-managed.

As she left Tadcaster, Margaret was met by Lord and Lady Latimer, accompanied by fifty ladies and gentlemen on horseback, all wearing the Latimer livery, as well as the two sheriffs of the city of York and 'many officers of the town'. They were soon joined by Lord Scrope of Bolton and Lady Conyars. But none of these could compete with the most important regional aristocrat, the earl of Northumberland, who met the Queen of Scots two miles outside the gates of York and accompanied her for much of the rest of her journey in England. The Somerset herald has left us a wonderful description of Northumberland which amply illustrates how the representative of the most important family in northern England took the opportunity to make a stunning statement about his position. What John Young probably did not appreciate was the compelling reason Northumberland had for doing so.

The earl was:

> well-horsed upon a fair courser, with a foot-cloth to the ground of crimson velvet, all bordered of orfèvrerie [a French word for goldsmith's work, which, in this case, refers to gold and silver embroidery]; his arms very rich in many places upon his saddle and harness, his stirrups gilt, himself arrayed of a gown of the said crimson. At the opening of his sleeves and the collar, a great border of stones. His boots of velvet black, his spurs gilt, and in many places he made gambades, pleasant for to see.[5]

The gambade was a low leap of a horse, in which all four feet leave the ground. But it was not just Northumberland himself, resplendent in his velvet, gold and jewels on his prancing horse, that caught the eye. His two footmen, the master of his horse, a company of 'many noble knights', his own herald and numerous other gentlemen wearing the earl's livery reflected his status and wealth. In all, there were 300 horsemen. Margaret is said to have been well pleased with this colourful display and the earl's accomplished horsemanship. Whether she knew much about Northumberland's real power is another matter. For, in truth, the earl was by no means the master of the north of England that he would have liked observers of this performance to believe. And his situation is revealing of how the first two Tudor monarchs sought to control the potential threat of a family that had wavered in its support for the crown since the early 1400s and would continue to do so into the middle of the seventeenth century.

Henry Algernon Percy, the fifth earl of Northumberland, was a young man of twenty-five in 1503 and recently married to Catherine Spencer, the daughter of a Devon knight. It was perhaps not the impressive match that might have been expected for a nobleman of his pedigree but it was the first step in re-establishing the local influence of the Percys, which had been brutally interrupted by the murder of Henry Percy's father, the fourth earl, when the boy was only eleven years old. The young earl was brought up at court in the south, while responsibility for administering the north of England fell to a council led by the earl of Surrey, ruling in the name of the duke of York, Margaret's younger brother. This was, of course, the very same earl of Surrey who now supervised Margaret's journey to Scotland. Surrey may have been as much a target for Northumberland's show of money and men as Margaret herself was. If so, it would not bring about any real change. Northumberland had already attained his majority and yet other men still governed the north of England. Surrey's role passed to the Archbishop of York, Thomas Savage, which essentially meant that the fifth earl was unable to recover the standing of the Percy family. He was a figurehead, albeit a very rich one. Predictably, his resentment of this type of insult festered. Less than a year after he welcomed Margaret Tudor to York, his men tangled with the archbishop's in an unseemly affray at Fulford, on the outskirts of the city, in which he was personally assaulted. In 1505 he would abduct Elizabeth Hastings, a wealthy Yorkshire heiress, who inconveniently died in his custody. Beneath his colourful attire and show of chivalry in the summer of 1503 was an insecure and resentful young man. He had been given the office of warden of the West Marches for his part in the ceremonial surrounding Margaret's time in the north of England, but it was only a temporary appointment, and was rescinded shortly afterwards.

For the present, however, he rode in front of Margaret's litter as she entered York through Micklegate Bar, with trumpets sounding a fanfare. Waiting to receive her were the lord mayor, Sir John Guillot, wearing crimson satin, and his aldermen, resplendent in their scarlet gowns. The procession wound through the city streets, watched by a huge crowd. People had vied for the best vantage points: 'All the windows were so full of nobles, ladies, gentlemen, damsels, burgesses and others, in so great a multitude, that it was a fair sight for to see.'[6] It took a full two hours for Margaret to reach York Minster, where she was greeted by the Archbishop of York and the bishop of Durham. Margaret kissed the cross that stood near to the font and then made an offering. Finally, she was able to retire to the archbishop's palace, with all the bells of the city's churches ringing out to acknowledge her.

The high point of Margaret's time in York came the next day, Sunday, 16 July. Wearing cloth of gold (as did the earl of Northumberland, who continued in prominent attendance on her), with a train so long that the countess of Surrey needed a gentleman usher to help her carry it, Margaret heard High Mass at the sumptuously decorated altar of the Minster. Young said that there were so many people in the church that it was impossible for them to be numbered. Perhaps he exaggerated for effect, but it must, nevertheless, have been a memorable sight. Margaret again made an offering after the mass, which she took from the earl of Surrey. Then, as now, royalty did not carry money.

The ceremonies were not yet over for a princess who had been constantly on show for two days. Back at the archbishop's palace, she received the countess of Northumberland, kissing her in welcome, as was the custom in England. Thomas Savage himself held open house for his many high-ranking visitors. Given their numbers, it must have been an enormous expense. Throughout the dinner that followed this reception music played and the company clearly enjoyed themselves.

Margaret left York on 17 July, again in formal procession, the mayor taking his leave outside the city walls. She continued north, making a leisurely journey through Yorkshire and then on to Durham, where her entry almost matched that in York for splendour and public interest. Once more, she changed her clothing before entering the town and again Northumberland was with her. This time he wore: 'a goodly gown of tinsel [cloth of silver], furred with ermine'. Clearly he was willing to put up with any discomfort that might ensue from wearing furs in the middle of summer. Once again, the ermine denoted his wealth and station in the eyes of the world. At Durham the bishop entertained as the Archbishop of York had done, at his own expense, providing 'double dinner and double supper to all comers'.[7] In Newcastle, her next major stop, Margaret was greeted by children singing hymns and playing instruments. On the evening of 26 July, while Margaret was still in Newcastle, Northumberland gave a banquet which lasted until midnight, accompanied by 'games, dances, sports and songs'. The next day, she arrived at Northumberland's main residence, Alnwick Castle. There, she killed a buck with her bow in his grounds. Margaret had always been keen on archery and was, no doubt, pleased to display her prowess. A little hunting must also have made a welcome change from the rigours of endless entries, processions and public spectacle, when all eyes were on her. In the spacious park of Alnwick, with her bow and arrow for company, Margaret could, just briefly, be herself.

Two days later she was on the move again, towards her final

stop on English soil. This was the border town of Berwick-upon-Tweed. Heavily fortified, it had a chequered history, passing between Scottish and English jurisdiction as warfare between the two countries, a constant reality of life in this disputed region, ebbed and flowed. The walls and castle bore witness to Berwick's turbulent past and its winding medieval streets, together with its situation on the coast, added to its appeal. Margaret stayed in the castle, where she was received by its chatelaine, Lady Darcy. During her brief stay in Berwick, Margaret 'had great cheer' and was 'given courses of chase within the said town, with other sports of bears and dogs together'.[8] Though sounding brutal to a modern ear, this would have been considered entirely appropriate entertainment for royalty in the early sixteenth century. Margaret was not a squeamish girl. She left Berwick with a large and impressive company, headed by the Archbishop of York and the earls of Surrey and Northumberland, the latter in a jacket of beaten gold and a purple cloak with a cloth-of-gold border. It is interesting to note that the Somerset herald never reports on what Surrey was wearing, preferring to concentrate on the splendour of everyone else present. Surrey may not have been over-bothered by appearances. He was a servant of the crown with a job to do, rather than a preening aristocrat with little real power. And the first part of his task, that of escorting Margaret Tudor safely to the Scottish border, was nearly accomplished.

'The said queen, very richly arrayed and adorned with gold and precious stones, sitting in her litter richly appointed', crossed into Scotland at Lamberton Kirk on 1 August 1503. There she was received by the Archbishop of Glasgow, Robert Blackadder, and the earl of Bothwell, both of whom she knew from her betrothal ceremony in the winter. The two men knelt down before her and did obeisance to her as their queen. With them came a large gathering of lords and gentlemen, all as richly dressed as their English counterparts. Having seen Margaret conducted to a pavilion especially constructed for the occasion, where she could rest and change her clothes, the English delegation partook of the generous amount of wine and food on offer, and made ready to depart. Northumberland's days of glory were over soon enough. But for the Queen of Scots it was necessary to mount a horse and ride over rough roads to the place where she would spend her first night in Scotland, the gloomily named Fast Castle, owned by the Homes, an important if not entirely reliable Border family. Reached by a drawbridge over a narrow ravine, the castle stood high above the sea and was known more for its impregnability than its comfort. Separated from her train for the first time since she left Collyweston three weeks earlier, Margaret Tudor had a dramatic introduction to the land which was now her home. She was thirteen years and eight months old and a very different life from the one she had known lay ahead of her.

Part II

The Queen of Scots, 1503–13

6

The King Comes Calling

'The king came arrayed of a jacket of crimson velvet
bordered with cloth of gold. His lyre behind his back,
his beard something long.'

Margaret's first sight of King James IV of Scotland,
described by Somerset Herald

On 2 August, Margaret emerged from the remoteness of Fast Castle and rejoined the rest of her train, who had spent the night in the more welcoming surroundings of Coldingham Priory. She then journeyed west to Haddington, a distance of nearly twenty-six miles. This would have been a full day's ride, through the lovely countryside of the Borders. The route took her past Dunbar Castle, which sounded its cannons to acknowledge her. Everywhere, there were crowds of people curious to see her. Sometimes a passage had to be made for her by force and the onlookers were rowdy, 'bringing with them plenty of drink'.[1] Over one thousand Scots had assembled at Lamberton Kirk when Margaret crossed into Scotland and their interest was clearly not diminished the following day. There had not been a queen consort of Scotland for sixteen years, since Margaret of Denmark's death in 1487, and the arrival of a young English queen certainly attracted attention, even if a considerable part of her attraction was the festive air of her procession and the availability of copious quantities of alcohol. Margaret spent the night in the more decorous company of the nuns of St Mary's Priory, just outside Haddington. This beautiful and ancient town was the first in Scotland to be given a charter as a Royal Burgh in the 1130s.[2] The priory was itself old, having been founded in 1158 by Ada, widow of Henry, earl of Northumberland, and Huntingdon, the younger son of King David I of Scotland.[3]

The nuns of Haddington were a Cistercian house. They owed their existence to the prestige attached to Cistercianism in the twelfth century but although the priory at Haddington broadly followed the rules of the order of White Friars, as the Cistercians were popularly known, it had never been under the jurisdiction of Cîteaux, the headquarters of the order in Burgundy. The nuns had acquired extensive property in the area, which should have given them financial security, but the situation of Haddington, so close to the English border, meant that the nuns were frequently victims of the depredations of war. If these hardships were not enough, the situation of the priory, on the left bank of the River Tyne, exposed it to the dangers of flooding, and a series of disputes with the burgh authorities in Haddington over payments which were due from the town's revenues soured relations between the nuns and local officials. There was also wrangling between the nuns and the vicars of various local churches over income which the priory claimed as its right. By the time of Margaret's visit, the nuns were experienced in fighting their corner and also in fulfilling the role of genteel boarding house for women of high status.[4]

The nuns of St Mary's in 1503 seem to have been good hostesses. Margaret left the next day, her company having had 'great cheer', and she 'was seen of the people in great mirth' as she departed.

From Haddington, Margaret travelled next to Dalkeith Castle, the seat of the earls of Morton. She was still performing the ritual of changing her wardrobe before these public entries in Scotland, as she had done in England: 'Half a mile nigh to the said town she appointed her richly, and her ladies and lords, and others of her company did the same.'[5] Waiting to meet her at the gate of his castle was its lord, John Douglas, second earl of Morton. Accompanied by many gentlemen, he made the reverential gesture of presenting her with the keys of the castle, to which she was welcomed as its lady and mistress. Morton's wife, Janet Crichton, waited between the inner and outer gate of the castle and knelt before the girl who was now her queen. Margaret raised her up and kissed her, before entering the castle's living quarters. But though her chamber was well appointed and her surroundings comfortable, it is unlikely that she found much time to relax. Despite the lack of any official announcement, Margaret knew that she was expecting a very important caller.

In the true romance of chivalry, of which both James IV and his future brother-in-law, Henry VIII, were enthusiasts, the King of Scots just happened to be out hunting in the neighbourhood of Dalkeith Castle when he heard of Margaret's arrival. As any ardent bridegroom might, he hastened to make a surprise visit. True, he was splendidly attired in a red velvet coat edged with cloth of gold and there was a lyre slung over his back, an unusual accessory for a casual hunting trip. He was also supported by all the great men of Scotland, his younger brother, Alexander, the Archbishop of St Andrews and the leading earls, Huntly, Argyll and Lennox. This was a carefully assembled group of dignitaries. Yet convention dictated that delighted astonishment at the king's sudden appearance was to be exhibited by Margaret and her party and that James was to be equally pleased with this unexpected opportunity to meet his young queen. It was all a pleasant game, albeit one that had been meticulously arranged in advance. It would hardly have been acceptable for Margaret to be genuinely unprepared for James's arrival.

They met at the door of Margaret's chamber, where 'he and she made great reverences the one to the other', James bowing low and Margaret curtseying deeply. James had done her the great honour of baring his head 'and they kissed together and [he] in likewise kissed the ladies ... and he in especial welcomed the earl of Surrey very heartily'.[6] These courtesies concluded, James and Margaret held their first private conversation apart from the rest of the company, the king continuing bare-headed and Margaret polite but animated, clearly, at least from the perspective of Somerset Herald, well able to deal with the situation – as she should have been, since she had been in training for this moment for much of her young life. A meal was then served, the couple washing their hands together and then sitting down to watch the entertainment that accompanied their dining. Supper was followed by further music and dancing, Margaret taking the floor with the countess of Surrey to demonstrate her skills as a dancer to James. Then the king took his leave, 'for it was late, and he went to his bed in Edinburgh very well content of so fair a meeting'.[7] As well he might have been, for his first meeting with Margaret, so expertly stage-managed, had gone without a hitch. What they privately thought of each other after this introduction we do not know.

James had seen enough to reassure himself that Margaret could well play the accomplished consort in public, though he could not fail to have noticed that she was not yet mature physically. The drawing said to be of Margaret at this age shows a serious and thin-faced girl, with a greater resemblance to her father than her mother. Though not unattractive, she appears to have lacked the beauty of her sister, Mary, who looked more like their mother, Elizabeth of

York. Margaret would not grow to be tall and frequent child-bearing made her stout but at this stage she seems to have borne out Henry VII's much earlier comment that she was small for her age. The King of Scots, on the other hand, so much her senior, was at the peak of his physical prowess. He was of middle height, high-spirited, athletic and fashionable, with shoulder-length reddish-brown hair. Margaret must have been relieved to find him charming and supportive. But what did she really know about this Scottish king with the long beard and his small kingdom, now her home, on the northern fringes of Europe?

James IV was thirty years old at the time of this introduction to his English wife, who was barely in her teens. His early life and upbringing had been very different from that of Margaret's father, Henry VII, but his path to the throne, if much shorter, was no less dramatic. He was born in 1473 in Stirling Castle, the eldest of three sons of James III of Scotland and Margaret of Denmark. It is worth noting that Margaret of Denmark was just twelve when she married, even younger than the daughter-in-law she never knew. She had admirably fulfilled the expectations of a queen consort and was a loving mother to her boys, who spent much of their time with her at Stirling. By the early 1480s, however, the royal marriage was running into trouble. The fact that the couple spent much of their time apart cannot have helped, even if it was not at all uncommon among European royalty at the time. But there were other problems. James III's personality and his policies made him unpopular, above all with the leading families in Scotland, who objected to his attempts to end the constant border warfare by alliance, rather than war, with England. They also resented his apparent preference for the company of courtiers who were considered to be low-born. James III lacked the sociability his son would later exhibit, preferring to spend his time in Edinburgh instead of travelling widely in his realm.

Whatever these perceived failings, he was a cultured man, keen on music, literature and architecture, and he did inspire loyalty in some senior advisers, notably his bishop of Aberdeen, William Elphinstone. He also cared about his dynasty sufficiently to commission the marvellous panel paintings in the Royal Collection, now on display at the National Gallery of Scotland, showing his family at worship. Margaret of Denmark, dressed in a beaded robe edged lavishly with ermine, is shown at prayer, guarded by the figure of St George, a saint more often identified with England than Scotland.[8] On a separate panel are her husband and eldest son, watched over by St Andrew. Both look suitably serious. But the little prince standing behind his father had more reason than the solemnity of religion to look glum. When he was nine a revolt led by James III's nearest brother, the duke of Albany, had compromised Margaret and her eldest son so badly in the eyes of the king that the rift was never repaired.

In fact, the queen seems to have become involved in an effort to save her husband's throne and safeguard young James's position, but her husband apparently did not see it that way. Contact was broken off, with the prince staying at Stirling with his mother. His peaceful childhood had come to an abrupt end. There was to be no reconciliation with his father, who took no interest in his education and, when Queen Margaret died in 1486, the prince and his two brothers were still at Stirling, under the guardianship of James Shaw, the keeper of the castle. Even more alarmingly, after his mother's death, it looked as though Prince James might be sidelined altogether. The king raised James's younger brother, the marquess of Ormonde, to the rank of duke of Ross and pursued a marriage for him with Princess Katherine of York, one of Edward IV's many daughters. There was no word of any such match for his eldest son.[9]

James III never really forgave those involved in the unsettling events of 1482, which had seen him imprisoned in his own castle in Edinburgh. Nevertheless, he was still king six years later, though discontent was again mounting among his nobility. Their objections to his style of government had never gone away and they had been watching with interest the advent of a new dynasty in England, in what must have seemed to them remarkable circumstances. Did they not have an attractive alternative to an unpopular king in the person of an overlooked heir who might be tempted to throw his lot, then so uncertain, in with them? We do not know what discussions were held or how contact was made, but James III learned in February 1488 that his eldest son had slipped away from Stirling Castle without permission, to join a growing band of rebels. If it was a blow to James III, it was also an irrevocable act on the part of his heir, who was just fifteen years old.

After unsuccessful negotiations and the gathering of sizeable forces by both the king and those opposing him, a military campaign ensued in the summer of 1488. At first it went badly for the rebels and young James found himself in flight from his father. But the tide turned conclusively on 11 June 1488, when the opposing armies met at Sauchieburn, close to the site of Robert Bruce's great victory against the English at Bannockburn. James III wanted a decisive victory. He rode into battle carrying Robert Bruce's sword and taking with him a chest which contained about a third of his annual income, presumably as some sort of financial surety in case the day went against him. Neither the sword nor the money did him any good. In circumstances that will never really be known, James III met his death. The most likely explanation is that the fighting was going against him and he was advised to leave the field but did not succeed in getting away. The Scottish chroniclers told fanciful stories about the king lying injured at a mill and asking for a priest, who, when he arrived, turned out to be an assassin and despatched him before he could be rescued. Only two things are certain: that James III died on or near the battlefield and that his son had given explicit orders that he was not to be harmed. These were clearly disobeyed but those responsible for his father's death were never brought to justice or identified. That James IV felt guilt for the murder of his father, an anointed monarch, is beyond doubt. He later wore an iron belt to which he added weight every year, as a penance. It seems unlikely that he wore this cumbersome accessory all the time, but the gesture was appreciated by his subjects.

Whatever the unpleasant truth behind his father's demise, there was also no doubt that James IV, at fifteen years old, was now king. He signed his first Royal Charter the day after Sauchieburn. Towards the end of June, he was taken to the Abbey of Cambuskenneth, on the northern bank of the River Forth, to attend the internment of James III. Margaret of Denmark was buried there and her husband was laid to rest beside her. The rift that had destroyed their marriage was healed in death. Their son would carry on the Stewart line. But for some time he would be dependent on the great families of the Borders who had put him on the throne. Like Henry VII in England, he had no experience of government. Like every Stewart monarch between 1406 and 1625, James IV came to the throne as a minor. Others would rule in his name, ostensibly until he reached his majority at the age of twenty-five.

In reality, James IV became actively involved in government well before that time. His intelligence and self-confidence made him a quick learner. He also became an inveterate womanizer, with a brood of illegitimate children. Those by

well-born ladies he freely acknowledged and he made financial provision for them. Yet these distractions and three serious
relationships with ladies of the court, Marion Boyd, Margaret
Drummond and Janet Kennedy (his mistress when he married
Margaret Tudor), never got in the way of his overall aim.
Possessed of a fine intellect and strong will, he was determined
that his country should make its mark in Europe and that, as
its king, he would not cede power to favourites. He would bind
the nobility to him, at a cultured, vibrant Renaissance court.
By 1503, he knew well that such a court needed a queen to
grace it and, of course, to bear him children. Margaret Tudor
was marrying a remarkable man.

The challenges that James IV faced in realizing his ambitions
were considerable. His was a small, poor country, regarded as
a chilly outpost by much of the rest of Europe. Its population
at the beginning of the sixteenth century was probably, at
the most, around 700,000, compared to a figure of around
3 million for England. It had only three towns of any size.
Edinburgh, the capital, with a population estimated to be
around 12,000, was by far the largest, though only a quarter
the size of London. Much smaller were Aberdeen, at 4,000,
and Glasgow, at a mere 2,500. It was an overwhelmingly
rural society, divided between the prosperous Lowlands of
the south and the rugged Highlands of the north and west.
Local loyalties were paramount. The Highlands were ruled
by clan chieftains who did not want interference from a king
in Edinburgh. This was a Gaelic-speaking area; culturally and
historically, it had more in common with Ireland, its near-
neighbour across the sea, than it did with lowland Scotland.
In the Borders no one, least of all a Stewart king from
the Lothians, could afford to fall out with the Homes, the

Hepburns or the Douglases, though James IV would soon have become aware of the tensions within different branches of these mighty lords. A canny monarch might exploit these to his advantage, without resorting to the extreme solution of his grandfather, James II, who stabbed Earl William of the Black Douglases in the neck during a heated argument about the latter's loyalty after dinner in Stirling Castle in 1452. If this initial blow did not kill the earl, the twenty-six stab wounds inflicted on him by the king's eager courtiers certainly finished him off. James IV would not follow such a path. He wanted to attract and contain would-be opponents, not murder them.

This was bound to be a long-term objective and not one that was likely to be achieved smoothly. But first he had to be crowned. The ceremony took place at Scone on 24 June 1488, barely two weeks after his father's murder and several days before James III's burial. Here was a chance for the king to show himself off in a ceremony full of symbolism and historical resonance, since the date was the anniversary of the Battle of Bannockburn and this was the first coronation for sixty years at a site regarded as sacred to Scotland and its kings. James rode on a horse decked in velvet and changed into a series of blue, black and crimson satin doublets at different stages of the ceremony, to underline his magnificence and prestige. Proceedings were conducted by the bishops of Dunkeld and Glasgow, and it was probably the latter, Robert Blackadder, who actually placed the crown on the young king's head.[10] James then took his coronation oath, to be 'a loving father to the people ... loyal and true to God and the Holy Church and to the three estates of my realm'. The obligation to act as a loving father to an entire country was a sobering one for a fifteen-year-old and a stark reminder of the responsibilities he now faced.

James had much to learn and in the first few months of

his reign he was constantly on the move. This was how he grew to understand his subjects and his realm. It must have been fascinating for a teenager who had spent almost all of his life inside the walls of Stirling Castle. He began what would become a regular round of the justice ayres, or assizes, at which Scottish kings regularly dispensed justice. The judicial system in Scotland was (and, in many respects, remains) quite different from that of England. It is hard to imagine the Tudor monarchs visiting all points of their realm and giving legal judgements on a frequent basis. Their governance and justice was centred firmly on London well before the early sixteenth century, based on a civil service and judiciary that was already well developed. But in Scotland these aspects of kingship were much more personal and the justice ayres allowed the Scots to see their king as a real, flesh-and-blood monarch, not some distant glittering figure partly hidden beneath a canopy of state. James IV soon came to relish this distinctive aspect of his role. There is no doubt that he was affable and that his subjects were eager to get close to their young king, to meet him in person, even to touch him. Henry VIII, who had a morbid fear of the diseases that could be caught from close contact, would have found such obligations not just irksome, but positively alarming.[11]

Many of James IV's later interests were piqued in these early phases of his rule. At Leith, Edinburgh's port, he watched the ships and learned about naval warfare on his first visit, not long after his coronation. The navy would become a lifelong passion, as would all things military, especially when it came to the latest technology. The restless boy who had been pent up in Stirling for so long now began to develop quickly. So much was new to him and, for the rest of his life, he would be unable to resist the allure of novelty. It would help him demonstrate to the wider world that he was truly a European king.

In foreign policy, however, he was more traditional. The 'Auld Alliance' with France, the famous 'antidote to the English', lay at the heart of his strategy. But he also courted the recently established Catholic Kings, Ferdinand of Aragon and Isabella of Castile, who now ruled Spain. A considerable amount of what we know about Scotland in these last years of the fifteenth century comes from Pedro de Ayala, the Spanish diplomat who spent some time in the 1490s at the Scottish court, and his Italian friend, the Venetian ambassador Andrea Trevisano, who knew Ayala when he moved south to London. It was from Ayala that Trevisano learned the major particulars of the geography, climate and society of Scotland. The kingdom was, he said, 'very rainy' but the people were welcoming and hospitable. 'The inhabitants of the country are called the wild or savage Scots, not, however, from the rudeness of their manners, which are extremely courteous.' They were 'extremely partial to foreigners' (a compliment seldom paid to the English then or now) and 'they all consider that there is no higher duty in the world than to love and defend their crown'. The nobility lived well, in 'excellent houses, built for the most part in the Italian manner, of hewn stone or brick, with magnificent rooms, halls, doors, galleries, chimneys and windows'. Trevisano was impressed by the ability of the Scottish kings to call rapidly on the services of up to 60,000 well-armed and trained men to support him at times of war. Such hostilities, he noted, were only ever with their neighbours, the English.[12]

Here, Trevisano had hit upon an inescapable truth. For James IV and his advisers, the relationship with England was a key part of Scottish policy, with profound implications for the crown. James III's desire to ensure peace by an alliance with England was merely one in a long line of attempts to stabilize relations between the two neighbours. Yet it had enraged important elements of his nobility and was unpopular with the Scottish people. Friction intensified by geographical closeness rarely had a positive outcome for long. The fact that the English claimed suzerainty over Scotland and could demand homage from the King of Scots was always going to be a sore point. The overthrow of James III did not exactly cause panic in London, but there was considerable unease. Henry VII's hold on his throne was far from secure in 1488 and there was concern about what the new Scottish regime's attitude to England might be, or even if it would survive at all. In the year following James's accession there were a series of challenges to the men who had put him in power, from disaffected lords who felt left out. The Lennoxes, a family based around their stronghold of Dumbarton Castle in the south-west of Scotland, were particularly aggrieved, but their attempt at an uprising failed in the summer of 1489, in a campaign fought along the upper reaches of the River Forth. James acquitted himself well in these series of skirmishes, proving that he was physically brave and not so easily to be written off as someone who could, because of his age, be manipulated by rival factions. This uneasy interlude taught him much about leadership and control.

By the mid-1490s, having taken the reins of government firmly into his own hands, he was ready to confront the English. In supporting the imposter, Perkin Warbeck, who claimed to be Richard, duke of York, the younger of the two Princes in the Tower, he demonstrated just how much trouble he could cause the new Tudor dynasty. Perkin, who took the title Richard IV, was welcomed at the Scottish court and even married to Lady Katherine Gordon, a member of the important Huntly family from northern Scotland, and a distant cousin of James IV himself. It seems unlikely that James really believed Perkin's claim, despite the acknowledgement by the permanently embittered Margaret of Burgundy, sister of the Yorkist kings, that this carefully coached Fleming was, indeed, her nephew. Perhaps the King of Scots did not trouble himself to think about it too much. It was a credulous age and the tales spun by Perkin and his minders about his dramatic escape from the Tower of London and years spent in hiding might well have appealed to his host's fondness for a good adventure story.

More important was the mischief this guest could do. For almost two years, between 1495 and 1497, Perkin was a guest of the Scottish king. By the summer of 1496, James was ready to demonstrate his determination to confront England. He took an army south, with Perkin in its midst. Alas, Perkin, for all the threat of the bombastic proclamation he had just issued against Henry VII, was no fighter. He left the Scottish host after just one day. James was made of sterner stuff. He pressed on, attacking properties in the Borders, enjoying the cut-and-thrust of skirmishing. Yet all this activity had more to do with image-building than any real conviction that he could win a war against England. He simply did not have Henry VII's resources. The conflict on the Borders continued into 1497, when the Scots besieged Norham Castle in Northumberland and the English, under the earl of Surrey, attacked Ayton Castle, which was owned by the Homes. This stalemate concentrated minds in London and Edinburgh. A seven-year truce was signed at Ayton, reflecting the cold-eyed realization that neither side could win this type of war. Henry needed peace and stability after more than a decade of challenges to this throne. James now felt that he had arrived on the European scene and would be taken seriously by his fellow monarchs. In due course, negotiations could begin for him to marry the English king's elder daughter. In the meantime, he could polish the reputation of his court, make sure that his nobility were brought to heel, and enjoy himself.

The Spanish diplomat Pedro de Ayala has left us a wonderful description of James IV some five years before he married Margaret Tudor. 'He is', Ayala wrote:

> of noble stature, neither tall nor short, and as handsome in complextion and shape as a man can be. His address is very agreeable. He speaks the following foreign languages: Latin, very well; French, German, Flemish, Italian and Spanish ... His own Scotch language is as different from English as Aragonese from Castilian ... his knowledge of languages is wonderful. He is well read in the Bible and in some other devout books. He is a good historian. He has read many Latin and French histories and has profited from them, as he has a very good memory ... His deeds are as good as his words. For this reason, and because he is a very humane prince he is much loved.[13]

The Spaniard had no doubt, however, of James's complete hold on the government of his kingdom. Even allowing for some of the inevitable obsequiousness of men like Ayala towards royalty, it is an arresting portrait. Margaret was soon to experience for herself the king's kindness and the place he held in the affections of his people.

7

'Welcome of Scotland to Be Queen'

*'He ... mounted upon the palfrey of the queen (with) the
queen behind him and so rode through Edinburgh.'*

In time-honoured fashion, James IV rides with his lass
through the Scottish capital

After their first meeting, James came to see Margaret
every day, dining with her, watching her dance and
playing his lute and clavichord, a stringed keyboard
instrument. It was said that Margaret greatly appreciated his
musicianship. She was no doubt also touched by his thought-
fulness in sending her several new palfreys when her favourite
horses unfortunately perished in a stable fire during her
second night at Dalkeith Castle. The king, hearing of her distress, rushed to comfort her, 'flying as the bird that seeks her
prey', according to John Young. This description was presumably meant to underline his swiftness rather than suggesting
that there was anything predatory in his manner. Margaret was
delighted with the gesture and they spent a long time before
supper talking together. Afterwards, Sir Edward Stanley sang
a ballad, which was much enjoyed by James, who called one
of his own gentlemen to sing a duet with Sir Edward. This
served, of course, to underline the importance of goodwill

between the English and Scottish groups. James was still following the courtly script in his own dress and gesture, leaping on to his horse 'without putting his foot within the stirrup'. His jacket was of velvet, edged in crimson and furred with white.[1]

By now, the wedding ceremony itself was fast approaching. Margaret left Dalkeith Castle on 7 August, 'placed in her litter, very richly adorned, and had on a rich gown of cloth of gold, with a purfle [border] of black velvet and a rich collar of pearls and stones'.[2] James came out to meet her halfway between Dalkeith and Edinburgh, bringing with him a courser with a splendid harness of cloth of gold and crimson velvet. The horse was intended to carry both himself and Margaret into the city of Edinburgh, but when James asked one of his gentlemen to mount behind him to test how the animal would react, it became evident that it was too high-spirited to be reliable. The king could hardly risk his bride's dignity, let alone the possibility of injury, if the horse misbehaved. It was necessary to improvise. So he mounted Margaret's palfrey, which had been following her litter, and, with Margaret behind him, entered his capital. He gave explicit orders that no one should go before them, 'that it might be seen that she was well accompanied, and richly'.[3] James IV's approach speaks of both spontaneity and informality, albeit within an otherwise carefully choreographed performance. Sharing a horse with James brought Margaret Tudor into much closer physical proximity with a man than would normally have been considered proper in England before the wedding of royalty. Later he would hold her closer still, guiding her through the mass they heard together at Holyrood Abbey with his arm around her waist. He knew that she was very young, and that Scottish custom must seem unusual to her.

The entry into Edinburgh continued the chivalric theme that James loved so much. A pavilion had been set up in a field just outside the city, where Sir Patrick Hamilton and Patrick Sinclair fought for the favours of a lady. After watching them joust with spears for a while, the king eventually stepped in to separate them, with Margaret behind him. Once in Edinburgh, they were met by processions of religious orders, the Grey Friars and the Jacobins, carrying crosses and relics for the royal pair to kiss. James, so John Young reported, was punctilious in letting Margaret go first and remaining bare-headed throughout. There were still several dramatic pieces to be played out before them, on richly decorated towers especially constructed for the entry, one of which had angels 'singing joyously for the coming of so noble a lady'. One of these angels presented Margaret with the keys to the city. Other tableaux showed Paris and Mercury giving the golden apple to Venus and the Angel Gabriel saluting the Virgin Mary. Finally, the royal party arrived at the palace of Holyrood, which they entered through the cloisters of the abbey. During all this time, James had never let go of Margaret. Now he con-ducted her to her apartments in the palace, where waited the earls of Scotland and many Scottish knights and gentlemen. They did reverence to Margaret and she to them.

Waiting in the nearby Great Chamber were the ladies of the court who had accompanied their husbands to the wedding. Letting go of Margaret for the first time in some hours, James watched as she kissed the great ladies of Scotland and received their homage. The bishop of Murray, Andrew Forman, guided her through this ceremony, giving her the names of each woman as she came forward to be received. Whether Margaret could possibly have taken all of this in is a good question. But for a while, during supper, James left her, allowing her to relax a little in her own rooms while he dined in his. But he was back after supper, to dance and then take his leave for the night. He 'bade her goodnight joyously'. She must, by this time, have been very tired and perhaps nervous about the wedding ceremony itself the next day. At least she now had a short breathing space to take in her surroundings.

James had spent lavishly on 'the king's palace near the abbey of Holyrood'. It had once been no more than a royal guesthouse before Edinburgh became Scotland's capital under the Stewart kings. They found the pleasant gardens of the abbey and the sense of space more attractive than the restrictions of Edinburgh Castle, where there was limited opportunity for expansion and the living conditions were described as 'windy and right unpleasant'.[4] James enjoyed spending Christmas there and wanted to make it a grander home, fit for a queen. However, pressures of manpower and money meant that the work had not started in earnest before the autumn of 1502 and was not completed for another year, so it must have had something of the aspect of a building site when Margaret first saw it.

Work apparently began on the queen's Great Chamber as late as October 1502, under the direction of Michael Wright. The chamber was probably largely constructed of timber, much of which came from the Baltic. The glass was also imported, as was the plaster, which came from France. By July 1503, just weeks before the royal wedding, the activity of construction had greatly increased, and the costs with it. Work continued during the autumn and even the winter but was not finally finished until September 1504, when Leonard Logy, the master of works, was granted a £40 annual pension (about £8,600 today) for 'his diligent and great labour made by him in the building of the palace beside the Abbey of the Holy Cross'.[5] The total recorded expenditure on the building works at Holyrood was £3,800 (about £846,000 today), though this did not include furnishings. Margaret had, it will be recalled, brought a splendid collection of beds, bed linen, carpets and tapestries with her from England, which would have partly offset her husband's expenditure in this respect.

The preparation of new accommodation for his consort in his favourite Edinburgh residence was a sign of James's determination that Margaret should have what was due to a queen. But to underscore the more intimate level of their relationship, he commissioned a wedding gift that she could associate with him as a person, that spoke to their shared values of faith and their commitment to each other. This was a superbly illustrated Book of Hours. It can still be seen in the Austrian National Library in Vienna.[6] How it got there is a story in itself, and we shall return to this later. Meanwhile, a facsimile can be seen in the British Library, which gives a vivid impression of the beauty of the original and how costly it must have been to produce.[7]

The two Flemish artists who collaborated on the Book of Hours have been identified as Gerard Horenbout of Ghent and Simon Bening, son of Alexander Bening, the master artist of Mary of Burgundy, who may himself have been a Scot. Both would go on to become court painters to Henry VIII, and two of Horenbout's children, Luke and Susanna, were celebrated Tudor miniaturists. Simon Bening was much younger than Horenbout, probably just nineteen, when he worked on the James IV and Margaret Tudor Book of Hours (Horenbout was nearer to forty years old), and his work shows his dependence at that time on his father's style and his comparative immaturity. The most elegant work in the Book of Hours is undoubtedly Horenbout's, though Bening's, particularly in the crowd scenes of his illuminations, is more earthy.

The frontispiece is the arms of Scotland, with the motto 'In my Defens' and the initials I (for Iago, or James) and M intertwined around the edge. The book begins with the Gospel of St John: 'In the beginning was the Word and the Word was with God and the Word was God.' A picture of James IV with St James is reminiscent of the Hugo van der Goes panel of the

Holy Trinity painted for James III, which I always marvel at every time I visit the National Gallery of Scotland. The Book of Hours then leads on to the Annunciation and the scene at the manger, with a very puny baby Jesus but a wonderfully characterful cow and ass looking on.

Later, there is a beautiful illumination of Margaret Tudor herself. She kneels at an altar bearing the words 'God us Defend' in gold lettering. It is probably a reasonable likeness of the young queen, when compared with the later Daniel Mytens portrait, which is itself a copy of an earlier work now lost.[8] It has been pointed out that Margaret's oval features and high forehead are common to both portraits. In the Book of Hours, we can see her auburn hair held in a caul. She wears a crown of gold and a small dog lies at the foot of the altar. Above it is a vision of the Virgin and Child, both looking down tenderly on her. She is presented to them by a young man in deacon's robes, perhaps St Cyriac, the martyr whose feast day is 8 August, the day of Margaret's wedding.

These portraits of Margaret and her husband, together with various scenes such as the Flight into Egypt, Christ among the Doctors and the Crucifixion, are all richly bordered with flowers, insects and fruits. James IV must have been very pleased with this lavish wedding present. He had given Margaret 'a Book of Hours of which any queen in Christendom might well have been proud'. Today, as has been rightly pointed out, it reminds us of the important ties between Scotland and Flanders in the cultural life of late-medieval Europe.[9] It also speaks to James IV's ambitions for his country in the wider European framework and the role he already envisaged for his wife as a queen worthy to grace his court and play a significant role in raising Scotland's profile outside the British Isles.

The monies expended on building works and Holyrood and the unknown sum James had paid for his glittering wedding present to Margaret pale into insignificance when compared with the overall cost of the wedding. This amounted to £6,125 (£1.36 million today). Perhaps, given the enormous amounts spent on royal weddings in the modern era, this sounds comparatively modest, but James did not enjoy an overflowing treasury. Like almost all monarchs of his period, he was always looking for extra sources of revenue. Nevertheless, an appropriate outlay on his wedding was an important part of his overall policy. He spent more than a quarter of his annual income on wine alone for the celebrations. He was not going to stint at this moment of triumph. Now the time had come for the final act in the extended negotiations that had formed part of Anglo–Scottish diplomacy for six years. Margaret Tudor had arrived in Edinburgh, been settled overnight in her own apartments at Holyrood and rose on the morning of 8 August in preparation to become, not just by proxy but in reality, the wife of James IV and Scotland's new queen consort. This was the fulfilment of a journey that had begun in Collyweston nearly four weeks earlier. The Scottish thistle and the Tudor rose would be united at last.

The chapel of Holyrood House, where the couple were married, is now an impressive ruin, but on 8 August 1503 it was full of colour, 'the sunlight streaming through the unshattered glass, glittered on the sculptured figures of saint and angel, and added a richer dye to silks and damask, to velvet and cloth of gold'.[10] This may sound like poetic licence but its accuracy is confirmed by John Young, who has left us a detailed description of the ceremony and the clothing worn by the bride and groom. Despite the seemingly insatiable obsession with Margaret's brother, Henry VIII, and his six wives, we have no surviving description of what any of these queens (or, indeed, Henry himself) wore at his weddings.[11]

This has gone largely unremarked by writers. For James and Margaret, on the other hand, we have detailed descriptions of how they – and many of their guests – were dressed. Let Somerset Herald set the scene. 'On the eighth day of the said month[August], every man appointed himself richly, for the honour of the noble marriage.' Between eight and nine o'clock, he said, everyone was ready, the ladies richly arrayed in gowns of cloth of gold, or crimson and black velvet. Others wore satin or tinsel (silk woven with gold or silver thread), as well as damask and chamlet (a woven fabric of goat's hair and silk). These were, Young said, 'of many colours, [with] hoods, chains and collars upon their necks, accompanied by their gentlewomen honestly arrayed after their guise, for to hold company to the said queen'.[12] They were, in other words, honouring Margaret by their own sumptuous dresses and jewels. In these descriptions, we can see that Mackie was not exaggerating when he painted such a vivid picture of the interior of the chapel and the bejewelled congregation gathered to witness the marriage ceremony.

Once the congregation was settled, the bishop of Murray, Andrew Forman, went to fetch the English party, the Archbishop of York, the bishop of Durham, 'and also the earl of Surrey, who was richly arrayed in a long gown of cloth of gold, with his rich collar of the Garter, accompanied by many lords'. These lords of the church, of the English nobility and their gentlemen were then brought into the presence of King James, who was standing in his Great Chamber. He desired them to sit, with the Archbishop of York on his right and the earl of Surrey on his left. James himself sat in a chair of crimson velvet, panelled with gold, under a blue velvet cloth of state, figured with gold. On James's right were his brother, the Archbishop of St Andrews, and all the leading prelates, while to his left were all Scotland's earls, lords and knights. The assembled company heard a short sermon from the English divine, Dr Rawlins, and then, after due reverence to the king, the company made its way to the queen's apartments. They did not tarry there long, as the time had come to conduct Margaret to the chapel of Holyrood. She and her party were expected to arrive before James himself.

As she moved to take up her position waiting by the font, Margaret was supported by the Archbishop of York, who held her right hand, and the earl of Surrey, who held her left. Neither man was likely to have been entirely congenial to her. Over the past month she had had more than enough of Surrey, and Thomas Savage, the archbishop, was not a humble, quietly reverent churchman but a larger-than-life figure who loved hunting. More reassuring was the presence of her lady mistress, Elizabeth Denton, whom she had known since nursery days and who was described on this occasion as being 'always nigh her'. It would have taken some time to dress her in her wedding outfit and the lavish jewellery that the occasion required. She and James wore matching outfits of white damask, Margaret's bordered with crimson velvet. John Young described her very rich necklace of gold, precious stones and pearls. On her head was a golden crown, liberally sprinkled with the same adornments. Her train was carried by the countess of Surrey, herself resplendent in a gown of cloth of gold. The train was so cumbersome that Lady Surrey needed the help of a gentleman usher to manage it, just as she had when Margaret had heard mass at York. Margaret's long auburn hair was caught in a rich coif, 'hanging down behind the whole length of the body'.[13]

Once the Archbishop of Glasgow had arrived, shortly after Margaret and her party, it was finally time for James IV himself to take up his place. Accompanied by his brother and all the holders of the major offices of Scotland, James came into the chapel and made reverence to Margaret, which she returned. He must have cut a dashing figure, for as well as his gown of white damask, figured with gold, 'he had on a jacket with sleeves of crimson satin ... under that a doublet of cloth of gold and a pair of scarlet hose. His shirt embroidered with thread of gold, his bonnet black, with a rich balas [ruby], and his sword about him.'[14]

Now all was ready for the ceremony itself. James and Margaret took their vows with Bishop Blackadder officiating. The Archbishop of York then read out the papal dispensation for the couple, who were distantly related, authorizing their union. 'This done', said John Young, 'the trumpets blew for joy'. James then conducted his wife to the high altar, where they knelt on cushions of cloth of gold to pray. Both then retired to separate sides of the church, he on the left and she on the right, and they heard the litany before the Archbishop of York began mass. Immediately after this, Margaret was anointed and crowned as Queen of Scots and given the sceptre to hold by her husband. The singing of the Te Deum completed the religious ceremonies. James led Margaret back to her chamber for a brief respite before a splendid meal to celebrate the wedding. They did not dine together, but Margaret was nevertheless honoured by being served before James.

Although he was more interested in what those attending the wedding wore and in explaining the roles of the different Scottish and English lords in attendance, John Young has also left us details of what was eaten at the wedding feast. Sitting in her lavishly decorated chamber, under a canopy made of cloth of gold, Margaret was served a wild boar, whose head had been gilded, then with 'a fair piece of brain and in the third place with a gambon [ham], which were followed by diverse other dishes, to the number of twelve, of many sorts, in fair and rich vessels'. Of course, this was a ceremonial feast and it is very unlikely that Margaret partook freely of all the food that was on offer. James dined in his own chamber, hung with red and blue, with his brother, the two English bishops and the ubiquitous earl of Surrey. The tapestries hanging on the wall told the story of Hercules and other heroes of Greek myth.

After the company had been served the various courses, it was time to cry *largesse*, a distribution of monies that was long associated with coronations and weddings in England and Scotland. James IV ordered his principal herald, 'Go ye, cry towards the queen first, that is to wit, LARGESSE.' So Margaret's title was called for all to hear: 'To the high and mighty Princess Margaret, by the Grace of God, Queen of Scotland and first daughter engendered of the very high and very mighty Prince Henry VII, by that same self Grace, King of England.' James's gift of forty gold crowns was then distributed. Then there was singing and dancing as well as games and a brief respite for Margaret when the king and his entourage attended evensong. The supper that followed was a lighter meal than dinner, though served with the same ceremony, and Margaret was given precedence again. James used the occasion to give his marriage gown to the English heralds. Young noted proudly that he and his companions carried it the next day in court, having thanked the king for his gift. Margaret, in a similar gesture, gave her wedding outfit the next day to the Scottish heralds.

Now this extraordinary day of colour, symbolism and pageantry was drawing to a close. But amid the spectacle, it is easy to lose sight of the fact that this had been, at its heart, the wedding day of a man of thirty and a girl who was not yet fourteen. It was of vital importance to both England and Scotland and their mutual need to try to find a way to live amicably as neighbours that the marriage was a success. James had done everything in his power, including stretching his exchequer to breaking point, to welcome and entertain the English guests and show reverence and support to his wife, at least in public. In private, he seems to have been unable to get away from the earl of Surrey, a man who never had the slightest qualms about forcing his company on anyone who would listen. But James and Margaret had one important duty to perform, to which John Young alluded tactfully. 'After the supper, the night approached, therefore each one withdrew him to his lodgings for to take his rest, and the king had the queen apart, and they went together.'

This is all we know about the wedding night of James IV and Margaret Tudor. There is no information on how Margaret was prepared for the marriage bed, whether there was the same ribald jollity that accompanied many weddings in those days. It would not be surprising, given James's character, if he simply eschewed all of these forced and sometimes embarrassing goings-on and, in the manner of his great-great-grandson Charles I a century later, simply removed Margaret and bolted the door to their chamber. Margaret would not have been completely innocent of what she might expect (ladies-in-waiting would almost certainly have given her some guidance) and it is reasonable to assume that some sexual activity took place, because both knew the importance, in law, of consummating a marriage. And Margaret, like Henrietta Maria in 1625, did not appear the next day; 'Touching the queen, I say nothing', remarked John Young, 'for that same day I saw her not, but I understand that she was in good health and merry.'[15] This last word did not have the same gleeful meaning that it does today. For, as a letter written to her father around this time indicates, she was not what we would call merry at all.

The rigours of weeks of being so constantly on public display, of the exhaustive round of engagements, the costume changes, the heavy jewellery, the unfamiliarity of a new court, with its own customs, a language which sounded somewhat like her own but was spoken with a strange accent and used many different words, all of this, taken with the obligations of marriage and the need to please a man she had only met days before her wedding, took its toll on the new Queen of Scots. It was universally acknowledged that she had performed her role admirably, with grace and diligence, conscious of who she was and what she represented. But she was also weary and homesick, uncertain about many aspects of her future and utterly exasperated with the earl of Surrey. He had interfered constantly, shown her insufficient respect, bossed her servants about and, by now, she was desperate to see the back of him and possibly of his lady wife and daughter, too, even as they laughingly shaved James IV's long beard the day after his marriage. Margaret had made it clear she did not like beards – her own father was clean-shaven – but she was too angry with Surrey to have much gratitude to the women of his family. She may even have seen it as a further sign that James would pay attention to them but not to her. In a remarkable letter to her father, she revealed the extent of her doubts and unhappiness and her deep-seated, underlying insecurity.

'Sir', she wrote:

> as for news I have none to send but that my lord of Surrey is in great favour with the king here, that he cannot forebear the company of him no time of the day. He and the bishop of Murray ordereth everything as nigh as they can to the King's pleasure. I pray God it may be for my poor heart's ease in time to come. They call not my Chamberlain to them, which I am sure will speak better for my part than any of them that have been of that counsel. And if he speak anything of my cause, my lord of Surrey hath such words unto him that he dare speak no further.

Here was an unvarnished account of the reality of Margaret's situation in the days immediately after the wedding, ignored and overlooked, deeply frustrated and anxious. Surrey's interference and his rudeness to Verney, her chamberlain, were a cause of great concern, as was his monopolizing of the attention of James IV at a time when Margaret was keen to spend private time with her husband, to establish herself and her household using the normal conventions of court practice, which, even at her young age, Margaret clearly understood. To say that Surrey was a thorn in her side would be to put it mildly. 'God send me comfort', she continued, 'that I and mine who be left here with me be well entreated.' That part of the letter was dictated to a secretary. The postscript, in her own large, sloping handwriting, is a poignant witness to the misery of a girl fully cognizant, perhaps for the first time, of the challenges that lay ahead of her.

> For God's sake, sir, hold me excused that I write not myself to your Grace, for I have no leisure this time, but I wish I were with your Grace now and many times more, when I would answer. As for this I have written … it is very true, but I pray God I may find it well for my welfare hereafter. No more to your Grace at this time, but our Lord have you in his keeping. Written with the hand of your humble daughter, Margaret.[16]

There was, of course, no going back. Her affectionate father would soon become a pleasant memory, consigned to the past with her much-loved mother and quiet upbringing on the banks of the River Thames. She was the wife of James IV and she would have to learn how to adapt to him and his country. The price of becoming a queen had been high for thirteen-year-old Margaret Tudor.

8

The Court of Queen Margaret

'Welcome to be our princess of honour,
Our pearl, our pleasance and our paramour,
Our peace, our play, our plain felicity
Christ thee conserve from all adversity.'

William Dunbar, 'The Thrissill and the Rois', a poem written
in honour of Queen Margaret

Margaret soon discovered that her worries about being overlooked and not treated with due respect and honour were unfounded. James IV was fully committed to making her a worthy queen, but he recognized that the transition from Tudor princess to Stewart queen would not take place overnight. There would inevitably be a period of adjustment. And what better way to begin this than taking his bride on a tour, so that she could meet the people of her new realm? James had already demonstrated the importance of regal visibility to Margaret by the manner of their entry into Edinburgh just before the wedding. Now he was to show her off, and enable her to acquire some familiarity with the Scottish countryside and the properties that were hers, as well as letting his subjects outside the capital see her.

They left with an enormous train, carrying all the gear they would need for comfort and display. By now, Margaret was used to travelling with a lengthy procession of carts, conveying her beds, furniture and a huge range of accessories, from horse harnesses to tablecloths. All of this stuff, and more, had rumbled along behind her as she journeyed north to Scotland. But she was soon to learn that her husband regularly travelled with up to thirty-five wagons, which could include almost anything that took his fancy, including, though not on this occasion, his favourite white peacock. Indeed, her most immediate impression of James IV, after he had shaved his beard at her behest and bade farewell to the irritating earl of Surrey, must have been of his restlessness and the breadth of his interests. She soon came to realize that he was an inveterate traveller, his desire to move about a product not just of his pleasure in meeting his countrymen, or even the mistress that he still hankered after, discretely removed to the faraway north of his realm. It was an essential part of his personality. He did not require, nor would he have wanted, Margaret with him on many of these jaunts, and she came to appreciate the time that she had to herself, with her ladies and household, in the palaces that she was about to inspect on their first royal progress together.

James had given the castle at Dumbarton, in south-west Scotland, to his wife the day after their marriage, a 'morrowing gift', as it was called, though they did not visit it during this first tour. As a residence, it seems to have had little appeal to Margaret and it was more of a stronghold than a home. There had been a fortress here since at least Viking times, sitting on a rock at the confluence of the River Leven and the River Clyde, and it remained in Norwegian hands until the 1220s, when the Western Isles came under Scottish rule. Too far removed from the centre of power and influence in Scotland by the time of Margaret's marriage to be attractive to a thirteen-year-old queen, it nevertheless would play a crucial part in the life of her granddaughter, Mary, Queen of Scots, who left for France from the castle in 1548.

With there being little of immediate interest to the queen in this less-than-welcoming location, James and Margaret's journey took them instead to Stirling, the dower castle of the queens consort of Scotland. A drawing from the late seventeenth century shows the castle perched high on a rock overlooking the town below, its impregnability from the south-east clear to see. The modern town has encroached on Stirling Castle's isolation but it remains an impressive site. The hall has been called 'the grandest secular building to have been erected in Scotland during the later Middle Ages'.[1] In size it certainly matched other great halls in English palaces and on the European continent. James IV had already spent lavishly on improvements, both to the domestic architecture of the palace and its fortifications, and would continue to do so throughout the rest of his reign. The one part of the building that does not seem to have been extensively changed, though it was kept in a good state of repair, was the Queen's Chamber. But then, James IV had been a bachelor when he started to make changes at Stirling, and could afford to please himself. It perhaps says something for Margaret's more guarded response to Stirling that she did not press for changes regarding her own lodgings in the castle. There may, however, have been other reasons for her lack of enthusiasm for her dower castle, as we shall see.[2]

Before returning to Edinburgh, the king and queen went to Linlithgow Palace in West Lothian, another of Margaret's properties. It would become her favourite home and she passed a great deal of time there when her duties did not require her to be at James's side, or when he was away. James spent large sums of money on it – some work there was going on almost every year of their marriage, but still Margaret seems not to have minded. One can understand why, since the palace occupies a most attractive site, on a promontory with a loch on two sides. The visitor today can appreciate it best by taking the circular walk which starts in the town and shows the ruins to best advantage. On a quiet day, the first visitors to Linlithgow can walk in through the outer gateway beside St Michael's Church as soon as the palace opens and have the place largely to themselves. Once inside, it is still possible to appreciate why Margaret, and subsequently her daughter-in-law, Mary of Guise, liked Linlithgow so much.

The first recorded royal residence there dates back to 1300 but was destroyed by a fire which engulfed much of the town as well. This gave James I of Scotland the opportunity to build the palace anew, to his own design, and work commenced in the mid-1420s. The assassination of James I in 1437 by disgruntled nobles took place before the building was completed and work thereafter was sporadic until James IV acceded to the throne. Like his great-grandfather, he wanted to make Linlithgow a royal residence, a domestic rather than military dwelling. This did not, of course, mean that it would be anything other than grand, but the work his master masons undertook there was one of rolling improvement and renovation throughout his reign. This remodelling included extensive work on the Great Hall, which was fitted with new clerestory lighting and a magnificent new fireplace. The apartments of the king and queen were also refitted and moved to the west courtyard range of the palace. Margaret would have found herself in surroundings truly fit for a queen, incorporating the latest architectural ideas from the European continent. Whatever the vagaries of climate, the necessity to adapt to short winter days and long nights of darkness, master new customs and a new language and familiarize herself with new courtiers and their families, by the time that she was enjoying the celebrations for her fourteenth birthday on 29 November 1503, Margaret Tudor knew that she was a queen indeed. The Scottish court, a small jewel but nonetheless brilliant for all that, was her new world.

In her husband's absence during that early autumn, Margaret had time to reflect on her situation. She could now take stock of her household and how it would function, and allow a breathing space for the English servants who had travelled with her to get used to their new surroundings and duties. After the fever pitch of the marriage celebrations, this would have been a welcome return to a more ordered life. The Treaty of Perpetual Peace had stipulated that Margaret was to have twenty-four English retainers in her household, though it was by no means exclusively a female preserve. Alongside the six ladies-in-waiting, headed by Lady Eleanor Verney, were Lady Eleanor's husband, Sir Ralph, the chamberlain who had clashed with the earl of Surrey; a treasurer, Edward Benestede; a clerk of the closet, Mr Carnavel; a master of the wardrobe, Piers Mannering (interesting that a man should be in charge of the queen's wardrobe),[3] who was supported by two English yeomen; a principal usher, Hamnet Cleg; John Camner, a luter; and Margaret's own *poursuivant* (herald), Bluemantle, who later became the Rothesay Herald and, though an Englishman, remained when the rest of Margaret's English servants left for home in 1507. He later served James IV in various diplomatic missions. In these evocative – even, to the modern ear, colourful – names we are afforded a glimpse of those who must now adjust to a different way of life and create, for their young mistress, a supportive household that needed to function smoothly within the wider Scottish court. There were other positions, of course, for Margaret had a full range of ushers, footmen, grooms of the chamber, pages, a master cook, laundresses and bakers, as well as the holders of more specialized offices such as her master of the queen's silver and the keeper of the pewter. In structure, her household resembled that of her mother, Elizabeth of York. The record for the households of earlier Scottish queens consort is scanty, but while it is possible that those of her predecessors were not markedly smaller in size, it is clear that Margaret's was comparable with that of other European queens consort in the early sixteenth century. James IV wanted his wife's household to reflect his own status as a Renaissance king.[4]

This raises the question of how the expenses of the queen and her household were met. The marriage treaty had stipulated that Margaret was to receive 'a marriage gift in kind and extent to the gift of any queen of Scotland at any time in the past'. Perhaps conscious still, even as late as 1502, of the underlying uncertainties surrounding the longevity of the dynasty he had founded, Henry VII was determined that his daughter should be given her due. Her dower was to be £6,000 (about £1.4 million today) per year with a further £1,000 (about £203,000 today) in grants and rents from her lands, as what amounted to personal spending money. Against this, it should be remembered that Margaret had come with a dowry of £35,000 (£6.7 million today), to be paid in three instalments. Though this was a welcome addition to the Scottish exchequer, especially at a time when James IV was spending freely, it was not an unusually large amount for a bridal dowry of this period and less than had been proposed for a marriage between his widowed father, James III, and Princess Cecily of York, Margaret Tudor's aunt.[5] Given the huge cost of royalty and the relentless drive towards conspicuous consumption among celebrities today, these sums seem rather modest, though direct comparisons are difficult.

Despite its distinctive character, however, Margaret's household was paid by her husband out of his own household expenses. There is evidence that she was separately funded for a brief period in 1508–9, when Sir Duncan Forester, her knight comptroller, kept separate accounts for her. It is not clear why this particular year should have been any different or whether there are other records which are now lost. However, Margaret's expenses were listed separately within James's own household records and it is significant that Forester became the comptroller of James's household as well as Margaret's in 1508, enabling him to combine his responsibilities in reporting the finances of the king and queen. While this may have made sense from an administrative perspective, it also meant that Margaret had virtually no experience of managing her own finances. This would make her life all the harder in the future.

Financial dependence was unavoidable, but in many other respects the marriage of Margaret and James was to be a successful partnership. The queen knew what was expected of her – that much was obvious in her frustration at not being able to work on their relationship around the time of her marriage. She had watched her own mother and learned from her in the year between her betrothal and Elizabeth of York's death. Margaret was to bring lustre to James's court and, with her ladies, to soften its masculine edges, so that it could fulfil its potential on the European stage. James had many mistresses and had even installed several of them, from time to time, in his palaces. They might live with him, but they had no acknowledged formal role. They could not meet ambassadors, dispense patronage, worship openly with the king or act as hostesses. Margaret could do all of these things, the social side of her life becoming increasingly important as she adapted to life at the Scottish court. It was the most significant way in which she could make her mark as a queen.

The queen's outer chambers, where both male and female courtiers could mix and be entertained, were often frequented by James and his friends. He and Margaret would play at cards (he often lost to her), listen to music and chat. Sometimes James would take part in plays, demonstrating his acting ability. In the winters, log fires were piled high and the queen, wrapped in furs, watched the firelight sparkle while listening to the tales of the makars, the Scottish storytellers who were part of the ancient Celtic tradition of poetry and performance. William Dunbar, the leading poet of James IV's reign, set many of his poems in the queen's chamber, leaving us a compelling image of its lively atmosphere. Of course, there may have been an element of flattery, but Dunbar was also frank about what he saw as the sometimes undisciplined nature of James IV's wider court.

> Sir, you have many servants
> And officials with different responsibilities:
> Churchmen, lawyers and fine craftsmen,
> Doctors in law and medicine,
> Soothsayers, rhetoricians and philosophers,
> Astrologists, artists and orators,
> Men of arms and valiant knights
> And many other excellent people,
> Musicians, minstrels and merry singers
> All kinds of soldiers,
> Makers of coin, carvers and carpenters,
> Builders of barques and small ships,
> Masons dwelling on the land,
> Shipwrights cutting wood on the shore,
> Makers of glass, goldsmiths and jewellers,
> Printers, painters and apothecaries

Dunbar went on to acknowledge the skills and contributions of this varied list, but he also painted an equally vivid picture of those he considered hangers-on.

Another company more miserable,
Though they are not so profitable:
Dissemblers, hypocrites and flatterers
Shouters, clamourers and chatterers,
Parasites and gunners,
Monsieurs of France, good claret tasters,
Inopportune beggars of Irish race
And stealers of foods, as if out of their wits

These 'Rogues not known to any respectable man' had nothing else to offer but to crowd James's doors, he concluded.[6]

This superb evocation of the vivid, bustling court of James IV and Margaret Tudor speaks powerfully to us over the centuries. Its frankness does not seem to have deterred the queen. In acknowledgement of Dunbar's writings, Margaret gave him a handsome doublet from her wardrobe. The makar was so delighted that he wrote two poems about the gift, though one poked fun at James Dog (the unfortunately named master of Margaret's wardrobe at the time) for being slow in releasing the gift to him.

Margaret had various forms of patronage at her disposal, in the form of grants of money, lands and gifts. Since her husband was the ultimate source of these favours, she worked with James to reward members of her household. That this was a partnership in which she had more than a passive role is perhaps best illustrated in the joint portrait of James and Margaret in the Seaton Armorial in the National Library of Scotland.[7] It is not great art, especially considering it is not even contemporary, but probably dates from the early seventeenth century. Margaret is wearing the arms of her father, Henry VII, on her skirt and a headdress that looks straight out of the fifteenth century. She and James are rendered almost like cartoon characters and both look far older than they must have been at the time of their marriage. Margaret appears to be well in her forties, though she has not yet acquired in this rendition the girth that was an inevitable result of her later pregnancies. James, wearing his favourite purple edged generously with fur, bears a somewhat closer resemblance to other portraits of himself, particularly his shoulder-length hair, but he looks haggard and his face has some traces of his father-in-law, Henry VII. This strange double portrait, evidently meant to convey the importance of the Anglo–Scottish marriage rather than any lifelike image of the two principals, is, nevertheless, the only one that survives of Margaret and James IV together.

Whatever its artistic failings, the Seaton Armorial does reinforce the image of partnership that underlay James IV's approach to Margaret's role in court and household matters. In the discussion and allocation of awards, the queen could influence the fortunes of members of her household and demonstrate that she was not a passive player in Scottish politics. One example is the grant of lands in Culcrieff in Perth and Kinross, in May 1507, to Margaret's usher Charles Maxton, 'remitted him at the instance of the queen, to whom he stands in service'.[8]

Margaret was also active in sponsoring marriages for her ladies. This was an important duty as head of her household and an effective way of showing the patronage she had at her command. Sometimes these matches were better than the young women could have expected at home, adding to their prospects and also further cementing, it was hoped, the relations between England and Scotland. In 1507, Elizabeth Barlow, one of Margaret's English maids-of-honour, made a splendid marriage to Alexander Elphinstone, a Scottish nobleman high in the king's favour. The couple continued to receive rewards from the king after their wedding. Since Elizabeth was from a minor gentry family whose standing had been compromised by her father's involvement in the Perkin Warbeck conspiracy, she was lucky to have been in Margaret's service at all. She had joined when Margaret was still a princess in England, accompanied her to Scotland, and was clearly close to the young queen. At the time of her marriage, Elizabeth received a new gown, a featherbed and bedclothes from the royal wardrobe. James IV also gave her a generous dowry in the form of the lands and the castle of Kildrummy in Aberdeenshire. This massive medieval fortress had once been the stronghold of the earls of Mar. As a gift to Elizabeth Barlow and Alexander Elphinstone, it clearly indicated the affection in which the couple were held by both James IV and Margaret.[9]

The Christian calendar also afforded opportunities to acknowledge the queen and her ladies. There were always great festivities at Christmas. Yuletide may have been the darkest time of the year but the atmosphere at James IV's court was always bright and lively. New Year's Day, for both the Tudor and Stewart courts, was traditionally a time of gift-giving, both between the monarch and his consort and through the distribution of rewards to the ladies and gentlemen who served them. Recent scholarship of the period continues to explore the importance, in terms of networking and fostering social relations, of gift-giving. It was more than a polite formality and though presents could be valuable there was none of the neediness of conspicuous consumption that has disfigured Christmas in the secular Western world. When James IV drew up his list of gifts to Margaret and her ladies in 1504, her first New Year's Day in Scotland, he did so partly out of personal generosity (he was a warm-hearted man, who liked to please people) but also with the intention of making the recipients feel welcome and valued in their new home. James established at this time a precedent of giving his wife New Year's gifts that were mostly jewellery. This first present was of two sapphire rings. Margaret's only recorded gift to James came several years later, in 1507. It was a salt cellar decorated with a figure of the Virgin Mary. James subsequently gave it away, as was common with New Year's gifts.

Like the queen, James gave her ladies presents of jewels. One of Margaret's chamberers, Margaret Dennet, received a gold chain with an image of Scotland's patron saint, St Andrew. Perhaps the gift touched Mistress Dennet; three years later, she married one of James IV's squires, Sir Alexander Ogilvy, another example of how the queen's ladies made good marriages at the Scottish court. Other ladies were given chains of gold with gold coins, a present often repeated over the years. One such chain given to Eleanor Jones cost £6.9s.10d Scots, worth over £1,000 today. One can imagine that Margaret Tudor's English ladies acquired a nice little nest egg in these golden gifts, though they may not have worn them much as necklaces. Some ladies, however, also received generous gifts of velvet, satin and damask.[10] To the male members of Margaret's household, New Year's gifts totalling about £21 (or something over £4,000 today) were distributed most years until 1508. It would seem that the ladies had the better of the New Year's gift-giving while they were in Scotland.

One aspect of Margaret's life as queen that has been overlooked in biographies is that of the obligations of public piety. This was an important part of pre-Reformation queenship. Margaret had demonstrated her devotion to the church and its rituals throughout her journey to Scotland, the most notable example of this being when she heard mass at York Minster, where her reverence was on show to a large congregation. The religious symbolism of her coronation, immediately after her wedding ceremony, completed her transformation from dutiful princess to queen, investing her with moral authority and also requiring of her the leadership in religious matters that was expected of a queen consort. She had been anointed with holy oil and thus entered, with her husband, into a partnership which was a visible emanation of the sacred nature of monarchy itself. Margaret's devotions were often conducted in public and she and James received ambassadors in their chapel after services. Such practices were part of daily court life in pre-Reformation Britain. Of Margaret's personal beliefs we know very little. She had a privy closet for her private devotions and her own chaplain to support and guide her. Educated at a time of growing interest in humanism, but before the advent of ideas that would challenge the very basis of the Christian church in Western Europe, Margaret does not seem to have followed the austere approach of her grandmother, Margaret Beaufort. She knew what was expected of her as a queen but was not ostentatiously pious.

She and James IV followed the faith that would soon be rocked to its very foundations, though Protestantism was late in arriving in Scotland and would not be espoused as a national religion until twenty years after her death. In 1503 the break with Rome could not have been foreseen. Instead, Margaret observed the rituals and activities that were part of a centuries-old tradition. She went on pilgrimages with her husband – James IV was a fervent pilgrim, often travelling on foot hundreds of miles to shrines in far-flung parts of Scotland, though he did not require this effort of his queen – distributed alms and participated in distributing the Royal Maundy on the day before Good Friday. In the case of Margaret and her sister-in-law, Katherine of Aragon, this was the most sacred public duty of the year and one in which they took part with their husbands. The solemnity of the ceremony was underlined by the dresses worn by the queen, either of blue or purple, the colour of royal mourning. In March 1504, for her first Easter in Scotland, Margaret's wardrobe records show that a gown of purple velvet and cloth of gold was ordered. This may well have been in anticipation of the Royal Maundy. Today in the United Kingdom we associate Maundy Thursday with the giving of special coins to carefully chosen recipients by the monarch. The custom in the early sixteenth century in Scotland and England was different. Clothing for poor women was distributed, the number of recipients depending on the queen's age. For Maundy 1504 in Scotland there were fifteen items ordered on Margaret's behalf, for each year of her age plus one, the year of grace. Although no contemporary record of the ceremony survives, it is not difficult to picture the young queen graciously bestowing the garments on the poor women as her husband looked on. She would probably also have washed the feet of the chosen women, while James IV washed those of a similar number of men. This ceremony, known as the *pedilavium,* was intended to remind watchers of Christ's washing of his disciples' feet before the Last Supper. It was thus deeply symbolic and Margaret's most important public activity of the Christian year.[11]

By Easter 1504, Margaret was well settled in her court and her role as Queen of Scots. It would be several years before she was able to demonstrate that she could fulfil that other, most vital function of a queen consort – the production of an heir.

9

Wife and Mother

'Few brides ever started their married life with fairer prospects: everything that James could do to please her was done.'

Sir James Balfour Paul on Margaret in 1503, in the preface to Volume 2 of *Accounts of the Lord High Treasurer of Scotland*

Queenship brought its rigours and expectations, and Margaret was well-schooled in these even before her wedding and coronation. But behind the public obligations of her role was a private relationship that needed to be developed between a mature man and a girl considered old enough to marry but who still had much to learn and who needed support and encouragement. James was an indulgent husband, generous to a fault. The treasurer's accounts for the early years of his marriage to Margaret show that he showered her with clothes and jewels, not just to buy her affection but to reinforce her confidence in her status as Queen of Scots and to deepen the bond between them as man and wife. There were great celebrations for her fourteenth birthday and the revels at Christmas 1503 were kept in Edinburgh with even more than their customary splendour. The presence of the queen and her ladies at court added a dimension that had been lacking in previous years, a gaiety and sparkle that made the period all the more enjoyable.

In the weeks before Christmas, Margaret's furrier and tailor were busy making gowns of satin, lined with miniver and ermine to keep out the cold. The work was so intensive that extra staff were needed in the person of 'a man to help the queen's furrier four days and three nights before Yule'.[1] For her bedchamber, beds were supplied from Flanders, 'two great beds of down and two great beds of Levant feathers with their bolsters and ticks of Brussels ... and two mattresses to lay under them'.[2] There is also ample evidence from the accounts of Margaret's love of hunting, an enthusiasm shared with her husband, who was also keen on hawking, and of the associated frequent necessity for everything from new bows and arrows to horses and all the paraphernalia that went with their equipment and care.

These were the groundings of a successful partnership but there was one area that Margaret, whatever reverence James did to her and no matter how many pleasant evenings they passed in each other's company, could not change: his weakness for women. Margaret was his wife; however, young and sexually inexperienced as she was, she could not compete with his mistresses. His favourite at the time, and the longest-established, was Janet Kennedy.

Janet was about nine years older than Margaret and had become the king's third serious mistress about four years before his marriage. Janet was the daughter of Lord Kennedy, whose estates were in Ayr in south-western Scotland. The family had useful connections at court and claimed descent from King Robert III. She had been married to a kinsman, Alexander Gordon, at the age of about sixteen and had borne him a daughter. The marriage seems to have foundered and by 1498 the alluring Janet was the mistress of a much older and more politically influential man, Archibald, earl of Angus.

He was then forty-seven years old and, like Janet, married, but in the relaxed atmosphere of the Scottish court such liaisons were commonplace and the church turned a blind eye to the fluidity of these relationships, sometimes even condoning remarriage. It was presumably while she was at court with her powerful lover that James IV saw Janet Kennedy and fell in love with her. He was already tiring of his current mistress, Margaret Drummond, so the progression to Janet was natural for him.[3]

'The Lady', as the accounts diplomatically described her, was soon set up in Stirling and had two children by James. He was a generous and attentive lover, as, indeed, he was to be as a husband, and Janet was always kept in a manner that reflected her importance in his life. But she was no foreign princess with titles, lands and prestige and her dubious marital status meant that she could never be considered as a wife for James IV. They both knew that, although the relationship might continue, it could not be as it was before. She was pregnant with their third child at the time he married Margaret Tudor. Just a few weeks before the wedding, she was moved out of Stirling to Darnaway Castle, in the far north-east of Scotland.[4] In the autumn of 1503, after their initial royal progress together, James IV left Margaret to undertake one of the pilgrimages of which he was such a keen adherent. This one would take him to Tain and the shrine of St Duthac. While in this part of Scotland, he also visited Janet Kennedy in her new home, some fifty-five miles distant. It seems likely that he spent time with her, perhaps chatting while they both embroidered, a pastime that this most remarkable of kings seems to have greatly enjoyed. It is hard to imagine Henry VIII plying his needle with silken threads, quietly watching Katherine of Aragon stitch his shirts.

James, who was always a swift traveller, returned to Edinburgh in time for Margaret's birthday. The child Janet was carrying, a daughter, did not survive, but Janet's son, the earl of Moray, lived on into the reign of his younger half-brother, James V, acting as a close confidant and adviser.[5] In 1505 James IV arranged a marriage between his mistress and John Ramsay, a favourite of his father who had turned traitor in the 1490s. This marriage, like her first, did not last long. Janet appears to have been an ideal mistress but an unsuccessful wife. She continued in quiet but not impoverished retirement, outliving both James IV and Margaret Tudor and dying in 1545.

It is unclear whether the little earl of Moray was living in Stirling Castle at this time, along with a half-brother, Alexander Stewart (the son of James IV's first mistress, Marion Boyd), and a half-sister, Lady Margaret Stewart, the daughter of Margaret Drummond. It seems more certain that the boys were in residence in 1502 and that Lady Margaret, who had been living at her family's seat, Drummond Castle, was brought to visit her father there shortly before James married Margaret. This does not necessarily mean that she was in residence when the king and queen arrived in September 1503, though she did move to Edinburgh Castle before the end of the year. Margaret is often represented as being appalled to find that her dower castle was being used as a royal nursery and that this discovery was the origin of her lack of enthusiasm for Stirling. There is no way of knowing whether she insisted that 'the bairns', as the treasurer's accounts describe them, were to be removed but, even if she did, this did not happen immediately. In 1504, when the king and queen visited Stirling again, James's children were still living in the castle and had to be temporarily lodged in the town while the royal couple were in residence. This suggests that a compromise of sorts had been reached the previous year. Eventually both the king's sons were sent abroad to study, their education being partly entrusted to the leading humanist scholar and thinker, Erasmus. Lady Margaret Stewart's household in Edinburgh Castle was conveniently separate from that of Queen Margaret's at Holyrood House. The child was given an education appropriate for a king's daughter and eventually made a good marriage.

The effect of the queen's discovery of the royal nursery on her relationship with James IV is hard to gauge. She had no bastard siblings herself as her parents' marriage had been loving and loyal. From this perspective, it might well have come as a considerable shock. There was no obvious or immediate rift, so perhaps James's charm and reassurance won the day. The past could not be undone and both husband and wife were committed to making their marriage work. For James it meant not just the security of his throne but the realization of his sweeping ambitions for Scotland. Margaret, only just emerging from the crisis of confidence brought about by the earl of Surrey's dismissive treatment of her household and herself, knew better than to engage immediately in warfare with her husband. In reality, she was not the disapproving stepmother at all. James IV's eldest illegitimate son, Alexander, became a close friend of the queen, often included at her table playing cards in the early days of her marriage, before his departure for Europe. He was only four years older than Margaret and was a quiet, bookish boy, devoted to his father. When he returned to Scotland in 1510, now appointed Archbishop of St Andrews, Alexander was given a prominent role in Scottish government. Margaret would have come to appreciate his qualities first-hand and there is some evidence that she gave him a Book of Hours, perhaps even the one that her father had presented to her when she left Collyweston in the summer of 1503.[6] The royal couple continued amicably together, though there are occasional hints that the queen could be stubborn. In 1504 she was staying at Dunfermline, the ancient capital of Scotland just north of Edinburgh, in the royal apartments attached to its magnificent abbey. Margaret seems to have liked Dunfermline and when she did not respond at once to a letter from James telling her to move because of the threat of plague in the town, he came down from Stirling to collect her.

There was also the need to comfort the king for the death of his much-loved younger brother (also called James, the Archbishop of St Andrews), who died in early January 1504. Scarcely were the celebrations for their first Christmas together over than the court was plunged into mourning. James ordered black garments for himself, including a riding gown, which he wore on a new black horse, itself decked out in black. James's youngest brother, John, earl of Mar, had died in the early spring of 1503. In the space of less than a year, James IV lost both his brothers, the companions of his childhood, and his immediate heirs. These grim reminders of the frailty of life, and the uncertainty of the Scottish succession, might have brought pressure on the king and queen to try and begin a family of their own, sooner rather than later. Yet Margaret did not conceive for two more years. This may have been accidental, but it seems more likely that James resisted the temptation to replace the losses too quickly. He did not need to compound his sorrow by risking the health of a wife who was just fourteen years old. Mindful of her age and of the concerns raised years before by Elizabeth of York and Margaret Beaufort, there was to be, as yet, no legitimate child for James IV. Instead, he encouraged Margaret to fulfil the other duties of queenship, while continuing to visit Janet Kennedy and perhaps finding solace in the arms of another, unidentified, mistress.[7] It was not until the early summer of 1506 that Margaret would have known for certain that she was with child.

We know nothing about the progression of Margaret's pregnancy. It was not the custom to comment on a queen's health at this time unless there was a miscarriage or stillbirth. Any indispositions or discomforts would have been dealt with by her ladies, within the privacy of her own chambers. Yet unlike their counterparts in England, Scottish queens did not undergo an extended withdrawal into darkened rooms, where only women were allowed to be present, weeks before the baby was due. Margaret was expected to be on view as the pregnancy progressed, her swelling belly a sign of pride and confidence, a reaffirmation of James IV's potency as king. The revels at Christmas 1506 were especially joyful, with James paying for minstrels and singers from England to come and entertain his wife.

He had made every effort to ensure her comfort. The royal wardrobe embarked on a flurry of activity, making new gowns to fit the queen comfortably as she grew larger. One of these appears in the accounts for early January 1507, a furred and lined nightgown of camlet (a kind of fine wool or goat's hair), which Margaret would have worn when relaxing in her own apartments, rather than a nightdress to sleep in. A new couch was also made for her, featherbeds and new sheets were delivered, and luxurious new bedding, including a crimson satin canopy which sat atop the red-and-green taffeta curtains of her bed of estate.[8] James IV had also given a splendid New Year's gift to his wife. It was a serpent's tongue, set with jewels, which may have belonged to his mother, Margaret of Denmark. The serpent's tongue was said to protect against poison and is a touching indication of the deepening of the bond between James and Margaret at a time when the birth of their first child was imminent. Ever considerate, and perhaps trying to lighten the combination of tension and boredom that often characterizes the final stages of pregnancy, James sent a lady to sing in Margaret's chamber on 15 February 1507. Chanting and singing over pregnant women could have a religious connotation as part of the rituals aimed at safe delivery. This lady's sweet tones seem to have produced the desired effect. Six days later, Margaret Tudor gave birth to her first child. It was a son, to be named James, after his father. The overjoyed King of Scots had, at last, a legitimate male heir.

The king immediately despatched a messenger to Henry VII in England with the news that his first grandchild had arrived. James also wrote to Louis XII of France and his wife, Anne of Brittany, with an enthusiasm that bordered on the tactless, since they had no male heirs of their own.

> Since there has been an alliance between his predecessors and the royal house of France for many years, and since there is a bond of blood between himself and Louis, he is doing nothing unworthy or contrary to family traditions if he announces by Rothesay herald events no less pleasing than advantageous that have happened to himself. Would that the birth of a son and heir to Louis were announced! Then he should have the pleasure that a friend should feel.

On the same day, 1 March, James sent a similar missive to Anne of Brittany, Louis XII's wife, saying that news of a son for her would give him as much happiness as could his own. 'And he must tell her of the arrival of the heir he desired, destined, if he lives, to revive the old intimacy with the royal house of France.' He added, somewhat quaintly, that 'if there is anything Scottish she could care to have, it shall be hers'.[9] He also informed his uncle Hans, king of Denmark, noting that 'you will be glad that one of your blood will rule in Scotland'.[10] The Danish king subsequently wrote to Margaret herself, acknowledging:

> her regard for him and her services in his interest

with her husband. He hopes that he will be able to repay her future kind offices. No greater good fortune in which he might have a share could befall her and her husband than the birth of a prince; and it will give the greatest pleasure among the Danish nobility.[11]

No expense was spared on the little prince's nursery and his wardrobe. Christened at Holyrood the day after he was born, he was carried to the ceremony wrapped up in white silk, in a cradle lined with ermine to keep out the cold of a Scottish February, his head resting on a pillow of cloth of gold. Taffeta from Florence was made into ruffs to decorate his other cradles, which were resplendent with scarlet covers and green ribbons. His cradle of state had a canopy of cloth of gold, held in place by gilt nails. In the summer and early autumn, he was dressed in clothes made of damask and satin, decorated with red ribbons. Surrounded by nurses and rockers and fed by a wet nurse, his early days were spent in luxury, with an attentive staff of his own. Yet if James IV was thrilled with the arrival of his son, he was far less sanguine about the health of his wife.

Margaret had apparently endured a difficult delivery of her boy and now she failed to rally. In fact, she lay extremely ill for some weeks, perhaps with puerperal fever. This bacterial infection was a great killer of mothers for many centuries, often setting in within a week of giving birth. Margaret was so ill, and James so anxious for her survival, that he took what for him was a characteristic step. He set off on pilgrimage to Whithorn in south-west Scotland, to the shrine of St Ninian, to pray for Margaret's recovery.[12] It was a journey of over one hundred miles and took him seven days on foot. Tradition has it that Margaret's fever began to break at the moment that her husband knelt in prayer at the shrine. In a credulous age, the queen's recovery would have certainly been regarded as a sign of divine intervention and James, known for his devotion to St Ninian, believed that his intercession had been successful. He was profoundly grateful. Later in the summer of 1507, Margaret herself went on pilgrimage to Whithorn to give thanks that she had survived the birth of her first child. James, ever the chivalrous knight, arranged a tournament in Edinburgh to celebrate the birth of a prince and the recovery of his queen. A Moorish girl in Margaret's service, known as 'Black Ellen', was the lady to be honoured at the lists. She was eventually 'rescued' from the unwanted attentions of a group of less-than-gallant knights by a 'Wild Knight', who turned out to be the king himself, poorly disguised but nevertheless wildly acclaimed by the spectators. What Ellen herself felt about being the centre of attention because of looks that seemed exotic to the audience we do not know.

The birth of her son marked a turning point in Margaret's life in Scotland. After 1507, most of her English servants went home. They were replaced by Scottish ladies and gentlemen, in a move that emphasized that Margaret was no longer a very young English princess who needed the comfort of familiar voices and faces. By now she had mastered the language and conventions of a different court and understood the domestic and international aims of her husband, as the king of Denmark's letter to her quoted earlier makes clear. She knew the geography of the country and had become visible to its people as she travelled, sometimes with her husband, sometimes by herself, through its dramatic countryside and small towns. Margaret Tudor was, in 1507, truly the Queen of Scots.

The joy of the royal couple lasted only a year. Their son died at Stirling a few days after his first birthday and the royal nursery, with all its splendid hangings, furniture and baby clothes, awaited another occupant. But from now on, regular pregnancies were to be at the centre of Margaret's life. She was pregnant again at the time of Prince James's death but her second child, a daughter, was born and died the same day in July 1508. By early 1509, the queen was carrying her third child. This was also a son, christened Arthur, born in October 1509. The choice of name may have been prompted by James IV's admiration for the legendary British hero or as a remembrance of Margaret's long-dead elder brother. But there was another factor in play here. Well aware of the implications of his wife's proximity to the English throne, James IV was also making a point about his new son's place in the British Isles.

Alas, like Prince James, Arthur died young. He only survived nine months. It used to be thought that the high rates of infant mortality before the modern period inured parents to the deaths of children. These came so frequently that surely they could not be unexpected and perhaps a degree of acceptance that it must be the will of God might have acted as a kind of shield. Nowadays social historians think differently. The surviving evidence suggests that the deaths of their young children affected our ancestors just as much as they would us. Margaret Tudor's babies had been born with every advantage of wealth, status and the best medical help available. James IV was fascinated by medicine and that his court was well supplied with doctors is shown in the accounts. But mostly their ministrations were unavailing when it came to infant deaths. Nor could the satin coats, taffeta ribbons and cloth-of-gold pillows save a sick baby's life. In the case of the king and queen's first child, they are the poignant evidence that he existed at all, and of the hopes that faded with his brief life.

Sad and perhaps increasingly desperate, James and Margaret again turned to pilgrimage as the solution for all their grief. In 1511 Margaret journeyed to the shrine of St

Duthac in the north, to pray for a child that would live – any child, even a girl, though it was naturally hoped that it would be a son. The queen's health had been endangered by each pregnancy; she seems to have encountered serious problems every time she gave birth. Now she was no longer the slim, homesick teenager who had married James IV in 1503. Death had taken early two of her sisters and two of her brothers, as well as her beloved mother, whose final attempt to secure a spare male heir for the fledgling Tudor dynasty had failed, at the cost of her own life. Margaret knew well, by this time, the heartache and dangers that were part of her life as Queen of Scots. But she also knew her duty. A childless queen, even if still a young woman, was a failure. She must hope that God would listen. James IV needed an heir.

Unlike her husband, Margaret did not go on pilgrimage without her full array of creature comforts. Her ladies in waiting accompanied her, as did the inevitable procession of carts carrying her clothes, bedding and the objects she used in her personal religious devotions. There was also an escort of knights and gentlemen. Even the court poet, William Dunbar, went along to record his impressions in rhyme. Margaret was received with great honour in Aberdeen and entertained as befitted a queen: 'Welcome our queen; the commons gave a shout; Be blyth and blissful, burgh of Aberdeen.'[13] After watching various religious and historical allegories, she continued on to St Duthac's shrine at Tain. There, she knelt in fervent prayer, hoping that, this time, she would be heard.

The following year, on 10 April 1512, Margaret gave birth to a third son. He was also called James but did not thrive for the first few months of his life. Finally, a wet nurse was found who seemed to suit the sickly little prince. The queen became pregnant again within months – a sign that the royal couple felt they could not afford to be confident that this child would survive any longer than his siblings had done. A daughter was born prematurely in 1513 and did not live. The life of the second Prince James was the thin, golden thread on which the Stewart succession hung. And by this time there were other, grave threats to the stability of Scotland. Margaret Tudor had been the personification of the Treaty of Perpetual Peace in 1503. Ten years later, relations between Tudor England and Stewart Scotland were characterized by mutual distrust and disdain. The prospect of warfare between the two nations seemed very real once again.

10

A Festering Rivalry

'It ill becometh a Scot to summon a king of England.'
Henry VIII to Lyon Herald, 11 August 1513

When Henry VIII became king of England in April 1509 Margaret had not seen him for six years. She knew nothing, except, perhaps, from private letters long since lost, of his transition from a bewildered child suddenly thrust into the limelight to the vibrant, self-confident eighteen-year-old who would come to play such a pivotal role in English history. Henry is often depicted at this stage of his life as the quintessential Renaissance prince determined to make his mark on the European stage, the focus of a glittering court steeped in the language and practice of chivalry. This was a place of swaggering young noblemen, Henry's boon companions, hanging on his every word as they jousted, danced and preened their way through the early years of his reign. The fair ladies who were the willing participants in this hedonistic lifestyle of disguisings, masques and tournaments were the women of the household of Katherine of Aragon, the abandoned widow of Prince Arthur, whom Henry married soon after his accession to the throne. He had also gained, through his queen, an influential and powerful father-in-law in Ferdinand of Aragon. Aligning his interests with those of Spain seemed natural to Henry. It played into his obvious desire to emulate Henry V by reviving the idea of war with France, speaking powerfully to his yearning for a past full of medieval chivalry and stirring battles.

Yet there were early indications that the king might not be entirely good-natured, or so certain of the path that lay ahead of him, as he might have wanted the world to believe. Just two days after his accession he gave orders for Richard Empson and Edmund Dudley, two of his father's closest advisers on financial matters, to be arrested and consigned to the Tower of London. They were both unpopular councillors who had profited from their roles, but so had many others. The pair were eventually executed more than a year later, victims of the new king's desire to dissociate himself from the swingeing tax regime of the last years of his father's rule.

Henry's marriage to Katherine of Aragon was under more stress, almost from the outset, than has sometimes been appreciated. In terms of intellect, it was definitely a marriage of equals. Katherine was an intelligent, well-educated woman and her difficult years of widowhood had given her a survivor's instincts as well as sharpening her character. She may well have inherited her steeliness from her formidable mother, Isabella of Castile, but Katherine was, by 1509, very much her own woman. She felt it her duty to counsel her husband on matters of state and, somewhat surprisingly in view of his general attitude towards women, he seems not to have resented this at the beginning of his reign, perhaps because Katherine's ideas on foreign policy conformed to his own.

However, she was six years older than Henry and though this may not have seemed a serious gap at the outset of their marriage, its implications for her childbearing potential could not be entirely dismissed. Katherine was twenty-four years old when she married Henry VIII. When Margaret Tudor was the same age she had already given birth to six children. Time was not on Katherine's side. She did become pregnant soon after the wedding, but her first child, a daughter, was born prematurely at the end of January 1510 and was probably a stillbirth. The ridiculous assertion by her doctor that the child might have been one of twins led the queen to encourage expectations that she might yet deliver a healthy child. Henry's disappointment was naturally considerable when nothing happened and did not improve his relationship with his wife. From the outset of their marriage, he seems to have taken mistresses whenever Katherine was pregnant. The birth of a son on New Year's Day of 1511 left both the king and queen of England delighted. In Scotland, James and Margaret still had no living children.

Henry's preparations to mark his son's birth matched those of his Scottish brother-in-law in 1507 in ambition and were even grander in reality. The little prince was christened with great ceremony on 5 January, though only one of his illustrious godparents, Archbishop William Warham, was present in person. Louis XII of France sent generous presents for his godson, as, one must presume, did Margaret of Savoy, his godmother, for whom the countess of Surrey stood proxy. Jousts were arranged over two days, on 12 and 13 February, to celebrate the new heir to the throne of England and fulsome poetry, notably lacking in literary merit (as was often the case on these official occasions), lauded the child's father.

> Our Royal Rose now reigning, red and white
> Sure grafted is on grounds of nobleness
> In Harry the VIIIth, our joy and our delight
> Subduer of wrongs, maintainer of righteousness
> Fountain of honour, exemplar of largesse.
> Our (e) clipsed Sun now is cleared from the dark
> By Henry our King, the flower of nature's work.[1]

A keen observer might have noted in the poem's first two lines a hint of uncertainty about the dynasty and its survival. Such misgivings were much nearer to the surface than Henry would have liked to admit. Nor did they ever really go away.

Henry's elation was fleeting. His firstborn lived for a far shorter span than his sister's, dying in his cradle on 22 February, a mere nine days after the tournament which celebrated his birth. Like the Scottish royal couple, Henry and Katherine would have to try again. They would not succeed for another five years, when Katherine gave birth to Princess Mary in 1516. And by that time much had changed in Scotland.

Though James IV had replied to Henry's early assurances of goodwill (written, it was noted, in Henry's own hand) with words that echoed the king of England's sentiments, the underlying stresses in their relationship would surface soon enough. These were both political and personal and were to cause Margaret Tudor much distress. The Treaty of Perpetual Peace had been signed with high hopes but much more limited expectations on both sides. There were inevitably flashpoints. The disputed area of the Borders was always going to be one of these. It is an area of outstanding natural beauty, peaceful now, but in the sixteenth century it was the scene of frequent raiding and violence, where livelihoods could be lost in one night of marauding and life itself was at risk. The Borders were the preserve of powerful local families, such as the Homes and Hepburns on the Scottish side and the Dacres in England. Special courts, with their own legal system, adjudicated on contentious matters, their juries composed of equal numbers of Scots and English when the charges were of homicide. The system, more sophisticated than the general picture of lawlessness on the Borders might suggest, had proved robust, even when relations between London and Edinburgh were strained. But periods of quiet tended to be short-lived.

Beyond the Borders, Henry VIII's courting of conflict with France was also a very sore point. Friendship between France and Scotland went back hundreds of years. The French were already describing the alliance as 'ancien' in the four-teenth century. Later, the Scots would refer to it as the 'Auld Alliance'. It was, at heart, a military pact, always aimed at England. 'Its theatres of war were northern England, south-ern Scotland, France and the sea.'[2] Yet the military side had taken on a long-lasting cultural dimension as well. Scots fight-ing in France settled there, particularly in the Berry, Touraine and Anjou regions. Arriving in large numbers as mercenar-ies in the fifteenth century, many had stayed and adapted to the French way of life. They built castles and became patrons of the arts, with one branch of the Stewarts settling in the area around Aubigny-sur-Nère in the Berry, ensuring that the name of the Scottish dynasty was respected and influen-tial far from home. The French, admiring the château built at La Verrerie by Bérault Stewart, called its owner 'a great knight beyond reproach'.

Yet these French Stewarts retained a keen interest in Scottish affairs and, as time would show, were willing to serve Scotland if called upon to do so. A leading member of the French branch of the Stewarts in the early 1500s was Lord Bernard Stewart, a kinsman of the king, who served on dip-lomatic missions between James and Louis XII. Regarded as the epitome of a valorous, chivalric knight, Bernard Stewart was the subject of a poem by the leading Scottish makar of the time, William Dunbar. In this *Ballad of a Right Noble, Victorious and Mighty Lord Barnard Stewart*, published in May 1508, Dunbar listed Stewart's victories (many of which had come in the Italian wars that so vexed Pope Julius II) and compared him to the heroes of antiquity. Printed to coincide with a great tournament in 1508, which may have been held in Stewart's honour, Dunbar paid tribute to this Frenchman with a Scottish lineage, in fine words honouring his:

> knightly name so shining in clemence
> For worthiness in gold should written be
> With glory and honour, laud and reverence.[3]

The English could not point to such a notable foreign presence of a key branch of their nobility, except for the awkward presence of Richard de la Pole, brother of the executed duke of Suffolk, now taking refuge at Louis XII's court. This was clearly not a connection that Henry VIII wished to advertise. Friendship, however, can come with a price. As Henry VIII moved closer and closer to the orbit of France's enemies, Louis XII of France would remind his Scottish ally of this. By 1513, James IV, growing increasingly tired of his brother-in-law's belligerence in word and deed, was finally convinced that his own interests would best be served by meeting his obligations under the long-standing French alliance.

From the beginning of his reign, James had been developing his military prowess. His own interests, particularly in building up his naval strength, were crucial in the development of his army and navy. The latter has been described as his obsession. Certainly it was something in which he had a passionate interest. This had been ignited by his first visit to the docks at Leith in the days immediately after he had come to the throne. During his reign James IV had a fleet of at least thirty-eight ships, some acquired as prizes or gifts, but most were the result of the king's determination to have a navy that matched in size and technology that of the greatest European states. It was not, of course, a Royal Navy in the modern sense, since no sixteenth-century monarch, let alone the ruler of a small kingdom, had the financial resources to build and maintain ships solely for warfare. Though the origins of the Scottish desire for a fleet that could defend the country and support Scottish trade went back into the fifteenth century, shipbuilding was a keystone of James's vision for his country. His achievement was remarkable but it came with a price. Towards the end of his reign, James's expenditure on the navy was the single largest drain on the Scottish exchequer.

The pride of his fleet was a huge warship, completed in 1506, and named the *Margaret*, for the queen. It was built at Leith by foreign shipwrights and used wood from various parts of Scotland as well as France and Norway. It rivalled the English *Mary Rose*, completed a few years later, in size and its cost (£8,000, almost £1.2 million today) was a quarter of James IV's annual income. He was thrilled with the *Margaret*, despite the expense, and came on board to dine even before she was floated. One can only assume that the queen herself was equally pleased but there does not seem to be any record of her having actually visited the vessel. Still, its naming was a great compliment to her, since work on the ship began well before Margaret herself was even pregnant with her first child.[4]

Prestige may have been a major factor in James IV's desire for an impressive fleet but defence was certainly another. And here the main foe was, predictably, England. Scottish traders, plying routes between Scotland and the European mainland, were frequently in combat with English ships. Tales of naval derring-do to rival those of later Tudor England are scattered through the narratives of Scottish chroniclers like Robert Lindsay of Piscottie. They are not strictly contemporary but they give a colourful picture of Scotland's sea-captains and of the importance of trade and political links with Scandinavian countries, reminding us that the significance of Scandinavia in British history is greatly overlooked. Yet there was another consideration in James IV's naval policy that would have implications for his steadily worsening relations with Henry VIII. The Treaty of Perpetual Peace did not prevent him from aiding foreign powers, even ones that might be at war with England, so long as he himself did not invade his southern neighbour. The implications of this were that James could build up a navy that might, if called upon, help him meet his obligations to his French ally, Louis XII. This may have sounded feasible on paper, but the tensions inherent in such an approach would eventually become all too apparent.[5]

Relations between the great powers of Europe had been in a state of flux since Charles VIII of France invaded Italy in 1494 and captured much of the peninsula. Despite recurring talk of further crusades against the Turks (an idea championed by James IV that owed more to his love of chivalry and professions of piety than practicality),[6] the language of war was becoming louder as the second decade of the sixteenth century dawned. At the heart of these diplomatic wranglings and shifting alliances was a dispute between Julius II (the Warrior Pope, as he was known) and the French monarchy, a hostility that wily players like the Habsburg Emperor Maximilian and Ferdinand of Aragon could exploit to their advantage. Ferdinand's daughter, Juana, elder sister of Katherine of Aragon, had succeeded to the throne of Castile on her mother's death in 1504. She was married to Philip of Burgundy, Maximilian's son, and dominated by her husband and father. Henry VIII, who saw France as a natural enemy, was inevitably drawn into the orbit of his father-in-law, signing a treaty with Spain in May 1510, just over a year after his accession to the throne.

The following year, there was an escalation of tensions on

the European continent when Julius II pressed for action to be taken to remove the French from Italian soil. He was indefatigable in his pursuit of liberating Italy, and, it might be added, expanding the territory of the Papal States. The Holy League, of which Henry VIII was a part, was formally signed in October 1511. In April 1512, the English declared war on France and despatched a fleet of 12,000 men under the marquess of Dorset. But Ferdinand of Aragon soon made peace with France, double-crossing Henry. It would not be the last time that the English king was let down by so-called European allies. Ferdinand's treachery, though an embarrassment, did not dent Henry VIII's resolve. In this he was encouraged by his wife and by his diplomats, notably Christopher Bainbridge, the xenophobic Archbishop of York who had been sent as envoy to Rome at the start of Henry's reign and who was soon appointed cardinal. Bainbridge actively encouraged Julius II's bellicose policy towards France, noting with evident satisfaction that a rival French cardinal in Rome was 'as partial a Frenchman as I am a Englishman. I pray God him evil triste.'[7]

In the spring of 1513, Maximilian was persuaded to join the Holy League, more than compensating for the withdrawal of Ferdinand of Aragon. Emboldened by the advent of this influential ally, Henry decided to renew the attack on France. He would lead from the front. But before he did so, in a sign of nervousness about the still-present threat of rebellion and rival claimants in England, he ordered the execution of the Yorkist Edmund de la Pole, earl of Suffolk. Leaving the organization of the logistics of war to Wolsey, who had risen rapidly in recent years, Henry landed in Calais on 30 June 1513 with a force of about 38,000 men, drawn from the retinues of his leading noblemen. Much of the aristocracy was enthusiastic about wars with France and continued to be so even during the reign of Henry's daughter, Mary I, half a century later. And there was to be a victory, albeit a very unimpressive one.

The Battle of the Spurs sounds wonderfully chivalric and rousing but was little more than a cavalry skirmish which resulted in the capture of the town of Thérouanne. Henry did not even take to the field himself. Unlike James IV of Scotland, he had absolutely no direct experience of battle. When he did go back to France with any army more than thirty years later, it was again primarily for show. By then he was, in any case, far too fat to be able to engage in combat even had he wanted to. In 1544, outside Boulogne, Henry had to be winched on and off his warhorse.

Under threat from all sides, Louis XII piled the pressure on his Scottish ally. In April 1512, he begged James to 'strengthen his forces in order to divert the king of England from his war against France', stressing that 'the King of Scots could do no greater service than by beginning a war against the king of England'. James's response was to prevaricate for some time. He asked for widescale help from Louis before he would commit, saying that he needed 'money, provisions, artillery, gunners, cavalry, infantry, engineers'. Unsurprisingly, Louis balked at this long shopping list, claiming that he had great expenses in France and in Italy. James had also made clear to him the vital, underlying factor for his reluctance. 'He has kept peace with the king of England, and if he breaks with him, he loses the reason of his marriage, the succession to the crown of England, to which he, by that marriage, is the nearest heir, apart from his ancient right.'[8]

For inextricably linked with the preoccupations of European powers was the underlying truth admitted by James IV in these diplomatic exchanges. He was ever mindful of Margaret Tudor's proximity to the English throne. Goodwill and respect between the Tudors and the Stewarts seemed to be vanishing with every passing year once Henry VIII became king. Beyond the Borders, the sea-fights, the distant plains of northern Italy, there was an intensely personal dimension and one that caused Margaret Tudor much anguish. The relationship with her brother was always going to be difficult. Margaret was Henry's heir-presumptive, though Henry seems never to have acknowledged this publicly. Should Henry die, the British Isles would, in effect, be ruled by James IV, in his wife's name, as he pointed out to Louis XII's envoy. James referred to his dynastic position in a meeting with Thomas Wolsey, then an up-and-coming servant of the English crown, as early as 1508, while Henry VII was still alive. In a fraught exchange of grievances, the King of Scots made clear his definition of what constituted a realistic assessment of the Anglo–Scottish situation.

> As to the renewal of the old league between Scotland and France, James says that as long as Henry treats him kindly, he will never break with him, nor renew the old league … His course of action is determined not by fear or *the possibility of succession* [my italics], but only by Henry's kindness and his own oath and promise. He thinks that so far Henry has not treated him like a son, but if henceforth Henry will be like a father to him, he would act in everything like his loving son.[9]

Henry VII did, of course, have a son and heir already. The omission of any mention of Prince Henry by James is striking. When he became king, Henry VIII found ways, both direct and indirect, of repaying his brother-in-law's effrontery.

Yet these smacked of frustration rather than conviction. James IV ruled 'with a confidence and ease which contrasts sharply with the frenetic efforts of Henry VIII to build up the prestige of Tudor monarchy, at home and abroad. James, like Henry was a man of imposing personality but an infinitely more charismatic one.'[10] Margaret's brother, it has been said, was 'a fusion of an able but second-rate mind with what looks like an inferiority complex'.[11] To the Scots, Henry's posturing may have looked pathetic but they could not afford to dismiss it entirely, especially in view of the deteriorating situation in Europe, and, moreover, when it involved a direct insult to their king.

The resurrection of England's claim to overlordship of Scotland came in January 1512, at a time when neither Henry VIII nor James IV had any surviving children. Given the tensions between continental powers, it was an impolitic move. James was unlikely to respond well to the English Parliament's declaration that he was 'very homager and obediencer of right to your highness', or the knowledge that Henry had been voted a generous amount of money to support his determination to invade France. He drew up a series of proposals for a new treaty with Louis XII within a week.

Margaret, meanwhile, was unswerving in her support for James. She had her own reasons for resentment against her brother. The legacies she was owed from the wills of Prince Arthur and her father had never been paid. Officially, Henry VIII chose to withhold them as a hostage for James IV's good behaviour but Margaret believed that there was a fair degree of spite and resentment on Henry's part. The queen had told Lord Dacre at the end of 1512 that she was sorry for what she termed 'any grudge' between her brother and her husband. That sounded reasonably mild-mannered but by the spring of 1513 she was much more forthright in direct correspondence with Henry VIII:

We cannot believe that of your mind or by your command we are so unkindly dealt with in our father's legacy, whereof we would not have spoken nor written had not the doctor [Henry's envoy, Nicholas West] now spoken to us of the same ... Our husband knows it is witholden for his sake and will recompense us ... We are ashamed therewith, and wish God word had never been thereof. It is not worth such estimation as in your divers letters of the same and we lack nothing; our husband is ever the longer the better to us, as knows God.[12]

Margaret was not one to mince words when fighting her corner, as her brother would come to realize in many of her letters to him.

She was also adept at dealing with English diplomats, treading a difficult path with aplomb. Nowhere is this more apparent than her interview with Dr Nicholas West in April 1513. By that time, though both the English and the Scots claimed that they wished to avoid outright hostilities, the war of words and its underlying menace were powerful indicators of the likelihood of conflict in the months to come. West, who at that time was dean of St George's, Windsor, was a rising churchman with a humble background, like Wolsey. He had been involved in diplomacy since 1502 and in 1513 was Henry VIII's envoy to Scotland. West's mission, ostensibly to try to settle the many points of contention on the Borders, afforded him the opportunity to assess James IV's intentions. It was not an enviable task. West was officious and he was also insistent. He pressed for assurances in writing that James would not take up arms against England in support of Louis XII. This James refused to do. He also made West linger in Scotland on the fringes of his court for two weeks. Though not unfriendly on a personal level to West, the King of Scots made quite clear through his secretary, Patrick Paniter, that he would not do Henry's bidding meekly: 'He [Paniter] concluded by repeating what many others had said at different times, that when we needed the Scots we made "importunate suit" to them, and when we did not need them, we despised them and did them all the harm we could.'

Thus rebuffed, West attempted to enlist Margaret's support. He asked her to intercede with her husband. Given her English background, he hoped that she might be able to use her influence to get a written commitment out of James. Margaret refused – and promptly asked about why her father's legacy was being withheld from her. She made her loyalties in the matter very plain.

Eventually, once Easter was over, West was permitted a face-to-face meeting with James IV, on 9 April 1513. He repeated his request and was again refused. James said he would lose the French king 'if he wrote so plainly' and reiterated his displeasure that Henry had accused him of saying one thing and doing another – 'that his words and his deeds did not agree'. Frustrated, West asked for permission to leave Scotland, which he said was given with good will. James advised him to travel to Linlithgow before he began his journey south. The queen was now there with her son and she had 'tokens' (gifts) for Henry VIII and Katherine of Aragon.

It was a Sunday when West rode out from Edinburgh to Linlithgow and he did not arrive till late afternoon. There he found Margaret fully apprised of the state of affairs between England and Scotland. She asked him at once how his interview with her husband had gone. Regretfully, West told her that James again refused to commit himself to paper. Margaret knew the reason for this very well and West, no doubt wanting to drive his point home, replied that James must stand in great awe of France, 'if he dared not show in writing the promise that he would keep his oath, and also that Henry would never reveal what he [James] wrote as long as he kept his promise'. Margaret had every reason to believe that her brother was unreliable but responded, tactfully, that she was sorry, 'as now Henry was in the right and James in the wrong. Without discussion of the legacy, or of any other matters, she gave him tokens for Henry, his queen and the princess [Mary, Henry's younger sister]'. Then, on her instructions, he was taken to see Prince James, 'a right fair child and large of his age'.[13]

There was more subtlety in this parting shot of Margaret's than West perhaps realized. She wanted him to see and report on her son as a reminder to her brother of the fact that, for all the 'tokens' she might send to him and Katherine of Aragon, they were still childless. She herself had a far greater gift – a healthy son and heir, at last, for the Stewart dynasty. And he was half a Tudor.

11

Flodden

'The battle began between four and five of the clock in the afternoon ... with marvellous slaughter of men.'

Contemporary English account of the Battle of Flodden,
9 September 1513

Although Margaret had spoken judiciously to Dr West when they met at Linlithgow, it is clear that the exchange rankled with her. She penned her bitter recriminations to her brother, quoted in the previous chapter, the very next day.

Margaret's eloquence was a typical Tudor trait. Henry VIII could, of course, match it. Nowhere was this more apparent than in the final diplomatic exchange between James IV and his brother-in-law. On 11 August, Sir William Cumming of Inverlochy, Lyon Herald, arrived at the English camp in France. He found Henry in his 'rich tent' and, undeterred by such impressive surroundings, delivered an uncompromising message. Henry was to 'desist from further invasion and utter destruction of our brother and cousin, the Most Christian King (Louis XII) ... and we will do what thing we trust may cause you to persist from pursuit of him'. Though not explicitly stated, James was informing Henry that he should abandon his French campaign altogether and 'be at home in your realm'.

Henry exploded. 'Tell your master', he said, 'that I mistrust not so the realm of England but he shall have enough to do whensoever he beginnith ... Tell him that there shall never Scot cause me to return my face.' It would surely be more fitting for James, 'being married to the King of England's sister', to count him, rather than Louis, as his ally. 'And now for a conclusion, recommend me to your master and tell him if he be so hardy to invade my realm or cause to enter one foot of my ground, I shall make him as weary of his part as ever was man that began any such business.' He went on to say that he was 'the very owner of Scotland and he [James] holds it through homage to me'. He called the King of Scots his vassal and a rebel. Nor would he leave Margaret out of it, claiming, 'I care nothing but for misentreating my sister, that would God she were in England on a condition she cost the French king not a penny.' Sir William Cumming knew his queen well enough to retort, on her behalf, 'If your Grace would give her your whole realm, she would forsake it to be entreated as she is.'[1] Though Henry was liberal with his insults, accusing James IV of being bribed by Louis XII, it is apparent from these bitter exchanges that the rivalry between James and Henry was intensely personal, and that the English king was determined to make his sister the focus of it.

In reality, he cared not a fig for how Margaret was treated in Scotland. His riposte to Lyon Herald effectively called his own sister a liar. It was already apparent that the rivalry was not just between James IV and Henry VIII, but between the Tudor siblings. As time would show, it never went away. Yet in the summer of 1513 Henry could not directly take part in any preparations for war against Scotland or any fighting that might ensue, no matter how much he threatened to expel

James from England when he returned. For the present, he had to leave the defence of England to Katherine of Aragon, his regent, and the council that advised the queen, led by Archbishop Warham. Most of Henry's leading military commanders had accompanied him to France and the admiral of the English fleet, Sir Edward Howard, had died in a foolhardy attack on the port of Brest in April. Henry's position was by no means as certain as his bombast had suggested. Just over a week after the fractious interview between Lyon Herald and the king of England, the main part of the Scottish army and its impressive ordnance marched out of Edinburgh, heading for the muster point in Berwickshire where the northern and Border lords would join them.

Before he left his capital, James had gone to Linlithgow to take his farewell of Margaret and Prince James. We do not know what passed between them and the dramatic fears the queen is said to have expressed were fabricated years later by chroniclers who wished only to diminish the king's memory. If Margaret experienced bad dreams and visions, or orchestrated the appearance of a strange man in blue prophesying disaster, while James was praying at the Church of St Michael beside the palace, none of these tales is corroborated in contemporary accounts. Perhaps she did have private misgivings about a war between England and Scotland as well as an inevitable degree of anxiety about her husband's welfare, but Margaret knew James well enough after ten years of marriage to understand that there was no future in trying to get him to back down against her brother now. For his part, James was sufficiently confident in the queen's sense and judgement to name her in his will as tutrix (or governor) to their son, as well as regent for Scotland, if he did not return. This was a high compliment to Margaret, who, as an Englishwoman, was not necessarily an obvious choice to hold the regency in the event of James's death. This position might have been expected to go to the nearest male blood relative. It is a testament to the strength of their marriage and their mutual respect, which had survived Margaret's understandable resentment at her husband's continued weakness for other women, that James deemed her capable of fulfilling such a role. She had proved a loyal wife and had suffered considerably in the quest to provide him with an heir. In fact, she was in the first weeks of yet another pregnancy when they parted, though it was probably too early for her to have known for sure that she was carrying another child.

Yet James did not seriously believe that Margaret would need to assume the responsibilities written into his will. He expected to succeed, to repel any force sent against him. His ultimate aim, ambitious but not necessarily unrealistic, was to press as far south as York, to establish an alternative government there for the north of England. Despite later claims, still repeated by some historians, that his council was divided and he had to strong-arm them into obedience, James was supported by his councillors and nobility, with just two exceptions. These were the elderly bishop of Aberdeen, William Elphinstone, a long-standing advocate of the benefits of peace with England, and Archibald Douglas, earl of Angus, who, at sixty-four years old, was no youngster himself. Angus and James IV had a history of difficult relations and the earl had been imprisoned for a while. He was also believed to be personally pro-English, though two of his sons accompanied James on the 1513 campaign.

James left Edinburgh on the evening of Friday, 19 August. His cannons, cast in bronze and superbly decorated, were examples of the very latest military technology from Europe. He also employed gunners and military strategists from the continent, though his master gunner, Robert Borthwick, was a Scot. The king had issued orders for the Scottish nobles and their retainers to muster at Ellem in Berwickshire.

This was a feudal levy (the last to be used in Britain) and the soldiers, unlike their English opponents, were unpaid. The nobility's overwhelming response to their monarch's summons is evidence of how successful James IV had been in uniting Scotland under his kingship. This campaign would, he believed, bathe the country in glory like never before, not even after Bannockburn. Small but potent under his leadership, Scotland would confirm its place as a leading European power. When the combined forces crossed the River Tweed at Coldstream on 22 August, in persistently damp weather, they were about 40,000 men. It was the largest force ever to invade England.[2]

The King of Scots's initial strategy was to follow the time-honoured pattern of Border warfare and attack the line of English castles that stood as a hopeful bulwark against such incursions in Northumberland. James met with some opposition, especially from the defenders of the bishop of Durham's fortress at Norham, but thereafter his progress was unhindered. The castles of Etal and Wark fell easily. He moved on to Ford Castle, which was surrendered to him by its chatelaine, Lady Elizabeth Heron, on 1 September. While considering his next move, James made Ford Castle his headquarters for four days. The weather was, if anything, worsening, there were early signs of desertion and the farther he got from Edinburgh, the longer were his supply lines. There was precious little in this part of England to feed a large army. He had time to take stock, as no opposing English force had yet appeared to challenge him.

Though his detractors subsequently claimed that James had indulged in a brief but passionate affair with Lady Heron, matched by a similar fling between his son, Alexander Stewart, and Lady Heron's daughter, there is no evidence to support these slurs, despite Sir Walter Scott's assertion in 'Marmion', his epic poem about Flodden, that 'O'er James's heart, the courtiers say, Sir Hugh the Heron's wife held sway.' Elizabeth Heron had never been to the Scottish court, as Scott asserts, as a hostage for her husband, though his release from prison seems to have been part of the terms she agreed for surrendering Ford Castle.[3] This suggests she was a loyal wife and effective negotiator rather than a seductive siren. The tale is salacious and bears witness to James's reputation as a womanizer, but, in truth, he had more to occupy his attention than his hostess's charms, real or imagined. Scrambling to respond to the Scottish invasion, the English were now preparing to defend the northernmost part of their realm. On Monday, 5 September their army was just twenty miles away from Ford Castle, at Bolton in Glendale. It was commanded by the seventy-year-old veteran the earl of Surrey, the very man who had escorted Margaret Tudor to her wedding to James IV ten years earlier. James IV's response was swift, and hardly that of a man distracted by a fair lady. He burned Ford Castle to the ground and moved on to join his own army, who were massing on Flodden Hill, an impregnable position just a few miles to the south-west.

Surrey was greatly distressed to have been left behind when Henry VIII, surrounded by men who were notably younger than the earl, set off for France. The exclusion seemed like an insult, a further indication that the taint of unreliability hung over the Howard family. Being told to keep an eye on the Scots was scarcely a compensation for the chance to crown his military career in France. On the surface, he put a brave face on this setback to his family's fortunes, responding to Henry VIII's command not to be negligent in keeping a close eye on the Scots with the words: 'I shall do my duty and your Grace shall find me diligent and to fulfil your will shall be my gladness.'[4] In truth, he was filled with much more despair than gladness. All he could see was tedious responsibility and perhaps, at the most, yet more border skirmishing. He had had enough of that years ago. There was no glory in it. Since he could not voice his displeasure to his own king, the embittered earl turned his venom on James IV. 'Sorry may I see him ere I die', he said, 'that is the cause of my abiding behind. If ever he and I meet, I shall do all that lies within me to make him as sorry as I can.'[5] It must have sounded like an empty threat, yet the Howards were a vindictive bunch and anyone who knew Surrey would have accepted that he meant every word, if indeed those ascribed to him in Hall's *Chronicle* are accurate. Perhaps they are nothing more than a chronicler writing years after the events described and producing a lively, rather than verbatim, account, designed to appeal to the reader.

For the next two months, it seemed unlikely that Surrey would ever have the opportunity to make good on such threats. He was given the title of commander of the north, with the remit of putting together a fighting force of men from among the levies of the northern lords. The early indications were that this would not even be needed. When Surrey enquired about the possibility of Scottish aggression, Sir Thomas Dacre reported at the end of June that he 'neither sees, hears nor knows of any such appearance or likelihood in the Scots'. He still found the Scottish Border officials that he worked with well disposed, giving him 'no cause of complaint'. [6] Dacre's confidence was misplaced. The reports of Scottish military preparations found their way down to London within a few weeks. By late July, Surrey was on his way north. At the beginning of August he was in Yorkshire, at Pontefract, where he held a council of the northern lords. Still Dacre urged caution. Surrey's force would simply not have the manpower to stage a counter-invasion. It could not be more than defensive, a means of keeping the Eastern Marches, as the border area of Northumberland was known in those days, protected. Until more was known about James IV's intentions the English response could not adequately be assessed.

In London, meanwhile, the outlook was very different. If Surrey had been frustrated and resentful at the thought of yet more inconsequential border skirmishing with the Scots, Katherine of Aragon was in her element. She felt that this was her moment. No longer merely Henry VIII's childless wife, she saw the opportunity to become a warrior queen, as her mother, Isabella of Castile, had been. Though dead for nearly ten years, Isabella loomed large in her youngest child's memory. While Katherine's sister-in-law Queen Margaret passed the weeks of late summer quietly with her toddler son at Linlithgow, the English queen's energy and enthusiasm for war were boundless. She would show her husband that she could galvanize his kingdom against the upstart Scots and relished the idea of taking the fight to James IV personally. Yet there is a hint of trying too hard in the frequent letters she sent to Wolsey in France. She exhorted him to ensure that Henry 'avoid all manner of dangers' and asked for regular news, since she was 'without any other comfort'. Perhaps this correspondence was a way of compensating for her very real concerns about her husband's safety. Both Margaret and Katherine were aware that if either of their spouses was involved in serious fighting, they could be killed. It was less than thirty years since Richard III had died on Bosworth Field. Such an outcome was even more alarming for Katherine than Margaret, because Henry VIII had no heir. And James IV had threatened to be in York by Michaelmas, 29 September. Katherine could not dismiss this as the empty promise of a man who had every reason to despise the Archbishop of York, Christopher Bainbridge.[7] If he could make good on his claim,

James would divide England while its king was still playing at war in northern France.

Katherine was nothing if not decisive. While Surrey was gathering men in the north, she and Sir Thomas Lovell were raising two separate armies, Lovell in the Midlands and the queen in the London area. She reviewed her troops at Buckingham, apparently intending to accompany them north if it became necessary. There is one report, from Venice, on Katherine and her welfare at this time which needs to be mentioned because it has attracted a great deal of attention in historical fiction, not least in television shows meant to entertain rather than inform. The assertion that Katherine was pregnant in the late summer of 1513, and that she gave birth to a son, is unsubstantiated. The same report in which it originates contains major errors, including the inaccurate statement that James IV had two legitimate children, a boy and a girl. It seems highly unlikely that Henry would have nominated his wife as regent if she was in the last stages of pregnancy, especially given her history of stillbirths. A queen who would have had to take to her chamber for weeks while awaiting a birth could not participate meaningfully in government, above all at a time of crisis. There is no other report of a child being born to her in 1513, so while it may look good on the screen to put Katherine on horseback at the head of her troops while wearing gold armour over her abdomen, this bears no relationship to reality. In the end, there would be no need of any extra troops. Katherine of Aragon's military adventure fizzled out in the Home Counties of England, amid the banners and badges which she had ordered for her troops. It would be Surrey and not the queen who engaged the King of Scots in battle on a Northumbrian hillside almost 400 miles away.

Surrey held a council of war with his English commanders on
4 September. He knew his army was much smaller in number
than the Scottish host and that his options were limited. A
pragmatist, the earl could not see any likelihood of victory if
he took on the entire Scottish army. On the other hand, it was
obvious that he could not stay for long in an area where there
were precious few supplies to be had. If a full-scale assault on
James IV's forces was not an option, neither was withdrawal.
The dressing-down (or worse) from the over-zealous Queen
Katherine in London was too hard to contemplate for a man
who shared the prejudices of his time when it came to females
thrust into positions of power. The best he could probably
hope for, when all the circumstances were considered, was a
limited action that might buy time and at least cause sufficient
disruption to the Scots that James's army would withdraw
back across the border. To achieve this, he had to get James
out into the open, and to do so as soon as possible. He would
even name a date for this confrontation to take place.

Surrey knew his quarry well, even if they had not met in
person for a decade. James was a true believer in the chivalric
code, whereas Surrey, not a romantic soul, saw it as merely a
means to an end. He had demonstrated his underlying contempt for chivalry in the way he had belittled Margaret Tudor
and her household during the journey from Collyweston to
Edinburgh and at the time of the marriage itself. Yet if he
followed the accepted form of things, he might yet be able
to play James to his own advantage. He sent his own herald,
Thomas Hawley, Rouge Croix, bearing two letters for the
King of Scots, one from Surrey himself and one from his son,
Thomas Howard, admiral of the English fleet. Hawley was
intercepted near Ford Castle, before he got close enough to
assess exactly what the Scots were doing up on Flodden Hill.
But he was treated honourably. The next day, Surrey and his
commanders heard the response of James IV, sent by Islay

Herald. James rejected all Henry VIII's assertions that he had broken the Treaty of Perpetual Peace. He was courteous in his reply, as befitted his rank and authority, and he seems to have ignored, at least in his public utterances, the contemptuous ramblings of the younger Thomas Howard, who had accused the Scottish fleet of fleeing before him by taking a long route to France around the coast of Ireland. Instead, James finished his reply with the words that Surrey wanted to hear: 'this we take for our quarrel and with God's grace shall defend the same at your affixed time, which with God's grace we shall abide'.[8]

Any relief that Surrey felt was short-lived. James was prepared to fight, but he had very wisely not specified where. He was now atop Flodden Hill, an impregnable position. The earl knew that there would only be one victor if he offered battle now – and it would not be him. Frustrated, and feeling that time was running out, he resorted to a calculated insult, berating James for not being true to his word.

> And by your herald Islay ye made answer that you were right joyous of my desire, and would not fail to accomplish the same and to abide me there, where you were at the time of my message ...

> And albeit it hath pleased you to change your said promise and put yourself into a ground more like a fortress or camp that any indifferent ground for battle to be tried ... I desire of your Grace for the accomplishment of your honourable promise your will dispose yourself for your part, as I shall do for mine, to be tomorrow with your host in your side of the plain of Milfield.

If these conditions were met, Surrey graciously promised that he would be 'ready to give you battle between noon and three o'clock in the afternoon, upon sufficient warning by you to be given by eight or nine of the clock in the morning'.[9]

Surrey's extraordinary cheek in summoning an anointed king to what sounds to modern ears like some sort of business meeting, with a detailed timetable and precise joining instructions, tells us a great deal about his bravado and perhaps also his mounting sense of desperation. James IV reacted with fury. He had had enough of this self-important English aristocrat. It was the very antithesis of chivalry to issue such a challenge to a king. 'Show to the earl of Surrey', came the reply, 'that it beseemeth him not, being an Earl, so largely to attempt a great Prince. His Grace will take and hold his ground at his own pleasure, and not at the assigning of the Earl of Surrey.'[10]

Realizing that James would not budge, Surrey was left with no option but to change the battleground himself. The appointed day for the fight was nearly upon him. The decision he made was that of an experienced soldier with nothing to lose. From midday on 8 September he moved his entire army across to the eastern bank of the River Till. In driving rain, his men marched north and west. By the afternoon of the next day they had all arrived at the foot of Branxton Hill. The terrain meant that these moves were not immediately obvious to James IV but when he received reports from his scouts he realized that Surrey was trying to disrupt his supply lines and cut off any possible retreat back into Scotland. The king's objective now was to get to Branxton Hill and place his formidable artillery along the line of the ridge before Surrey arrived. Though striking such a large camp and moving its guns was no straightforward task, he gave his orders without hesitation. He believed he would have the old man at his mercy.

In the mid-afternoon of 9 September 1513, King James IV of Scotland stood atop Branxton Ridge in Northumberland, looking out over what was soon to become the field of battle below. It would not have been easy to have clear sight of the land as the weather was atrocious. There had been almost incessant rain since he left Edinburgh and now the sodden hillside was swept by wind, which blew sheets of moisture across in drifts. The smoke of campfires diminished visibility even further and the mud coating the tracks between Flodden Hill and Branxton Ridge had impeded the progress of his guns, though they were finally now in position.

James was satisfied that all was ready. He was splendidly dressed, a gold-and-scarlet surcoat decorated with the royal arms of Scotland covering his full suit of armour. At forty years old, he was still very fit and fully able to support the rigours of hand-to-hand fighting, should this become necessary. At his side was his standard-bearer, carrying the king's red-and-gold banner. The king and his commanders, also richly arrayed, had discussed their battle plan and were ready for combat. The Scottish army, composed of four different groups or 'battles', as they were known, was drawn up awaiting James IV's orders. On the left were 10,000 men commanded by Lord Home and the earl of Huntly, a combined force of Borderers and Highlanders, perhaps not kindred spirits, and not always speaking the same language, since Gaelic was common in the Highlands. Yet overall they were a formidable fighting unit, whose two leaders had, for some time, put their personal differences aside and were now co-operating in support of their king against the hated English. In the left-centre were the earls of Erroll, Montrose and Crawford, commanding 7,000 men from central Scotland and the Lowlands. To their right was the main 'battle', some 15,000-strong, commanded by the king himself and with his household troops at its core, fighting under the banners of

St Andrew and St Margaret. To James IV's right was a smaller force of 5,000 men, led by the earls of Argyll and Lennox. These were mostly Highlanders and their chieftains, joined by a small group of Frenchmen.[11]

This army of around 35,000 men was formidable by any standards. Nor was it notable merely for its size. The flower of Scottish nobility had come to serve the king, proud of his achievements in raising Scotland's status in the world and looking to share in a glorious victory. They were committed to the Stewart cause and willing to put their lives on the line for it. When James gave the order for the first volley of gunfire at about three in the afternoon, not one of them could have anticipated that anything other than a resounding victory over a disrespectful young brat of an English king, conveniently far away in France, could be the outcome. If there were any misgivings about the lack of familiarity with the terrain, no one seems to have voiced such doubts. There was some discussion about whether James himself should stay to the rear, to safeguard his royal person. James gave such fears short shrift. He had been fighting since he was fifteen years old and was not about to skulk behind his troops now. His willingness to hazard danger had caused anxiety in the past. He did not expect to win merely by recourse to artillery. The guns were, quite literally, an opening shot, designed to signal the commencement of battle. His highly trained pike formations would then move forward to sweep the English off the field.

It was only when the unpredictable, billowing wind temporarily cleared that Surrey got the full picture of what he was facing. He made quick adjustments to the disposition of his own, much smaller force, which numbered about 26,000 men. His son Edmund commanded the right, facing Home and Huntly, while Thomas, the admiral, who had only arrived belatedly, was opposite the forces of Crawford, Erroll and

Montrose in the centre. The earl himself was on the left, with Dacre's force of mounted 'prickers', as the light cavalry of the English side of the Borders was known, in reserve. Sir Edward Stanley and his longbowmen were not part of these initial manoeuvres; their moment would come in the latter stages of the engagement.

The Scots, shooting downhill, soon realized the difficulties of finding the right range. Most of their shot went right over the heads of the English army, whereas Surrey's gunners, with lighter ordnance that could be more easily moved, had more success shooting uphill. James IV had not expected that his first artillery barrage would settle anything but neither had he anticipated how ineffective his great guns would be. So now it was necessary to give the order for the pikemen to move down towards the enemy.

On that gloomy afternoon, the English army watched as Huntly and Home's men moved down towards them, in tight formation and in total silence, as they had been trained by their European experts in field warfare. Many were barefoot, in order to get better purchase on the muddy slope. The sight must have been more eerie than even the most ear-shattering war cries or Gaelic imprecations. It seemed like the Scots were sending a wall of quiet death down Branxton Hill. As Huntly and Home's men swept on, Edmund Howard's men, panicked by the pikemen and their supporting bowmen and swordsmen, broke and fled. Howard was left fighting for his life. He was eventually rescued, having been knocked to the ground three times, by the Bastard Heron, the brother-in-law of Lady Elizabeth Heron of Ford Castle, whom the Scots had wanted to capture since he had murdered one of James IV's Border officers. The Scots knew well who Edmund Howard was and had failed to push home their advantage by trying to capture him for ransom. This gave Surrey time to call up Dacre and for the momentum of the fighting to change dramatically. This, however, had little to do with Dacre, effective though his 'prickers' were. Instead, it was the result of something that James IV and his remaining generals could not have anticipated – the nature of the ground on which the rest of the Scottish army would now find itself in deadly hand-to-hand fighting. For Huntly and Home, from their position to James IV's left, had taken a different route downhill. It was longer, but over firmer ground, and it gave no real indication of the difficulties that would be encountered by Erroll, Montrose and Crawford.

The ground at the bottom of the slope was more than a marshy morass. As thousands of Scots, with their unwieldy pikes in tight formation, advanced and were harassed by their English opponents, it became a sea of mud without any surface at all. The men were encumbered by carrying their pikes in tight formation and their leaders soon exhausted by wearing such heavy armour that they could only fight for a few minutes at a time. They sank deep into the ground and were despatched by the English, whose lighter weapons made it easier for them to recover and move around. For, as the Scots were to discover, the English bill, a hedging instrument much shorter than a pike but even more deadly in such dire circumstances, could kill swiftly, brutally and much more effectively.

James IV, observing that the advance of his earls was faltering but still unaware of the full horrors that the terrain would wreak on his army, then moved his own 'battle' forward and downhill. He still hoped that he could get the upper hand but must have had increasing misgivings. As the afternoon turned into evening, he would have realized how desperate his situation was. The Scots fought on, their king in their midst, with remarkable bravery, but they were drawn ever further into a quagmire of death. Home and Huntly had withdrawn when their first, successful, part of the attack was over. They were now being held at bay by Dacre's forces and were unable to intervene directly, for which they have been criticized. Home had not given up, however, and continued to put up resistance well into the evening, when he tried, unsuccessfully, to harry the English and rescue James IV's guns. Argyll and the Highlanders, now without orders, did not move forward and their indecision proved costly when Stanley's men stole up the hill and outflanked them, inflicting heavy casualties with the arrows from their longbows.

By six in the evening, most of the Scottish commanders were dead. James gathered his household troops and fought on, hoping that if he could kill Surrey the English might yet crumble. It was said that he got to within a spear's length of the man who had brought him his bride. His standard-bearer was killed next to him and his much-loved illegitimate son, the short-sighted Alexander Stewart, fell in the thick of the fighting. James himself was wounded by an arrow that lodged in his jaw, and his left hand was almost severed before he, too, was slashed across the throat by an English soldier wielding a bill. As his blood seeped into the sodden ground, he must surely have wondered, with his dying breath, what would happen to the Scotland he had ruled so brilliantly and the English princess who had become his wife so young and played her part irreproachably in his success.

Flodden is one of the most important and least-known battles in British history. Its battlefield is also one of the best preserved in Europe. Anyone who wants to see where a great monarch died can visit the site, and walk up Branxton Ridge to look out, as James IV did, over the fields below. The land at the bottom is still damp and, even without the benefits of the twentieth-century science of hydrogeology, if the Scots had been given more time to scout the landscape before battle was joined, it is possible that James would have used his forces differently. Surrey, a wily old soldier who was spurred by the bald realization that he must succeed or face the fact that his family's fortunes would not be recoverable, deprived King James of that possibility by shifting his English army under cover of concealing terrain and appalling weather conditions.

In 1513, what is now peaceful countryside was the scene of slaughter so appalling that, at its height, the loss of life rivalled in intensity some of the actions of the Somme campaign in the First World War. The defeat was overwhelming for the Scots and left a deep scar on their history for centuries. The words of 'The Flowers of the Forest', the famous lament for the fallen of Flodden, are not contemporary, though its melody may be based on a much earlier tradition. The sentiments are certainly true: 'The pride of our land lay cold in the clay'; 10,000 Scots, including a bishop, two abbots, twelve earls, thirteen lords, five eldest sons of peers and up to 300 other men of rank, perished with James IV. It was said that more than eighty members of the extended Hay family fell that day. Nor should it be forgotten that 4,000 Englishmen died too. Astonishingly, no monument was erected on the battlefield until 1910. It bears the simple but heart-breaking inscription: 'To the brave of both nations.'[12]

There is no contemporary Scottish account of the battle but the English, predictably, were keen to put quill to parchment to enthuse over their victory. Their poets, too, poured scorn on James IV or presumed to describe the feelings of his lonely ghost as it contemplated the wreck of his dreams.

Of Scotland he said late I was king
With crown on head and sceptre in hand
In wealth and honour I lacked nothing

In peaceable manner I ruled my land
Order my realm I could with a white wand
Now I am exiled from land and liberty
King without realm, lo now where I stand
Miserere me deus et salva me[13]

The poet William Dunbar called James IV 'the glory of princely governing'. This gives the idea of his spirit, wandering lost and alone, unaware even of what has happened to him, a desperate poignancy. There is in it an echo of the belief that was clung to by some of his subjects that he had somehow escaped the carnage and gone on pilgrimage to the Holy Land. But there is no question that he was dead. Dacre identified the king's body, stripped naked, as had been all the Scots by plunderers from the English side, the next morning. His loss would have the gravest of implications for the British Isles, which were not fully played out for the rest of the sixteenth century. Yet in 1513 there was one person, above all, for whom his loss was overwhelming. Two months before her twenty-fourth birthday, Queen Margaret, by now certain that she was again pregnant, was left to contemplate the collapse of her world. Even in the desolation of her first grief, she could not have imagined the difficulties that lay ahead.

Part III

The Struggle for Power, 1513–24

12

Aftermath

'The lords think it expedient, and it please the queen's grace, that the king our sovereign lord be crowned on ... the 21st day of this month of September in the church of the castle of Stirling.'

The Lords of the Council of Scotland to Queen Margaret

Popular legend has it that Margaret had kept watch for the returning army from a turret room at Linlithgow and that her screams reverberated around the palace when the messenger arrived with the news of her husband's death in battle. This is dramatic but obviously fanciful. Margaret may have been strong-willed but there is no indication that she was ever hysterical. Nor can the news of the defeat have been entirely unexpected, since rumours of what had befallen James IV and the Scottish host reached Edinburgh the day after the catastrophe at Flodden. There was sufficient concern for the local authorities to put the capital immediately on a defensive footing, in case the English attempted to push further into Scotland. We do not know precisely when the news reached Margaret at Linlithgow, or who imparted it to her. Her private grief must have been considerable; James IV, for all his womanizing, had been a supportive and generous husband and their relationship had strengthened over the ten years of their marriage. Margaret was twenty-three years old and pregnant with their sixth child. She might have been forgiven for thinking that her world had collapsed, leaving her vulnerable and uncertain. Instead, she acted with firmness and decision.

It was of the utmost importance to safeguard her son, dangerously exposed to further English incursions if he remained at Linlithgow. Margaret moved with despatch to take him north to Stirling, originally her dower castle but now hers by right as queen mother. Stirling's lofty walls and improved defences offered the best hope of security for the child-king and his pregnant mother. Ten days after Flodden, a general council of the Scottish lords, sitting at Stirling, approved Margaret's appointment as regent and governor of the kingdom, as James IV had laid out in his will, which stated that 'he constitutes and ordains Queen Margaret … his most dearest spouse, tutrix testamentare'. Margaret was to rule with the aid of a council, and always with a minimum of 'three spiritual and three temporal [lords] as it liketh the queen to command'.[1] This gave the queen power to direct all aspects of government, from military expenditure to religious appointments and the vexed question of foreign policy, as well as the upbringing of the king, whose education was to be entrusted to the aged William Elphinstone, the faithful servant of the child's father and grandfather. Margaret would retain the leading role in government and responsibility for her son, so long as she did not remarry. In September, as the queen and her advisers struggled to deal with their sorrow and the day-to-day demands of running a demoralized country, the possibility of her remarriage did not seem an immediate concern. The priority was to arrange the coronation of James V on 21 September.

Scottish kings were traditionally crowned at Scone near Perth, but it was felt safer for the ceremony to take place at

Stirling in such uncertain times. The seventeen-month-old king, supported by his mother, was crowned by the Archbishop of Glasgow, James Beaton. The boy could not have understood what was going on, or anticipated the difficulties that would lie ahead during his long minority. As Beaton held the crown over little James's head – it was, of course, too big for him to wear – many of the congregation shed tears to see the hopes of Scotland embodied in such a young infant, so heedless of the import of what was going on around him. Most coronations are, by nature, celebratory events but the circumstances of this one, so soon after the disaster at Flodden, became known as the Mourning Coronation. Yet it would be far from the truth to suppose that Scotland was left rudderless after Flodden. The country had been dealt a terrible blow with the loss of its charismatic king and many of its leading men, but it had by no means ceased to function.

Margaret was advised by a full council and there was considerable continuity in respect of the major office-holders. James Beaton was appointed as chancellor by the end of September 1513. The role had most recently been occupied by Margaret's stepson, Alexander Stewart, who died fighting beside his father at Flodden. Beaton was then about forty years old, an active and able administrator as a churchman, who now found himself in one of the most powerful offices in the land, quite an achievement since, unusually, he had no connection with any of the leading noble families of Scotland. Beaton was committed to Scottish independence and was determined to ensure that his country would not be bullied by England. The touchy area of Anglo–Scottish relations would, within a year, create friction between Beaton and Margaret.

Serving alongside Beaton was Alexander Home, one of the survivors of Flodden, who retained the role of chamberlain while also, in view of his affinity, being given responsibility for the pacification of the Borders. Archibald, fifth earl of Angus, a long-time thorn in James IV's side, was appointed to a prominent role in charge of justice south of the River Forth. Angus attended James V's coronation and some council meetings but died at the end of October. There was continuity, too, in the key roles of Lord Clerk Register, keeper of the Privy Seal and the principal secretary, filled by Gavin Dunbar, William Elphinstone and Patrick Paniter respectively. All of these men were experienced in the various functions of government and in the conduct of diplomacy. The preponderance of churchmen in these highest offices of state is typical of the times. They had, however, to work alongside an influx of newcomers on the council, brought about by the deaths of so many leading nobles at Flodden. These men were the younger, inexperienced representatives of their grieving families. Theirs was a crash course in politics and most took the responsibility seriously. Popular histories of Scotland in the sixteenth century have tended to depict the Scottish nobility as all being violent thugs. Some certainly were, at least at times, but the majority wished to serve their country and it is a tribute to their collective determination that Scotland survived and functioned as successfully as it did, despite long minorities of its Stewart monarchs and the ambitions of England (and, later, France) to subjugate the Scots.[2]

Much of the Scottish council's work for months after Flodden was taken up with attempting to provide assistance as quickly as possible to the many widows, of both great men and small, who were suddenly left without access to the income of their dead spouses. Ladies of all classes needed to ensure the title of their sons (often young children) to inherit their fathers' estates. The register of the council's meetings, often referring to decisions taken 'at command of the Queen' or 'at the Queen's instance', records the determination of Margaret and her lords to give redress as speedily as possible to those who had suffered such grievous losses. One such petitioner, heard at Perth on 5 November, was 'Isabel Dunbar, widow of Patrick McClellane of Gelstoun who was slain "in our sovereign lord's army and under his banner". Their son and heir is aged four and there are other five children, the eldest within seven years of age.'[3] It is in such poignant documents that the full scale of the tragedy of Flodden is revealed.

Margaret's 'daily' council was made up of a minimum of either six or eight lords, selected from the larger group, to be evenly divided between lords temporal and lords spiritual. She certainly did have a say in the choice of those who were 'to give her counsel and assist with her grace in such matters and actions as shall occur for the time', as is shown in her dismissal of Patrick Paniter, the long-serving secretary, in the spring of 1514.[4] It is not at all clear how many council meetings she was able to attend in person and historians have assumed, though without direct evidence, that the fact that she was pregnant must have acted as a constraint, particularly as the date of her delivery grew closer. Her appointment to the regency in James IV's will has been described as 'the only example of a sixteenth-century regent provided with an unambiguous, legally watertight and widely accepted statement of monarchical delegation to underpin her rule'.[5] The reality of governing Scotland, however, was not nearly as straightforward.

Although the sixteenth century in Europe saw many royal women emerge as powerful consorts, regents and even rulers in their own right, it was still a patriarchal society, one in which women were regarded as inferior to men and therefore not fit to take on serious responsibility. Of course, many did, often as a result of being widowed. In that respect, Margaret Tudor was not so different from Isabel Dunbar, or many of her European counterparts. The women of the Habsburg family were frequently sent as regents to distant parts of a growing empire, where they toiled unceasingly, in circumstances of great material comfort, it is true, but without the ultimate power that came with simply being male. In Margaret's case, the precedents for a female regent in Scotland were decidedly mixed.

There had been two female regents in fifteenth-century Scotland, Joan Beaufort and Mary of Guelders. Joan was an English noblewoman, the wife of James I of Scotland. She lost her husband in even more horrendous circumstances than Margaret. James I, an increasingly unpopular king, was hunted down by disaffected nobles, headed by his own elderly uncle, and assassinated in the sewers below the Blackfriars monastery in Perth. He had been attending a council meeting with his wife. Joan herself was wounded but managed to escape back to Edinburgh Castle, where she speedily secured her son, the six-year-old James II. Yet though she claimed the right to rule in her son's name after these events, which took place in late February 1437, her supporters were few in number. The fact that Joan was English by birth and had been married to a king hated by most of his own aristocracy did not help her cause. By the early summer, when Archibald, fifth earl of Douglas, was named lieutenant-governor of the realm, Joan's hopes of being formally recognized as regent evaporated. She did, though, retain control of her son. Two years later, in 1439, she married again, to Sir James Stewart, the Black Knight of Lorne, with whom she had a further three sons to add to the eight children of her marriage to James I. The little James II was taken from his mother's care very soon after her second marriage. Though Joan struggled sporadically to regain power, she unfortunately backed the wrong factions and was under siege in Dunbar Castle when she died in 1445.

Margaret must have known something of this earlier English Queen of Scots's attempts to establish her position and retain custody of her son, though she could not have drawn much comfort from them. The example of Mary of Guelders offered more hope. The wife of James II of Scotland was a Burgundian noblewoman who had amply provided her husband with sons when he was tragically killed at the siege of Roxburgh Castle in 1460. A cannon that the king was standing next to exploded, leaving his widow as regent for their eldest son, James III, who was then eight years old. Mary proved herself an effective ruler, anxious to promote Scotland's place in Europe. The outbreak of the first phase of the Wars of the Roses in England greatly weakened one of the major threats to Scottish security and Mary offered refuge to Henry VI and Margaret of Anjou after the Battle of Northampton. Her rule was cut short by her early death in 1463.

Neither of these examples offered clear guidance as to what Margaret might expect in her own case. Her first priority, with the advice of her council, was to ensure good government and stability in Scotland. Beyond that, the way forward was far from clear. The queen knew that relations with England and the rest of Europe had to be addressed. Her brother's policies and those of France would inevitably impinge on her capacity to rule effectively in Scotland. Margaret wanted peace with England and in this she was certainly not alone. But how could she pursue such a policy without inevitably being identified as pro-English? She was, after all, a Tudor by birth and her brother's army had just inflicted a humiliating defeat on Scotland. Yet if Margaret hoped for understanding or a constructive relationship with Henry VIII she was to find, not just in 1513 but in all the years to come, that she could expect nothing but interference, opposition and a barrage of wounding personal criticism in respect of her handling of Scottish affairs and her personal life.

The opportunities offered by a Tudor brother and sister ruling in harmony over the British Isles might seem obvious in retrospect but the sibling rivalry that lay beneath them has been overlooked by historians. Margaret understood that she needed her brother's help but was, naturally for a spirited Tudor woman, unwilling to allow herself to become an accessory rather than an equal. After ten years in Scotland she knew the country and its politics far better than Henry, who viewed the Scots with contempt and, as far as Margaret was concerned, pursued the attitude which underlined his entire kingship – that if you were not with him, you were against him. When Margaret wrote to Henry asking for a permanent peace, he replied, 'that the Scots should have peace or war with him according to their own choice and behaviour'. This dismissive response set the tone for all the frustrations that were to come. He would never seek her advice or listen to her on Scottish matters. On a personal level he did, as we shall see, have at least some degree of fraternal concern for Margaret's physical wellbeing (it would be a blow to his prestige if his sister was ill-treated), but beyond that he soon came to see her as an obstacle and not an ally. She was not someone that he could turn to for support in dealings with his Scottish and European neighbours. No documents survive to show whether he wrote to her after Flodden, though Katherine of Aragon certainly did.

Henry's Spanish queen had crowed to her husband that only the sensitivities of her advisers prevented her from shipping James IV's dead body over to France, so that he could share her gloating. On 16 September, by which time the news of the King of Scots's death would have reached Margaret in Linlithgow, Katherine wrote that she was sending a piece of James IV's bloodied surcoat as a trophy:

In this your grace shall see how I can keep my promise, sending you for your banners a king's coat. I thought to send himself unto you, but our Englishmen's hearts would not suffer it. It should have been better for him to have been in peace than have this reward.

She concluded, piously, that 'all that God sendeth is for the best'.[6] In a more conciliatory gesture, she sent a friar to Scotland to comfort her sister-in-law for the loss of her husband. Margaret, who had religious advisers of her own well able to fulfil such a role, sent a polite but terse reply.

The contradictions inherent in Margaret's desire to be her own woman while having, from time to time, to call on Henry's support never went away. They were also inextricably caught up in Scotland's policy towards France, the old ally that had drawn James IV into war with England and, inadvertently, sealed his fate. James IV had committed his splendid navy to the French cause in the 1513 war and sent the earl of Arran and Lord Fleming with the ships. The fleet had, however, arrived too late to play any part in the war in Europe. It would probably not have been needed in any case, but Arran was blamed for the delay because he had taken the western route via Ireland and stopped off unnecessarily in that country. He and Fleming were still at the French court when news of Flodden arrived.

Louis XII expressed his grief extravagantly in his instructions to Alexandre de la Bastie, his diplomatic representative in Scotland. He said that he:

grieves so much that he will never be content till he has shown the love he bore to the late King, which he will try to show also to the young King his son. Though such tragedies cannot be mentioned without sorrow to those whom they touch most deeply, [his] love to the late King of Scots was so great that he cannot hide it, and though he cannot bring him back from the dead, yet he would wish to make his memory everlasting in all the world as a great and virtuous King, worthy of all honour and glory, and to raise, preserve and guide his noble descendants and preserve them from their enemies.

He went on to mention the rumours that James IV was still alive – though he probably knew better than to give them much credence – and to ask for confirmation from Margaret and her council. Then he reassured them that he would, of course, maintain all his alliances with Scotland and charged de la Bastie to 'show to the Queen and Council the trouble which would come were the said kingdom [Scotland] to fall into the hands of their enemies, whereby would be lost the noble race of the Kings of Scotland'. Margaret and her advisers would have noted, however, that Louis was not disposed to let Arran and Fleming, or any of the Scottish ships, return just yet, claiming that he would 'guard them for the young King'.[7]

The self-interest in this declaration would not have been lost on Margaret, but her situation as regarded Louis XII and France was not a straightforward one. The next in line to the Scottish throne, at least until the child she was expecting arrived in the spring, was John Stewart, duke of Albany, James IV's first cousin and son of Alexander Stewart, the rebellious younger brother of James III. John (or Jehan, as he signed himself, in the French fashion) was born in France during his father's exile there and was a loyal and useful servant of the French crown. As the nearest male relative to James V, he was a serious contender for the regency, and therefore a potential threat to Margaret's position. It was true that he had no personal experience of Scotland or its politics, having never set foot in the land of his father's birth, but his upright character and military expertise made him a viable alternative, in the minds of some of the council, to a Tudor queen. As early as 26 November 1513, the general council of lords meeting at Perth gave formal support to Louis XII's request for the continuation of the Auld Alliance and requested Albany to come with men and munitions, so that Scotland could be better defended against future attacks by England. There was also the suggestion of a division of power between the queen, who would remain as keeper of the person of the young king and his unborn sibling, and Albany, who would be responsible for the day-to-day government of Scotland. Margaret, who was determined not to cede any of her power to a French rival (a move which offended her own sensibilities as much as she knew it would incur her brother's implacable opposition), was saved from having to face such an unpleasant challenge by Louis XII's refusal to let Albany come to Scotland. He always had one eye on relations with England and it was already apparent that Henry VIII did not want Albany in Scotland. So, for the time being, the threat to Margaret receded. It must, however, have preyed on her mind as her pregnancy progressed.

Early in 1514 there was speculation that Margaret might marry Louis XII when his wife, Anne of Brittany, died. Lord Dacre remarked, with all the gallantry of a man who had kidnapped his own heiress wife and forced her into marriage, that Louis was welcome to Margaret. The idea, perhaps never really given any serious consideration, faded. By the summer of 1514 it was Margaret's younger sister, Mary, who was selected as the new bride for the ageing French king. A Tudor triumph, perhaps, but not one that favoured Scotland. Despite his fair words, Louis made peace with England. He had not bothered to consult the Scots, nor did Henry VIII think it necessary to consider the implications of an Anglo–French alliance for his elder sister. But by then, Margaret had made a fateful decision about her own future. Exactly a week before Princess Mary Tudor's elaborate proxy wedding to Louis XII, on 13 August 1514 at Greenwich, Queen Margaret married for a second time.

13

The Second Husband

'A young, witless fool'.

His uncle's dismissive judgement of Archibald Douglas,
sixth earl of Angus

On 8 April 1514, Lord Dacre reported to Henry VIII that Margaret had taken to her chamber in Stirling to await the birth of James IV's posthumous child.[1] The queen had maintained a keen interest in government until a few weeks before this, dictating a letter to be delivered by the Lord Treasurer to a meeting of the Lords in Council which she ended by thanking them 'of the great diligence and labours you take for the common good of our realm, our son and us'. It was signed 'Margaret R'.[2] Three weeks after she retired from public view, Margaret gave birth to another son, on 30 April. He was named Alexander and given the customary title of the second son of a Scottish king, duke of Ross. Both mother and child did well; indeed, Margaret seems to have recovered more quickly from childbirth than she had with most of her previous pregnancies. She soon doted on little Alexander, the favourite of her children. The arrival of a second son might have been expected to strengthen the queen's position but, as the summer went on, she apparently did not see this as sufficient security for her continued role as regent.

It is not clear why Margaret felt her hold on power becoming more uncertain. She was soon attending council meetings again but the continued scepticism of some of her advisers, who had always been unconvinced of the wisdom of an Englishwoman directing Scottish government, could not have been lost on her. The brief records of council meetings do not give any flavour of discussion or dissension but there were undoubtedly mixed feelings and Margaret's active involvement in the choice of candidates to fill vacant church appointments continued to be a source of disagreement. This may have been at the root of her dismissal of Patrick Paniter as secretary.[3]

Appointments to benefices were, however, an aspect of monarchical power which previous rulers had viewed as being of the utmost importance. It did not help Margaret that challenges to her nominations, which could not be concluded without papal approval, had come from Henry VIII himself. This could hardly have improved the queen's standing in the eyes of her councillors. The key vacancy was that left by the death of Margaret's stepson, Alexander Stewart, Archbishop of St Andrews. At the end of 1513, the queen, with the council's support, proposed William Elphinstone, who, though elderly, was much revered for his life of service to the Scottish crown. Yet by the following spring, his appointment was still unconfirmed, following interference from Henry VIII, who had written to Pope Leo X as early as 13 October 1513 requesting him 'not to dispose of any of the Scottish bishoprics, rendered vacant by the slaughter of the prelates who were in the battle [Flodden], armed and without sacerdotal habit, until Henry has expressed his wishes with regard to them'. This was, he said, because 'the affairs of Scotland concern him nearly'.[4] The fact that the pope was also keen on promoting his own nephew to the see of St Andrews merely added to the delay and to rising Scottish frustrations.

Margaret was also well aware that there was continued support for the duke of Albany among the leading men of Scotland, though it was by no means universal. The Borders remained insecure, with Lord Dacre determined to keep up pressure and cause as much disruption as he could. A peaceful resolution of this constant cause of instability was high on the queen's priorities, but an effective military presence to give force to her intentions was not yet possible. Albany's arrival, with soldiers at his back, could strengthen Scotland overall but what his authority might be vis-à-vis that of the queen regent was a very grey area. It is hardly surprising that Margaret felt threatened by continued talk of the arrival of a foreigner with his own army. Where would this leave her?

In late spring, aware that rumours of disagreements among the council were fuelling disorder and the perception that the exercise of justice in Scotland was feeble, an order was given requiring all sheriffs to act diligently in enforcing the law in their districts. Dacre, an inveterate stirrer, reported in early June to Henry VIII: 'Sir, of a surety there is neither law, nor reason, nor justice at this day used nor kept in Scotland, but get as get may.'[5] This was almost certainly an exaggeration, but the measures taken at the time show that the situation was causing anxiety at the heart of Scottish government. The rumours of faction in the council also reached Albany in France. He wrote to Margaret encouraging her to 'make a point of fostering unity'. A further act in July used strong language to reinforce the Scottish government's determination to adminster justice in 'the most extreme ways throughout the realm'.[6]

Aware that doubts about the queen's authority were troubling not just to Margaret herself but to international perceptions of good government in Scotland, the council issued what appeared to be an unequivocal declaration of support for her regency on 12 July: 'Madame', it began:

we are content to stand in one mind and will and to concur
with all the lords of the realm to the pleasure of our master
the king's grace, your grace, and for the common weal,
and to use none other bands now nor in times to come in
the contrary.[7]

Yet Margaret was not reassured by this show of approbation
and deference. Her unease had been growing throughout
the spring of 1514. In the summer, she took a fateful step that
would have profound consequences for Scotland as a nation
and for herself as a woman in a man's world.

There is no reliable contemporary account of the precise date
or place of Margaret Tudor's marriage to Archibald Douglas,
sixth earl of Angus. Earlier biographers have given the date
as 6 August 1514, following John Lesley's *History of Scotland*,
written in 1578, but not printed until the early nineteenth
century. Lesley's date is conjectural and he does not give a
location for the ceremony.[8] The tradition has grown up, and
been repeated by recent writers about Margaret, that the wedding took place in secret in the church of Kinnoul, then a
village outside Perth on the bank of the River Tay. Kinnoul
is now a residential area of the city itself. The current parish
church dates from 1827, though it is known that there were
several earlier churches in Kinnoul. The present one does not
claim any connection with Margaret Tudor or her second husband on behalf of its sixteenth-century predecessor. All that
can be said with certainty is that the wedding took place sometime between late July and late August 1514, by which time
the queen's second marriage could not be kept secret. So who
was Archibald Douglas and why had Margaret chosen him as
a spouse within a year of the death of James IV at Flodden?

Archibald Douglas was the grandson of the fifth earl of Angus, who had died at the end of 1513. His own father was one of the many aristocratic casualties of Flodden but it was not until the early spring of 1514 that Angus joined the Scottish council. Like many other young men who were thrust into positions of influence by the disaster at Flodden, he had no direct experience of government. The Douglases, however, had a long and chequered involvement in Scottish affairs. Originating from Lanarkshire, they were the most prominent family in lowland Scotland for more than two centuries. Such power and influence would inevitably have led to resentment among the other great noble houses of Scotland and potentially caused friction with the monarchy, even if the Douglases had attempted to tread a careful path through history. As it happened, they were neither collegiate nor notably loyal to the crown. Anyone who tries to get even a basic grasp of the fortunes and personalities of the Douglases in medieval Scotland (and in France, for, like many noble Scots, they were also active there) enters a world of treachery, murder, tangled illegitimacy, affairs with sisters-in-law and violent deaths in battle which makes *Game of Thrones* look sedate. A family whose leading men sported names like Archibald the Grim, James the Gross and Hugh the Dull cannot easily be overlooked. It is marvellous stuff, but not easily disentangled. Yet an explanation of the Black Douglases and the Red Douglases is necessary to understand the background of Archibald Douglas and why his peers reacted to him – and his marriage to the widowed Queen Margaret – in the way that they did.

The original split between the Black Douglases and the Red Douglases took place in the fourteenth century, when the two divisions of the clan held separate earldoms. The Black Douglases were descended from the first earl of Douglas's legitimate son, James, while the Red Douglases were the product of the first earl's liaison with his sister-in-law,

Margaret Stewart, fourth countess of Angus. Margaret's title passed to George Douglas, her illegitimate son by the first earl. He died in 1400 and, thereafter, his descendants were given the title of earls of Angus and known as the Red Douglases. Relationships between the two branches of the family were seldom cordial, but in the mid-fifteenth century they grew worse. The Black Douglas earls fell foul of King James II and their disagreements resulted in the infamous murder of William, the eighth earl of Douglas, in Stirling Castle in 1452.

Understandably wary after the entrapment and summary beheading of his young cousin and namesake, the sixth earl, at the so-called Black Dinner twelve years earlier, William Douglas had tried to combine extension of his power in southern Scotland with staying out of James II's way by going on pilgrimage. He discovered, on his return, that the king had taken steps to curb his power and confiscate some of his lands. This was a serious source of disagreement in itself but James believed that Douglas was involved with rebels, and summoned Douglas to Stirling to explain himself. When Douglas refused to give ground, James II, a man not noted for his placid temperament, stabbed the earl in the neck with a dagger. Douglas, who had come under safe conduct, was then finished off by the king's courtiers. Such behaviour by the monarch did not inspire loyalty in William Douglas's brother James, the ninth earl, who rebelled against the king but was defeated at the Battle of Arkinholm in 1455 by a force led by George Douglas, fourth earl of Angus, himself a Red Douglas. The antipathy between the two sides of this great family resulted in the forfeiture of all the Black Douglas lands and the execution of the youngest Black Douglas brother, Hugh, earl of Ormonde.[9] James Douglas fled to England, where he remained in exile for many years, eventually returning to Scotland during the reign of James III and effecting a rapprochement of sorts with his Red Douglas cousins. Such was the heritage of the man who became Margaret Tudor's second husband in the summer of 1514.

Archibald Douglas himself was then in his early twenties. He was probably born in the same year as Margaret, though the precise date is unknown. His mother was a Drummond, which gave him links with another of Scotland's most prominent families. Nothing is known of his education, or what prompted his uncle's harsh judgement. Like his new wife, he had been married already, and widowed. In fact, his first wife, Margaret Hepburn, was the daughter of Patrick Hepburn, first earl of Bothwell, who had represented James IV at Margaret Tudor's proxy marriage. The couple were married in 1509 but Margaret Hepburn had died, probably within the last twelve months. Archibald's availability was therefore providential. Certainly his ambitious relatives, on both the Douglas and Drummond sides, saw it that way and encouraged him to abandon his engagement to Lady Jane Stewart of Traquair, an arrangement he had entered into shortly after the death of his first wife. Indeed, the impetus to propose Archibald as a prospective bridegroom for Queen Margaret may have come as much from his Drummond relatives as his Douglas kindred. He had ambitious uncles on both sides.

All of this suggests that Margaret may have been put under pressure, at a time when she was concerned about the viability of her position, to conclude a match with a man she certainly did not know well and whose apprenticeship in government was only just beginning. It would have been easy to prey on her fears and represent the young widower as the solution to her difficulties, despite the fair words she had so recently received from all the leading men of Scotland. Quite how the courtship, brief though it was, could have been carried out under the eyes of suspicious churchmen and nobles who had strong reservations about the Douglases is a mystery. Royalty led very public lives in those days and frequent meetings between the queen and her suitor would surely have attracted attention. Household staff, however loyal, might also have been expected to chatter among themselves, leading to inevitable rumours, but if Margaret's servants did, indeed, have some idea of what was afoot, their discretion seems to have been exemplary.

There is, though, one significant clue that perhaps affords an explanation of how Margaret's relationship with Angus evolved: on 1 May 1514, John, Lord Drummond, an active and wily seventy-six-year-old, was appointed as keeper of Stirling Castle and of the person of the king. He was Archibald Douglas's maternal grandfather. Drummond was now in a position to encourage and facilitate contact between the queen and the earl, and to do so with subtlety. The lack of firm evidence about the date and place of the marriage itself merely adds to the impression of calculated subterfuge. How could Margaret and Angus have arrived for the marriage ceremony at a church near Perth unremarked without careful planning? One possibility is that the wedding took place at an unsocial hour, either very early in the morning or late at night. Margaret's chief residence at the time was still Stirling, which is thirty-four miles from Perth, more than a day's journey by horseback. The officiating priest at the wedding is said to have been Drummond's own nephew.

A clandestine wedding is the stuff of romantic novels but the evidence suggests that this particular union was, on both sides, more pragmatic than love-struck and that the queen may have found herself under pressure that was hard to resist. Besides, Margaret did not wish to find herself on the European marriage market once more. Continued widowhood meant that she could still be a pawn in Henry VIII's diplomatic manoeuvres, whether as a bride for the French king, Louis XII, his equally elderly Habsburg rival, Holy

Roman Emperor Maximilian, or even the Italian Francisco Sforza, duke of Milan. To any of these rulers, Margaret, personable and evidently fertile, might have represented an attractive choice of wife. She could have exchanged the chilly and far-from-wealthy Scottish court for the luxuries and prestige of becoming a queen consort on a far greater stage. But this was not what Margaret wanted. Her guiding motive in remarrying in Scotland was to retain hold of her two sons and to shore up her own power as regent. She must have known that whoever she selected would be unpopular with other Scottish lords but, in truth, there were not many candidates apart from Angus.[10] So she agreed to marry him. She knew the risks but evidently believed they could be managed. No one had seriously expected that she would remain unwed. Indeed, some, most notably the poet William Dunbar, encouraged her not to languish too long in the single state.

> O fair sweet blossom, now in beauty's flower,
> Unfaded both of colour and virtue
> Thy noble lord that died has done *devoir*
> Fade not with weeping thy visage fair of hue.

Dunbar finished by exhorting the queen to 'live in lustiness', a term which in the sixteenth century would have suggested something more akin to healthy enjoyment of life rather than sexual voracity.[11]

Margaret has been heavily criticized for this second marriage, notably by female historians, who have fallen over themselves to depict her as a thoughtless, selfish young woman overpowered by sexual attraction for Angus. This character assassination began in earnest with the prim Victorian historian Agnes Strickland, who combined a moralizing tone with a shaky grasp of history and a penchant for hindsight in her many ill-informed judgements about Margaret and other women rulers, most notably Margaret's granddaughter, Mary, Queen of Scots, and James VI and I's wife, Anna of Denmark. Strickland remained an authority for many years and has coloured interpretations of Margaret Tudor ever since. 'In one moment of womanly weakness and romantic folly', wrote Maria Perry in 1998, 'Margaret Tudor had effectively destroyed her own power base'.[12] Such sentiments are enough to make the modern cohort of vibrant young women scholars of the period shudder. Womanly weakness and romantic folly are not part of their vocabulary, nor should they be. Indeed, Margaret was looking to shore up her power base and build upon it. Yet that the marriage of Margaret Tudor and Archibald Douglas was a disaster that blighted many lives is beyond doubt.

14

The Queen at Bay

*'To my lord duke of Albany, to come home in this realm
of Scotland in all possible haste. For the defence of the
same and for good rule to be put and kept in the said
realm in all parts.'*

Invitation to John Stewart from the Lords of the Council
of Scotland, 18 September 1514

The marriage of Queen Margaret and the earl of
Angus had taken place quietly but was evidently
known within two weeks, possibly even earlier.
Indeed, there would have been little advantage in keeping
it secret. Margaret had acquired a second husband to demonstrate her determination to retain power and exercise
it with the support of one of Scotland's leading families.
When the council met on 26 August, Angus was described
as 'her spouse'. Perhaps the couple would have liked a
little longer to hone their strategy but it was soon obvious
that they would not get their way. Attempts by Margaret
and her husband to deprive the chancellor, James Beaton,
of the Great Seal were firmly rebuffed, revealing even at
this early stage that their marriage had always been a power
play, not a moment of romantic folly. Indeed, the queen

ELIZABETHA · VXOR
HENRICI · VII ·

Anno h̅ o i̅ 20 octobꝛ ꝑmago henricth vii tannrtus erge vltertlim[...]
oꝛdinata ꝑ hensaiti smck tu ergit   albenum ·

1] Henry VII in 1505.
This portrait, by an unknown
artist from the Low Countries,
shows Margaret's care-worn
father two years after her
marriage to James IV of
Scotland.

2, *above right*] Elizabeth of
York, Margaret's mother.
The eldest child of Edward
IV was fully committed to
the new Tudor dynasty and
much-loved by her husband
and children.

[3] Lady Margaret Beaufort,
the grandmother of
Margaret Tudor. A pious
woman of great resolve,
she influenced Margaret's
upbringing. It was from
her house, Collyweston in
Northamptonshire, that
Margaret began her progress
to Scotland.

[4] The beautif[ul]
manuscript of t[he]
1503 Treaty of
Perpetual Peace,
which laid out t[he]
future of Anglo-
Scottish relation[s]
and the terms
of Margaret's
marriage to
James IV.

The entry of...
Princess Margaret
into York. 1503.

[5] A Victorian depiction of Margaret entering York through
Micklegate Bar on her white palfrey.

Maguerite Dangleterre Jvyne l'eleure fans dhihuny Dmc
2 vi Dangleterre femme de Jaques IV Roy bescosse

[6] A drawing of Margaret at about the time she married James IV.

[7] Stirling Castle, the major dower castle of Scottish queen consorts, was frequently Margaret's residence.

[8] James IV of Scotland, Margaret's charismatic first husband. Killed at the Battle of Flodden in 1513, he was an affectionate, if unfaithful, spouse, confident of his wife's abilities.

[9] Margaret's entry into Edinburgh, riding behind her husband, imagined by Victorian artist William Brassey Hole.

[10] Holyrood Abbey, where Margaret and James IV were married on 8 August 1503.

THO.ˢ HOWARD EARL OF SURRY

The Original late in the Torington Collection.

The Autograph of Thoˢ. Earl of Surry.

[11] Thomas Howard, earl of Surrey, who was responsible for delivering Margaret to Scotland. She resented his high-handed manner.

[12] The sumptuously illustrated Book of Hours of James IV and Margaret Tudor, a wedding gift from the king to his young wife.

[13] Henry VIII, Margaret's younger brother. Their relationship was marked by an almost lifelong sibling rivalry which had dire effects for both Anglo–Scottish relations and Margaret's own welfare.

[14] Katherine of Aragon, first wife of Henry VIII and Margaret's sister-in-law. They first met in 1501 when the Spanish princess married Prince Arthur, Margaret's elder brother.

[15] The Flodden Memorial at the foot of Branxton Ridge in Northumberland. Only erected in 1910, it bears the simple inscription 'To the dead of both nations'.

[16] Queen Margaret, sheltering her bewildered little son, James V, refuses to hand over her children to the custody of a delegation of Scottish lords at the gates of Stirling Castle in 1515.

[17] John Stewart, duke of Albany, governor of Scotland from 1515 until 1524. The nearest in the line of succession to James V was born in France and knew little of Scotland. His relationship with Margaret was volatile but he attempted to rule Scotland honourably.

[18] Archibald Douglas, earl of Angus, Margaret's second husband. Theirs was more likely to have been a marriage of convenience rather than a love-match. It soon descended into acrimony.

[19] James V of Scotland, Margaret's only surviving son. His mother's devotion to him was a constant in his life, despite their often being apart physically during his childhood. He grew into a handsome and energetic king.

[20] Margaret's daughter-in-law, Marie de Guise. Marie was the second wife of James V and she seems to have forged a good relationship with Margaret.

[21] Princess Mary Tudor, Margaret's younger sister, seen here with her second husband, the Tudor courtier Charles Brandon, duke of Suffolk. The sisters saw each other again in 1516–17, when Margaret spent a year in London.

was compelled to agree to the wording of the request that Albany should come to Scotland as its governor. Beaton and Lord Home, who was still a powerful force in the Borders and southern Scotland and therefore a natural enemy of the Douglases, moved that Margaret be deprived of the regency, citing that she had broken the terms of James IV's will by marrying again.

They were supported by a majority of the council, meeting at Dunfermline on 21 September 1514, where it was stated that:

> the queen's grace has tynt [forfeited] the office of tutrix of the king's grace our sovereign lord her son, and shall cease from the using of the same in times coming and shall not intromit [interfere] with any matters pertaining to the crown and decernis [determines] the lords of the council to provide therefore, because she has contracted marriage ... through the which the office of tutory ceases in her, conforming to the laws of the realm.[1]

This meeting was attended by an unusually large group of the lords, an indication of just how badly the news of the queen's second marriage had been received. Forty of them signed the statement which deposed Margaret from the regency and which also required her to desist from using crown property and jewels to bolster her position and reward her supporters in what was characterized as her 'unjust quarrel'. They also announced that she had no authority to call the parliament that she had summoned for 20 November. It seemed that the queen and her new husband had conclusively lost this first tussle with the angry nobility of Scotland.

She and Angus retired to Stirling to consider their future actions. The challenge could scarcely have been unexpected. They knew that the situation was not necessarily as dire as it seemed. Though the opposition was formidable, it was not universal. There were significant supporters in the queen's party, including the earls of Crawford and Glencairn, Robert Shaw, the abbot of Paisley, and others who believed that peace, rather than confrontation, with England was the best policy. Margaret still had physical possession of her sons and hoped that she could call upon her brother for help if needed, and also her sister, Mary, now the queen of France and wife of Louis XII. More importantly, despite the earnest request to Albany, he still did not come. It seemed, to cooler heads, that there might be room to compromise in the autumn of 1514. That optimism, however, proved illusory.

The main stumbling-block was Margaret herself. She and James IV had been united in their goal of elevating the prestige of the Scottish crown. She was not willing to see their success disappear. Given the reins of power, she proved herself a true Tudor, with a clear and determined vision of her role. In all the adversity of the decade that lay ahead she never lost sight of her goal, which, put simply, was to govern in the name of her son until he became of age – and, it might be added, to continue to influence him even after he gained his majority. It is easy to say, in hindsight, that this was an unrealistic and selfish aim, and to suggest that Scotland might have been better served by co-operation rather than confrontation, but compromise in politics was often considered weakness in the sixteenth century. Margaret Tudor knew that success was derived from strength and visible displays of majesty. In her eyes a ruler only reached accommodation with opponents when it could be turned to perceptible advantage.

The international reaction to her second marriage would

have confirmed her assessment of her situation. Although somewhat muted, for the two kingdoms of the British Isles were still viewed as peripheral players by the European powers, the response had been generally favourable. Italian commentators evidently felt it perfectly reasonable that a young and attractive queen should not remain single for long. They did not know much about Angus himself and one report claimed that he was a Scottish duke. Throughout his long and chequered career Angus might well have aspired to such a title, but he never attained it. The only duke in the Scottish aristocracy was, traditionally, the duke of Ross, second son of the monarch. Still, the fact that Angus had been 'elevated' in this way by foreign commentators speaks to the acknowledgement that the Queen of Scots was expected to marry a man of significance.

Henry VIII's reaction was also broadly favourable, even though Margaret had remarried without his permission. He had arranged the splendid match for Mary, his younger sister, with the king of France, and was now at peace with that country, but there were still tensions and Scotland figured largely in these. The Douglas family were considered to be pro-English, so Margaret's choice, even when made secretly and without consultation with her brother, was an acceptable one. A Scottish lord who was known to be strongly independent in outlook, or, even worse, pro-French, would have caused consternation in London. Yet if Henry believed that Margaret would always see her interests as identical to his, the English king was soon to be disabused. Indeed, it is a measure of how little he valued her judgement that he always put the advice of Lord Dacre before anything that he received from his sister. In Henry's eyes, Dacre was a rugged Border lord whose assessments were much more to be trusted than those of a woman who was, he believed, overly emotional in her reactions. He would take his lead from Dacre and Angus, now the earl was his sister's husband. It never occurred to him to treat Margaret seriously as a fellow monarch.

Holding fast to the ideas of kinship and what she believed were shared interests, Margaret did not, at first, realize that her brother would, in effect, bypass her and be guided by others. In the uncertain atmosphere of the autumn of 1514, she wrote appealing to him for aid. The loss of the regency deprived her of a key source of income and the instability of Scotland made collection of rents from her lands increasingly difficult, especially as her rights to a number of her properties were now being challenged by her opponents.[2] It was military support that she felt would swing the balance of power back firmly in her favour, as she made clear when she addressed Henry.

> I commend me to you with all mine heart. I have received your loving and comfortable writings from a man of Lord Dacre's ... wherein I perceive your fraternal love and kindness. I and my party were in great trouble of mind, till we knew what help you would do to us ... My party-adversary continues in their malice and proceeds in their parliament, usurping the king's authority, and as I and my lords were of no reputation, reputing us as rebels, wherefore I beseech that you would make haste with your army by sea and land.[3]

There is an air of desperation in this letter. It was, of course, unrealistic to expect Henry VIII to interfere in Scotland by invading at the start of winter, even if he had the men and the desire to do so. Margaret had also left her brother in no doubt that his northern neighbour was the prey of faction and that, though not beaten, she was certainly no longer in control of government. Nor was he likely to do very much about her financial difficulties, even if she was, as she put it, 'super-extended'. Fearful that she might be besieged in Stirling and subsequently compelled to sign documents against her will, she told her brother that if he received any letters purporting to come from her but signed only 'Margaret R and no more' he would know that she had signed under duress. But she did assure Henry VIII of the continued good health and spirits of her sons, describing the boys as 'right life-like'. She was, no doubt, hoping that one of the boys would ultimately be Henry's heir, as her brother and Katherine of Aragon remained childless. His nephews' continued wellbeing, and how to safeguard it, gave their uncle food for thought. The following spring he would propose that his sister and her children leave Scotland altogether and live under his protection in England. Margaret was, understandably, implacably set against such a move. She feared her son would lose the crown if he left his kingdom and the Scots would give it to Albany instead. Henry's idea showed how little he understood Scottish affairs. Meanwhile, the dawn of the year 1515 brought a further twist in this tortuous period of Margaret Tudor's life.

Mary Tudor had been queen of France for barely three months when Louis XII died on 1 January. She had married, at the age of eighteen, a gout-ridden man more than thirty years her senior. A pawn in the European marriage game since her childhood, she had been betrothed previously to the future Holy Roman Emperor, Charles V, destined for the Burgundian court and, ultimately, to the throne of Spain when Charles inherited Castile from his mother. Such grandeur would have left her sister, Margaret, and her sister-in-law, Katherine of Aragon, well in her wake. When Henry VIII deemed it advantageous to end the war with France, the Habsburg alliance was quickly forgotten. The death of Anne of Brittany, Louis XII's first wife, conveniently widowed the French king. What could be more appropriate than to seal the new-found amity between England and France by uniting the two royal families? Louis had only daughters from his marriage to Anne and they could not, by Salic Law, inherit the French throne. A young wife might provide male heirs and rejuvenate a monarch who was certainly not in the best of health. Mary was also a renowned beauty and Louis was greatly smitten when they met at Abbeville in northern France. On 9 October 1514, a magnificent wedding took place. This was followed by Mary's coronation several weeks later at the abbey church of St Denis outside Paris, where French queens were traditionally crowned.

Despite an early rift between the royal couple, when Louis dismissed most of her English attendants, Mary had settled with impeccable demeanour and behaviour in France, delighting many in a court that was by no means convinced of the benefits of such a close alliance between England and France. Graceful, queenly and speaking fluent French, Mary was committed, as Margaret had been when first in Scotland, to playing her part in representing English interests in a foreign land. The five-year difference in the age at which they first became queens was definitely in Mary's favour and she was more confident than Margaret had been, effortlessly able to win the besotted affection of Louis XII without fear of mistresses lurking in the shadows. It is true that Louis seems to have valued her almost ostentatiously as a pretty ornament on which to hang priceless gifts of jewels, rather than for her undoubted intelligence and quick wit, but Mary, like her sister, was perfectly happy to demonstrate this public show of royal wealth and prestige. Her constant attentions to her husband made the autumn of 1514 pass in a kind of idyll. Yet as the Christmas festivities began, it was evident that Louis's health was declining. Determined to enjoy the season, he continued to ignore his physicians' advice to take life rather more quietly, whether in bed with his wife or among the entertainments of the court. His end came suddenly.

> He so fervently loved [Mary] that he gave himself over to behold too much her excellent beauty bearing then but eighteen years of age, nothing considering the proportion of his own years, nor his decayed complexion; so that he fell into the rage of a fever, which drawing to it a sudden flux, overcame in one instant [his] life.[4]

We know that Margaret had written to Mary in the autumn of 1514 but this correspondence does not survive.[5] It is reasonable to assume that she sent messages of condolence to the younger sister who would, for the rest of her life, be known in England as the French Queen, and that she would have learned with interest that Mary would keep to her determination to 'marry where my mind is' now that she was widowed. Like Margaret, Mary's second marriage was to an aristocrat, in this case Charles Brandon, recently ennobled as duke of Suffolk. And like Margaret and Angus, Mary's marriage to Brandon, a dubious chancer who happened to be a boon companion of Henry VIII, may have been less of a love-match than is often supposed. Mary was anxious to clarify her situation as quickly as she could once it was evident that she was not pregnant by Louis XII and to extricate herself from a French court that was unlikely to show her much support now the king was dead. She had known Brandon since her childhood and he had been sent to France by Henry VIII to bring Mary back home. His very presence in France made him an obvious, perhaps the only, choice. The decision to marry in secret relieved Mary of any further concern that she would continue to be wafted around the European marriage market at her brother's whim. Henry VIII was furious when he found she had out-manoeuvred him, but eventually relented. Mary settled down to a quieter life as a country duchess, raising a family and attending court from time to time. Margaret did not have the luxury of this more pastoral existence and it is unlikely that she would ever have wanted such a life. Yet she, just as much as Mary, was to find her life changed by Louis XII's death. For Margaret, the loss of a brother-in-law she never knew would not lead to tranquillity, but even greater uncertainty. The new king of France was Francis I, a cousin of Louis XII and married to Louis's daughter, Claude. His view of the benefits of closer ties with England was very different from that of his predecessor and he now prepared to send John Stewart, duke of Albany, to Scotland at last. A showdown between the queen and her opponents would now centre on the person of this foreign-born Scot, who was a stranger to them all.

15

Confrontation at Stirling

*'The Duke of Albany, by reason of his might and power, did
take from me the king and duke, my said tender children.'*

Queen Margaret to Henry VIII, October 1515

wo Frenchmen were now to enter Margaret's life and
together play a crucial part in it over the next decade.
These were the new French king, Francis I, and John
Stewart, duke of Albany, her late husband's first cousin. They
were very different men, in appearance and character, and if
their aims for Scotland were not precisely the same, they were
united in the belief that the future of this small, currently
unruly country had a key role to play in maintaining the
balance of power in northern Europe. It was a long-standing
ally of France and a convenient thorn in the side of England.
Scotland was not, though, quite important enough that men
or money could be committed to it whole-heartedly, and this
stop-start approach explains much about the often-confusing
period of the minority of Margaret's son James V. Nor was
there much consistency in Henry VIII's policy towards
Scotland, which was reactive rather than based on any positive strategy and always complicated by the English king's
increasingly fractious dealings with his own sister.

Margaret never met the saturnine Francis, whose panto-mime-villain looks, emphasized by a very large, long nose and full, sensuous lips, suggested at first glance that he might be more interested in the pleasures of the table and the bed than in government. Beneath this unprepossessing exterior there was, however, a determined dynast, whose expectations of becoming king of France must have seemed a near certainty when he married Claude, the elder daughter of his cousin Louis XII. The marriage of Louis and Princess Mary Tudor brought an anxious check to the hopes of Francis and his ambitious mother, Louise of Savoy, who had devoted her life to ensuring that her son would succeed to the Valois throne. The danger of Francis remaining forever a high-ranking Prince of the Blood if Mary produced a son soon passed, though the young widow could not immediately leave France after her husband's death until it was established beyond all reasonable doubt that she was not pregnant. It would have been ironic if both of Henry VIII's sisters had given birth to posthumous sons, but Mary was not to match Margaret in this respect. Besides Francis, there was no shortage of more distant male relatives who could succeed in France, a stark contrast to England, where Henry VIII was still without any children at all. The nearest male relative to Henry was, of course, his nephew James V of Scotland, but his ambivalence towards Margaret's son was a permanent feature of Anglo–Scottish relations throughout James's life.

While Francis had no immediate wish to tear up the peace treaty with England that his predecessor had so recently nego-tiated, he wished to establish at the beginning of his reign that he had a different view of how Scotland could serve French interests. He demonstrated that he was willing to extend more than bland assurances of amity to his country's ancient ally by sending a new ambassador, Jean de Plains, to Scotland within two months of his accession. De Plains brought with him a commitment that some of the Scottish lords had been waiting to hear ever since the death of James IV and which Margaret learned with bitter regret: Francis would, indeed, send the duke of Albany to Scotland, to restore good order and safeguard the king and his brother. In vain did the English ambassadors in France object to this development, pointing out that Albany was 'the most suspect person that might be sent for the surety of the two young princes and the Queen, for he not only pretended title to the crown of Scotland, but also he was called thither by the young King's adversaries and also makes himself party with them'.[1] Margaret would have been even more appalled if she had known that the instructions to de Plains contained the further suggestion that the little duke of Ross should be sent to France to be educated there.

Henry VIII, alarmed about the wider implications of potential hostilities and a new invasion from Scotland if Albany were to arrive imminently with a substantial force of men, suddenly discovered a concern for Queen Margaret that he had hitherto not evinced, at least not publicly, remarking that it was only natural for him to ensure that his sister was not 'oppressed'. So safeguards against an invasion of England ever taking place 'with the consent of the ruler for the time being in Scotland' were built into the renewed treaty with England. The wily Francis was perfectly happy to play the English just a little longer while he prepared to renew the wars with Italy begun by his predecessor, Charles VIII, in the closing years of the previous century. His commitment to Scotland would always be contingent on how that country could serve French interests and indirectly restrict those of England. But, in the immediate term, while grateful that the peace with England was secured, Margaret was not happy with the price she herself would have to pay. For almost two years it had haunted her and now it could no longer be avoided. On

18 May 1515, Albany landed at Dumbarton on the west coast of Scotland. What this would mean for both the duke himself and the nervous Queen of Scots was not at all clear.

The duke of Albany may not be a familiar figure even to those who profess an interest in the sixteenth century, but he is an interesting man who played a significant role in giving this confused period of Scottish history what little cohesiveness it had. Indeed, had he been permitted to stay for the entirety of James V's minority, the king's childhood would probably have been much more settled and his education and training for kingship given proper attention. Instead, the regent's attempts to assure good governance of Scotland were doomed to failure because he was never there for long enough to impose his authority.

John Stewart was in his early thirties when he first set foot in his father's native land. His precise date of birth is conjectural, but likely to have been around 1482. He was born in the Auvergne in south-western France, a beautiful region of hills and ancient towns, where his mother, Anne de la Tour, was a younger daughter of the local count. This peaceful setting was the haven of his father, Alexander, duke of Albany, the second son of James II of Scotland.

The elder Albany fled Scotland in 1478 following a bitter dispute with his brother James III, which had seen him become a figurehead for the anti-English faction among the nobility. The Stewart dynasty had little trouble producing heirs but relations between the male siblings were often far from cordial. Alexander was seen as a real alternative to his brother the king, but his supporters were not strong enough to remove James III. From his exile in France, Alexander learned in 1480 of the mysterious death of his younger brother, John, earl of Mar, whose demise, it was widely held, had been ordered by James III himself. Far from frightening him, this seems only to have convinced him of the need to return to Scotland when the time was right. The opportunity came in the crisis of the summer of 1482, when James III was seized at Lauder in the Scottish Borders by a group of nobles, including his own half-uncle, and returned a prisoner to Edinburgh Castle.

Supported by the future Richard III and an English army of 20,000 men, Alexander returned to Scotland. That he was aiming for the throne seems beyond doubt but he drew back from deposing James III after consulting with the queen, Margaret of Denmark, at Stirling about his future role and the education of his nephew, who would become James IV. As the months passed, Alexander realized that his goal could not be achieved, partly because of growing anti-English sentiment among the ever-changeable nobility, but also because the unexpected death of Edward IV in 1483 deprived him of the certainty of ongoing English support. So he returned to France and his French wife, where an injury sustained in a jousting tournament (Alexander, like James IV, loved chivalric sports) brought an end to his tumultuous life in 1485. His son and heir, John, was just four years old.

Once his early childhood was past, Albany moved to the French court at the age of twelve, where his education was completed. Much of it was military and he was part of the entourage that accompanied the victorious Charles VIII when the French king entered Milan in 1499. Later Albany served in Louis XII's Italian campaigns. As a young man, he was a courtier and a soldier, but much of his experience was in European warfare rather than politics. He was also very wealthy following his marriage in 1505 to his first cousin, who was the count of Auvergne's heiress.[2] She was a mere child of about eight years old at the time, but would have been in her late teens at the time her husband first arrived in Scotland. She did not accompany him and no explanation has been given for this. Her presence might have been construed as even more of a threat by Margaret, who was unhappy enough at Albany's coming without having to cope with a potential rival to her position as the first lady in Scotland. Although there is no indication that Albany's marriage was unhappy, it remained childless.

Such was the family background of the man who now arrived in the land of his father's birth to govern in the name of a child he had never met. Before John Stewart could assume the role of regent, his father's title and lands, forfeited by rebellion, needed to be returned formally to him. The embarrassing history of his family was an impediment that many, but by no means all, of the Scottish lords were content to overlook in exchange for his assuming the government of Scotland. It says much for the febrile nature of Scottish politics, and the entrenched patriarchal attitudes of the times, that the rule of an unknown Frenchman of dubious heritage was believed to be preferable to that of an Englishwoman who was familiar with Scottish politics and the customs, geography and language of the country, and married to a Scot. Margaret's sex and her choice of husband were deemed greater barriers to good government and stability than the arrival as the head of government of a complete stranger.

Yet despite the fact that he knew next to nothing about Scotland and that neither he nor his monarch were fully committed to his remaining in the country for any great length of time, those who now met John Stewart for the first time were impressed by his bearing and his evident wish to govern well. He was a good-looking man, with a passing resemblance to James IV, soldierly but also diplomatic, direct without being rough and authoritative without being overbearing. Happily for the Scots, and unusually for the times, he was basically a decent man with a strong sense of duty. He had every intention of putting the interests of the little king first and foremost and standing above faction. His initial goals were straightforward: he needed to establish his regency through the appropriate ceremonial proceedings and induce the queen, by persuasion, if he could, to give him control of her sons.

Margaret's first impressions were not unfavourable. She found Albany's French manners charming, could converse with him easily in French and liked his deference to her rank in his dealings with her. She also accepted that it was inevitable that the duke would call a parliament, which he did in July 1515, and that his status as governor would be confirmed during the session. He made an impressive entrance on 11 July, as the ever-watchful Lord Dacre, who had spies everywhere, reported to Henry VIII: 'the sword was borne before Albany to and from the Parliament by the earl of Arran and a coronet set on his head by Angus and Argyll and he was appointed Protector till the king came to the age of eighteen'. Dacre was almost certainly misinformed about Angus's participation in the ceremony, which is not verified in the parliamentary record. Angus was never Albany's man and he already knew that his wife would only give up her sons under extreme duress, even though he might, personally, be willing to sacrifice them.

Albany's move to bring the boys under his physical control was not long coming. On 26 July 1515 the Scottish parliament enacted legislation whereby the king and his brother were to be given to the safekeeping of eight Scottish lords. Margaret was given the right to choose three from among them but when a deputation arrived at Stirling to apprise the queen of this decision she lowered the portcullis of the castle and refused even to let them in. Angus was still with her at the time but slipped out soon afterwards. The fortunes of his family had seemed set fair at the end of the previous summer, when he and Margaret were first married, but both his uncle, Gavin Douglas, whose appointment to the bishopric of Dunkeld was now in dispute, and his grandfather, Lord Drummond, had swiftly fallen foul of Albany. Concerned, above all, with safeguarding his own position and estates, he left his younger brother, George Douglas, to protect the queen and her children at Stirling. Events would soon prove just how ineffective George Douglas was.

Margaret now countered Albany by putting forward the names of four lords who would be acceptable to her as guardians of her sons, providing she was allowed access to the boys. These were her husband, the earl Marischal (William Keith), Lord Home and Sir Robert Lauder. Albany was never going to agree to any arrangement that involved an official role for Angus and by now his patience was wearing very thin. Rumours were circulating that Angus might attempt to kidnap his stepsons with English help and remove them to England. Dacre had been busy with a flurry of correspondence, cooking up a scheme that was doomed to failure. With the assistance of Lord Home, who resented being sidelined by Albany, he conceived the idea of putting together a small raiding party that could spirit Margaret and the children away across the border. Dacre believed that dark forces were at work in Scotland. Could the future safety of Henry VIII's nephews really be assured by a man who himself was so near to the Scottish throne? He recalled the unknown fate of the sons of Edward IV, who had disappeared inside the Tower of London in 1483, never to be seen again. Likening Albany to Richard III was extreme but not entirely implausible.

The removal of the boys to England never happened. Home's force was a mere forty men, quite unable to break through the regent's force, which was by now besieging Stirling Castle. And aside from the sheer impracticality of the scheme, there was another serious stumbling-block, namely Margaret herself. She did not think it was in the best interest of her sons. If James V was taken to England he might never regain his throne. The Scottish lords, determined to have a strong leader, would gift the throne to Albany instead. On 4 August 1515 Albany arrived at the gates of Stirling with 7,000 men and an artillery train that included the famous cannon Mons Meg. Margaret's dower castle was a formidable fortress but she could not hope to defend it with just her brother-in-law and his small group of fighters. She must deploy the only weapons left to her – her own courage and the little king himself.

What followed was a piece of pure Tudor theatre. Margaret knew she had no option but to submit but she would do so with as much flair for the public occasion as any exhibited by other members of her family. She had the portcullis raised and, clad in full regal attire, issued forth, holding the hand of the three-year-old James V and followed by a nursemaid carrying the duke of Ross. While Albany stood on and watched, she gave the keys of the castle to her son, reinforcing publicly that he was the keeper of the castle and the monarch of Scotland. As the child clasped the keys in his little hand, she told him to pass them to the regent. The significance of this gesture was not lost on Albany. He handed the keys back to James, acknowledging that he was, indeed, the ruler. He could hardly have done otherwise in the circumstances, and, of course, Albany was no Richard III. He never wanted the Scottish throne and had no intention of depriving this child of his birthright. James V, no doubt schooled by his mother as to what was expected of him before they came out of the castle, behaved with a touching solemnity. Even though he was so young, the incident must have left a powerful impression on him. Looking back on it as he grew up in his troubled kingdom, he must have wished that his ambitious stepfather could always have acted with the dignity and restraint of the duke of Albany.

Margaret had taken the moral high ground, but she had lost her sons. The boys were left at Stirling, where the castle's new keeper, Lord Erskine, shared their care with Lords Fleming and Borthwick and the earl Marischal. The earl was one of Margaret's own choices for their guardianship, the only crumb of comfort that the queen, now removed to Edinburgh Castle, could take from the situation. She must, nevertheless, have hoped that the parting from her children would not be of too long duration. She loved both of them dearly, especially Alexander, who seems to have been her favourite. But much turmoil lay ahead for Margaret Tudor, now heavily pregnant with Angus's child. It would be two years before she could, once more, hold James V's hand. She never saw his brother again.

16

Flight

'Her Grace was delivered and brought to bed
of a fair young lady.'
Lord Dacre to Henry VIII, 18 October 1515

The duke of Albany wasted no time in reinforcing his authority after Margaret's capitulation. Outwardly, she seemed to have accepted her fate, writing positively of recent developments to her brother and Lord Dacre. Yet these letters, as the queen later explained at length, were dictated by Albany's secretary and signed under duress. Recent research on the correspondence has revealed that Margaret's subsequent protestations about the pressure exerted on her in August 1515 are fully justified. While a dispute about who wrote what might seem, at first sight, somewhat arcane, the unravelling of this by a scholar working on Margaret's correspondence is a marvellous historical detective story. It tells us much about the queen's predicament and helps to explain her subsequent decisions and the sense of grievance about how she was treated – and traduced – at this time. Her later indignation, which is sometimes dismissed as a further indication of her changeable, constantly complaining character, is revealed as fully justified.

Four letters were written with Margaret's signature (or, in

one case, apparent signature) in just eleven days, between 20 and 31 August 1515. Three were addressed to her brother, Henry VIII, and one to Lord Dacre. They show a sharp change of tone from the fears voiced in her recent correspondence. Gone is the concern for her boys, to be replaced with the encouraging information that 'I have presence of my children at my pleasure and opportunity to leave or enter when ever I will.' She went on to refer to the wider international environment and her support of the peace treaty between England, Scotland and France, thus demonstrating her desire to work amicably, and in a constructive fashion, with the duke of Albany.

> Brother, I am resolved that I and my said cousin [Albany] shall take one part, for I know it is most for my profit … the king of France has sent me writing … and prays that I will entreat and do my diligence to keep the peace between the realms, which I pray you to do likewise.[1]

This all sounded most positive, but it was far from the truth. Margaret's signature on this letter to Henry VIII appears to have been genuine, but on at least one of the other letters, to Lord Dacre, it was forged by her secretary, James Inglis. He, of course, knew it well enough to make a convincing copy to anyone who did not examine the signature minutely. But lest the contents of this missive be accepted as truly representing her views, Margaret sent a letter written in her own hand (a holograph letter) and several verbal messages, via servants whom she evidently trusted implicitly, to Lord Dacre. These left him in no doubt that recent correspondence purporting to be sent of the queen's free will had been dictated to Margaret and, even where her signature was legitimate, sent under duress. 'The queen of Scots', he wrote to Henry VIII in early September, 'lately … advertised [warned] … that the duke had enforced her to subscribe sundry letters directed to the pope's holiness, your highness and the French king … And therefore saying the said subscribing was expressly against her will and mind.'[2]

The queen herself made this pressure abundantly clear when she wrote to the French ambassador to Scotland, Jean de Plains, at the beginning of October: 'Truly, when I was in Edinburgh the said duke [Albany] caused my secretary to make writings which for fear I subscribed and other was subscribed by my said secretary feigning my hand, whereunto I was never agreeable.'[3] She also wrote a brief note in her own hand to Dacre in late August or early September, sent by her messenger, Robin Carr, saying that he could trust the account Carr would give of her predicament, claiming that she had been 'constrained to do against my will'. The letter is surprisingly legible, given the general perception of Margaret's handwriting as being impossible to read, and is signed clearly 'Your friend, Margaret R'. A summary of Carr's wider, verbal explanation to Dacre of the queen's predicament at this time survives. It makes quite clear that Margaret was being kept in Edinburgh against her will and was not allowed to see her children or contact her friends.

The role of Albany in the composition of these letters remains conjectural. Since his English and Scots were virtually nonexistent, he could have done no more than indicate what he wanted Margaret to be saying. The precise wording of the correspondence may well have been dictated by someone among the Scottish lords who supported him. What is absolutely clear is that none of what was said had been written of her own free will by Margaret Tudor. This makes her subsequent course of action, which might otherwise seem ill-thought-out, perfectly comprehensible. Realizing that she was now powerless, heartbroken to have been parted from her sons, with no guarantee when, or even if, she would see them again, and also fearful for her own safety, Margaret took a desperate decision. She must flee Scotland and take refuge with her brother in England. He could do little other than welcome her. Whether he would support her returning to Scotland with an army at her back was quite another matter.

Leaving Scotland was not an option that greatly appealed to Margaret, but she was seven months pregnant and feeling very vulnerable as the result of treatment which she considered harassment. Nevertheless, Albany needed her support, or he would not have made such efforts to bend her to his will. Once he had firmly established his authority it is conceivable that he might have relented in his attitude, especially as regarded some sort of access to James V and the duke of Ross. He wanted to present himself as the unifier of a deeply divided Scottish polity, not as some sort of foreign ogre hellbent on destroying the happiness of the Queen of Scots. He had, though, succeeded in isolating Margaret, which meant that she could only turn for support and advice to her contacts in England and to disaffected Scots like Lord Home. Her husband, always mindful of his own interests, found himself caught in the middle. His own part in the dramatic events that were to follow is strangely opaque. Angus had been married to Margaret for barely a year but was already realizing that his interests as a Scottish landowner might not always coincide with his wife's priorities as queen mother. This underlying tension in their relationship would become much more obvious over the next two years.

Margaret may have felt stifled and belittled by Albany, but she was now to be played by two men, Lords Home and Dacre, neither of whom cared much for her welfare. To them she was a potential asset to be exploited. Dacre had been joined by Henry VIII's chaplain, Thomas Magnus, and together they put pressure on the queen to abandon Scotland altogether. Dacre, never the most reverent of men, did not hold back from reminding Margaret that she should have followed his advice from the outset: 'Madam', he wrote, 'all these premises the king my master and his most honourable council hath at all times heretofore supposed this great trouble and danger would ensue unto you, unless you would have followed counsel, which you would in no wise do in time convenient'. To add salt to the wound he went on to claim that her actions had jeopardized the situation of her children, which he dramatically characterized as 'the utter destruction of the King and Prince, your sons, my master's nephews'. Of course, the boys were safe – Margaret had no reason to suppose otherwise at this point – but Dacre's suggestion that they might be in extreme danger had echoes of the disappearance of the two sons of Edward IV, the Princes in the Tower, thirty years previously. Margaret had lost the opportunity to bring them to safety in England, so Dacre reminded her. Now her only hope for herself and her unborn child lay with himself and Lord Home, who was to give her shelter at Blackadder Castle once she had got away from Edinburgh. From there she could be brought to the border at Coldstream and escorted to Dacre's main residence, Morpeth Castle.

Margaret was not a woman given to dithering, whatever scarcely veiled insults Dacre might direct at her. She had shown firmness in the face of opposition to her regency and made certain that her brother knew that she was being coerced. But with her confinement fast approaching, she felt that the longer she remained in Scotland, the less likelihood there was of an acceptable solution to her dilemma. So she agreed to the plan suggested by Dacre. Having announced earlier that she intended to go to Linlithgow Palace for her lying-in, she applied to Albany for permission to leave

Edinburgh. This was granted, and on 11 September she set out with her husband, ostensibly to prepare for her seventh confinement in the place where she had given birth to her other children.

This was the first move in a protracted, sometimes hair-raising journey made in conditions that would have been challenging for the healthiest of women. Given Margaret's advanced stage of pregnancy, it was to prove a harrowing ordeal that she never forgot. Yet previous writers – and notably female historians – have often been far from sympathetic to the queen's plight. Albany's biographer, Marie Stuart, never less than scathing about Margaret's character, asserts that 'with feminine cunning Margaret made her approaching *accouchement* an excuse for withdrawing from public life into an inviolable privacy where she could hatch plots as fast as her fertile brain wished'.[4] The outcome of these 'plots', in other words, Margaret's itinerary, is then inaccurately described, but we learn 'that such adventures were most unsuitable for a lady in her delicate condition'. The condescension is quite remarkable.

Albany was apparently unsuspecting at this stage. He would, in any case, have been on shaky ground if he tried to deny a queen of Scots the right to give birth in her own palace. No watch was kept on Margaret and Angus, so that they were unobserved when they slipped away from Linlithgow at night on 14 September. The plan had originally been to go straight to Blackadder Castle but it was too far for Margaret to reach in one ride. Instead, she and her husband stopped at the seaside fortress of the Douglases, Tantallon Castle. It is as dramatic a location as any that could be imagined. Perched on the edge of the cliffs, with the North Sea thundering below, the castle looks out over the Bass Rock, home to multitudes of seabirds. Although it would have had a reasonable level of comfort in the sixteenth century, the Douglases seldom used it as a home. It was built as a refuge, to withstand siege and assault, since it could be provisioned from the sea. Yet for a woman in turmoil, fearful for her life and the future of her sons, remaining there for any length of time must have seemed a dire prospect. In fact, it soon became apparent that her stay there would be just a staging-post on the journey into England. Albany learned of Margaret's flight on the evening of 14 September and knew he must stop her if he could. Margaret and Angus soon moved on to Blackadder Castle, which had been prepared for her coming. Lord Home had burned his boats in offering her refuge and facilitating her escape. He was a true Borderer, supremely conscious of his own interest, and he had become disenchanted with Albany, whose policies he thought would disadvantage him if the duke established a firm hold on Scotland.

Albany, however, had far from given up. He believed that, with appropriate concessions on the part of himself and the Scottish council, it would be possible to persuade Margaret to stay. The French ambassador, de Plains, whom Margaret seems to have trusted, was willing to act as an intermediary. Albany offered the queen his protection, stating, 'do her all that accorded to be done upon reason'. He exhorted her to 'be a good Scotswoman, as accords her to do, for the great love she should have to her son, the King, his realm and lieges'.[5] It is possible that Margaret might have been persuaded by these professions, which were intended to soothe her and restore her confidence. But Albany knew that there was another person deeply implicated in all of these doings, who had his own motives for wishing Margaret out of Scotland, and that was Lord Dacre. He even went so far to assure Dacre that there was no intention of invading England and that the presence of armed men in the Borders was merely to enforce law and order, not repeat the events of 1513. He concluded his memorandum with a clear statement that he hoped would be conciliatory: 'My lord protested solemnly that in case he passed to the borders for the pursuit of the tresspassers fore-said [lawbreakers and dissidents such as Home, though he did not give any names] that his mind was not nor in any way to hurt or violate the peace made between the realms of Scotland and England.'[6]

Margaret never received these assurances. She had already been frustrated, after leaving Blackadder Castle, by being turned away from Berwick by the town's governor because she did not have official leave to enter England. This was a remarkable oversight by Dacre, who sent to London to remedy it as soon as possible. Margaret, frustrated and exhausted by all the gadding about, the uncertainty and stress, had no option but to return back across the Tweed to Coldstream Priory, where she was looked after by the Cistercian nuns. When Henry VIII's permission for his sister to enter England was received by Dacre, he lost no time in spiriting her away from Coldstream into Northumberland. She was in the land of her birth at last, but at what cost? Henry VIII had specif-ically excluded Angus from the pass issued to Margaret; he was to remain in Scotland. Dacre had intended Margaret to press on to his main residence at Morpeth. It was a grand northern castle and an appropriate place for a queen to give birth. Margaret, however, simply could not go any farther. She was in severe pain and knew, as someone who had given birth six times already, that her labour was fast approaching. Instead of the relative comforts of Morpeth, she could not get beyond Harbottle Castle, a border property of Dacre's that was scarcely more than a military outpost. And it was here, on 8 October 1515, that Queen Margaret gave birth to a daugh-ter. The baby was given her mother's name and seemed likely, despite the notable absence of comfort in her first surround-ings, to survive. There was much less confidence about her mother, who was still not quite twenty-six years old.

Margaret announced her daughter's arrival to Albany using language that seems to us, centuries later, quaint and rather charming, though it emphasizes both her strong faith and that the baby was a queen's child. She had, she wrote, given birth to 'a Christian soul, being a young lady'. This new Margaret would have a life almost as eventful as her mother's and inherit in full the keen intelligence of the Tudors and the sheer capacity for survival of the Douglases. Time would tell how much she would need those qualities. Yet at the beginning of her life, in the chilly surroundings of Harbottle Castle, there was difficulty even in finding a wet nurse. Aristocratic ladies then and for centuries to come did not breast-feed their own babies. The benefits, both to mother and child, were unknown. Dacre was nonplussed by the situation. He could provide only the basic necessities and it was difficult to get hold of a doctor in whom he had any confidence. A splendid layette for the baby and a complete wardrobe of new clothes for her mother had been hastily despatched from London by Henry VIII and Katherine of Aragon, who was, yet again, pregnant herself and no doubt felt especial concern for her sister-in-law's predicament. But these remained at Morpeth to await a time when it was felt that Margaret was strong enough to move.

Ten days passed before she could even sit up in bed. The memory of previous pregnancies and their aftermath would have been potent, above all that of her first, ill-fated Prince James, who had brought such joy to his parents. Then she had been a teenager and, though dangerously ill, her youth and, it was believed, her husband's pilgrimage to pray for her survival had triumphed. Angus, compelled to remain in Scotland by her brother's order, was not there to support her. He was, in any case, no James IV. Henry VIII had despatched a trusted courtier, Sir Christopher Garneys, to Morpeth with the necessities deemed suitable for his sister and niece and letters of comfort from himself and Queen Katherine. The letters were sent on to Harbottle but the clothes and furnishings remained at Morpeth to await the queen's recovery. Dacre kept the English king informed of Margaret's progress. It was, he said, very slow: 'The queen lieth yet in childbed and shall keep her chamber these three weeks at least.'

Indeed, it was not until mid-November that Margaret left comfortless Harbottle, desperately in need of a warmer welcome in Morpeth. Even then it was a slow journey, done by careful degrees. Margaret was initially still in too much pain to be taken over uneven tracks in a horse litter and her bed was hoisted onto the shoulders of Dacre's servants. It is hard to imagine the discomfort of such a mode of travel. And she could not, on that first day, go more than four miles to the house of Sir Edward Ratcliffe at Cartington. She was still so weak that she did not move on for five days. By 21 November she had travelled a further five miles to Brinkburne Priory, where she was formally received by Lord Ogle and the abbot of Newminster. Ogle was a local landowner and Newminster a Cistercian abbey, an offshoot of Fountains Abbey in Yorkshire.

Sir Christopher Garneys gave a detailed account of the stages of Margaret's removal from Harbottle to Morpeth, emphasizing the agony it caused her and thus the need for careful management of her health. Garneys was a gentleman usher of the King's Chamber and a personal confidant of Henry VIII. He was tactful and genuinely concerned for Margaret's recovery and it is from him and the more hardnosed Dacre that we have a vivid picture of the queen's mental and physical state at this time. Sir Christopher saw a woman who had been through a great ordeal and had lost not just the trappings of queenship – her wardrobe, her jewels, her luxurious beds and furnishings – but her confidence and identity as Queen of Scots. Dacre saw Margaret differently. To him she was a pawn in his political ambitions and though he seems to have neither liked nor respected her, he was compelled to protect her and offer hospitality, at considerable expense. He both wanted to be rid of her and yet to maintain what he perceived as his influence over her, which was most easily done while she remained under his roof.

By the end of November, Margaret's excruciating journey along the unforgiving roads of Northumberland was over. Lady Dacre received her royal guest at Morpeth Castle, where Margaret could at last try to ease her pain in Lord Dacre's own bedchamber and hope to derive some entertainment from the preparations that were beginning for Christmas. Elizabeth Dacre, née Greystoke, came from a wealthy family and had been a royal ward when her husband abducted and married her in 1487. Whether or not this was done with her foreknowledge (Dacre later claimed that there had been a pre-contract), Elizabeth was a great prize and the marriage made Dacre a substantial local magnate. The union produced five surviving children, though there was also an illegitimate son, which suggests that relations were not perfect between the couple. Nevertheless, Elizabeth Dacre was well placed to act as hostess to a fugitive queen and seems to have handled the role with aplomb. The Dacres knew very well that their reputation in the Borders would be enhanced by Margaret Tudor's approbation. And Lady Dacre had other important guests arriving from Scotland to enjoy her hospitality. Morpeth Castle that Christmas entertained Angus, who had been allowed to join Margaret for the festive season, the Scottish chamberlain, Lord Home and his wife and various other local dignitaries from both sides of the border.

Christopher Garneys paid tribute to the efforts made by the Dacres to entertain these guests.

To say of all the hangings of the hall and chambers with the newest device of tapestry ... his cupboard all of gilt plate, with a great cup of fine gold ... with the board's end served with all silver vessels, lacking no manner of good victuals and wild fowl to put in them, that can be gotten for money.[7]

The Dacres had clearly spared no expense in decking their hall or feeding their guests. Nevertheless, underneath the seasonal bonhomie, there were currents that ran deep. Dacre and Home were both Borderers and knew each other well. They could be outwardly convivial while still harbouring suspicions of each other's motives. Home expressed to Garneys his desire to be thought well of by Henry VIII and offered to serve the English king. Yet he was in the house of the man detested by many Scots for his role at Flodden. Dacre knew very well that Home was, like himself, a man who would serve his own local interests first and foremost. They may have shared a Christmas cup of wine together but there was no real warmth between them.

We know nothing of what passed between Margaret and Angus during this brief reunion.[8] It was the first time he saw the daughter for whom he would subsequently show scant affection. Margaret's morale, at a time when her physical recovery remained slow, was greatly bolstered by seeing the clothes that Henry VIII had sent her; here were material markers of her queenship. Garneys had arrived with this portmanteau rather like the wardrobe master to some play. Indeed, Margaret's reaction was highly theatrical. Carried out of her bedchamber in a chair, she surveyed the beautiful dresses that were laid out before her with emotion and fervent thanks. When she had seen everything she bade the Lord Chamberlain (Home) and other gentlemen come in and look at it, saying, 'So, my Lord, here ye may see that the

King my brother hath not forgotten me and that he would not I should die for lack of clothes.'[9] In fact, she liked the gowns of cloth of gold and cloth of silver so much that she had them sent for several times a day and held up so that she could appreciate them more. These additions to her wardrobe inspired Margaret to order further garments, some sent for from Edinburgh and others to be made new. It is not clear where the twenty-two gowns that Garneys reported her owning at this time came from – they could not all have accompanied her on her flight from Scotland – but still more were now ordered: a gown of purple velvet lined with cloth of gold and a gown of crimson velvet furred with ermine as well as three kirtles of satin. Even the indulgent Garneys was quietly amused. 'These five or six days', he wrote, 'she has had no other mind than to look at her apparel'.

Margaret has been reviled for such apparent flightiness and self-absorption but this is to misunderstand the importance of appearance to royalty. Clothing set them off from everyone else, even the aristocracy. In Margaret's case, rebuilding the splendid wardrobe she had enjoyed as Queen of Scots was necessary to her self-esteem and the image that she wished to project and which was equally expected of her. Perhaps, as Garneys hinted, her enthusiasm was somewhat extreme but it was a reaction to her vulnerability, her loss of status and the uncertainties which she knew she now faced. It may also have been a compensation for the continued weakness and extreme pain she was still enduring. Garneys's sympathy for Margaret's suffering is in marked contrast to the scorn of later commentators who have criticized her lack of self-control.

I think her one of the lowest brought ladies, with her great pain of sickness, that I have seen ... her grace hath such a pain in her right leg that these three weeks she may not endure to sit up while her bed is a-making and when her grace is removed it would pity any man's heart to hear the shrieks and cries that her grace giveth.[10]

It would seem that the main cause of Margaret's discomfort was sciatica, probably brought on by so much riding while in an advanced state of pregnancy. Anyone who has been afflicted by this condition will know how excruciating it can be.

Gradually, the physical debilitation lessened, only to be replaced by an equally severe emotional torment. Alexander, duke of Ross, Margaret's younger son, had died earlier in December 1515 after a brief illness. Fearful that the news might prostrate the queen even as she showed signs of improvement in her overall health, she was not told of her loss till after Christmas. The heartbreak did cause a relapse, but she rallied bravely. Alexander had been her favourite – more so than little James V, according to Garneys – but he was also something more than just a child lost to the high infant mortality rates at the time. He was the last gift that James IV had given her. Alexander's death could not have been a more potent reminder of all that she had lost on Flodden Field.

17

A Year in London

*'I am in right good health and as joyous as any woman may
be in coming to her brother ... as I am most desirous now to
come to your presence and to have sight of your person, in
whom, next God, is my only trust and confidence.'*

Queen Margaret to Henry VIII, 27 April 1516

While Margaret remained just over the border
in Northumberland, the duke of Albany held
out some hope that she might be persuaded to
return to Scotland. Though he had the support of the majority of the Scottish lords and was generally respected in the
land where he was regent, the court of public opinion in
Europe, beyond France, was much more censorious. These
criticisms were fuelled by the English, in what nowadays
would seem a classic case of briefing against someone whose
power and standing they tried to diminish at every turn.
The tragic death of the little duke of Ross played into Henry
VIII's hands. It was easy to drip-feed into the ears of foreign
diplomats innuendo about the child's death. What were the
circumstances? He had appeared healthy when his mother,
now so bereft, parted from him. The suggestion that it had
been a suspicious death, with little or no attempt made to

save Alexander, provoked an even darker thought. How safe was the four-year-old King James V himself? Though Thomas More's partisan history of Richard III was not published until many years later, the disappearance of the two sons of Edward IV, the Princes in the Tower, was as celebrated a mystery in 1516 as it is today.

The Venetian ambassador, keen to demonstrate how closely he had his ear to the ground, recorded the following extraordinary outburst by Thomas Wolsey during a meeting with the cardinal, who told him the following.

We cannot but admit that his Majesty has the affairs of Scotland much at heart, for were he to hold them in small account he would be 'una bestia', seeing that his sister, the Queen, owing to the Duke of Albany, is yet most grievously ill, having been prematurely delivered of a daughter, who subsequently died; she having been expelled her kingdom, deprived of all her friends, part of whom are imprisoned, whilst others have been put to death. He, moreover, has taken the entire administration of the kingdom out of her hands and what more immediately exasperates his Majesty is the fact that he removed the two princes from their mother's guardianship and placed them under his own charge, since when one of them has died, and there now remains an only child, in the event of whose death the kingdom would fall to the said Duke.

Warming to his theme of the wicked, conniving relative who sought power for himself at the expense of the lives of two innocent babes, Wolsey continued: 'Think what reason, divine or human, can palliate such great cruelty and whether his Majesty, remembering that he is a King, can tolerate the like.' It was for Francis I to remedy this grievance and, if he did, Henry would remain on friendly terms with the French king, even though 'Francis exhibits little gratitude for the faith kept towards him by his Majesty'.[1]

Though Margaret could exaggerate with the best of them and undoubtedly did feel a strong sense of injustice at her treatment, it is hard to believe that she would not have raised an eyebrow at this impressively inaccurate catalogue of her woes. For one thing, her daughter, Lady Margaret Douglas, was very much alive and Margaret also knew well that it was her enemies among the Scottish lords (curiously missing from Wolsey's description of her situation), not Albany, who were the instigators of her misfortune. The cardinal studiously avoided any mention of the repercussions of Margaret's second marriage. And he also let slip, at the end of his tirade, that what lay beneath all this righteous indignation was really the state of relations between France and England, in which his monarch, of course, had never strayed from the path of rectitude.

Meanwhile, the inhabitants of Morpeth Castle were themselves far from certain of the manner in which their current dilemma would resolve itself. Margaret was anxious to see her one surviving son and to retrieve her lost authority, not to mention her jewels, clothes and the rents from her dower lands. Still in communication with Albany, her declaration that she was determined to go south to her brother's court, often taken on face value as a sign of her continued hostility, may have been intended to put pressure on the duke to agree to her return to Scotland on her terms, not his. In late February 1516, she wrote to Albany acknowledging his latest letter. Her response mingled a degree of conciliation with firmness. She did not, she said, 'remember the words of Albany at their last interview, but acknowledges she has often had goodly and pleasant words as well as letters from him, and though his conduct has not always corresponded to them, yet, as now matters are being accommodated, hopes he

will reform it'. Her confidence would be the greater, she went
on, if Albany released Gavin Douglas, the bishop of Dunkeld
(her husband's uncle).[2]

Margaret's continued correspondence with Albany made
Lord Dacre nervous. It is evident that Dacre was not at all
sure of her still and was very anxious to get her to London
as soon as her health and that of her daughter permitted.
Given the state of roads in winter at that period, it was realistic to assume that her immediate departure was most unlikely,
which increased her host's anxiety. He and Thomas Magnus
set about reinforcing Margaret's sense of all that she had suffered – and making it official – by drawing up a memorandum
of complaint against Albany. The original of this document is
held in the British Library and begins with the uncompromising heading: 'Hereafter ensueth the great, manifest and
detestable injuries and wrongs done and committed to me,
Margaret Queen of Scots, by John Duke of Albany, since his
coming and repairing into the realm of Scotland.'

It was an impressive list of grievances, but presented hap-
hazardly, and any one of them could have been challenged.
Margaret began by accusing Albany of depriving her of
government during the minority bequeathed to her by James
IV and, she asserted, 'confirmed by the Pope'. To achieve this
nefarious end, the duke had 'besieged her in Stirling Castle
when she had no men about her, but only gentlewomen,
taken her children from her and put her out of the castle'.
Stirling Castle was, she claimed, part of her dower, paid for by
her father. There were, of course, problems with both these
statements. Her first husband had made the role of regent
contingent on Margaret's not remarrying and Stirling had
long been the dower castle of Scottish queens consort, so
to claim that Henry VII had paid for it in any specific sense
was disingenuous. But the loss of Stirling and the profits that
came with it had left her in 'great debt and danger', which

had caused her to flee. Albany had ignored her piteous entreaties to be allowed to see her children and 'deprived her of her jewels and other riches' left behind at Tantallon and Edinburgh.[3] This was signed 'Margaret R' but although she had agreed to its contents, she had not drafted them personally. There followed a long list of outrages on the Borders committed by the Scots, which emanated from Dacre, the author of both parts of the document.

One might well ask where in all of this was the earl of Angus, Margaret's husband? His name and that of Lord Home were included in the overall complaint as having been unjustly accused by Albany of intending to foment rebellion and 'cause an invasion of Scotland by England for the destruction of the King and realm'. They had, in effect, been branded as traitors. Yet Angus was already back in Scotland by the time that Margaret's grievances were formally aired in March 1516. The earl was in a difficult position and he needed to watch the situation in Scotland carefully, since his own future depended just as much on it as on any decision that his wife might make about her own future. At the beginning of 1516 the earl of Arran (a man of inconstant loyalty) had broken with Albany and raised a rebellion in western Scotland. At Kittycrosshill near Glasgow, sometime in the second or third week of January – the precise date and even the location are unknown – Albany's men met a force of about 6,000 men led by Arran. There was a major confrontation, but no actual fighting. When Albany unfurled the royal banner, his opponents decided not to attack, knowing that to do so would leave them open to a charge of treason if they failed. Albany had sufficient support and was known for his military prowess. Thus there was no battle, though this strange incident is often referred to as the Battle of Kittycrosshill.

This further cementing of Albany's authority left Angus in a quandary. If he stayed too long by Margaret's side in

England, his lands might be confiscated and he would find himself proscribed as a traitor. His precise movements and whereabouts at this time are unclear, but he was evidently in contact with the regent of Scotland by mid-February. Dacre referred to him as 'having entered with Albany' at that time, though there was not a formal reconciliation until the end of the following month, caused by continued problems for the duke of Albany in western Scotland. Angus was not going to commit until he was absolutely sure that might was on Albany's side. From the duke's perspective, the appearance of unity in Scotland, even with aristocrats as unreliable as Angus and Arran, was vital to his international standing and his hold on the country that he governed in the name of the young king. Finally, on 7 April 1516, a full pardon and restitution of lands was made to both Angus and Home. Angus returned to Scotland, leaving Margaret in England. Albany had given him permission to visit his wife in London if he wished but the earl did not avail himself of the offer. He would not see Margaret again for more than a year, and by then much had changed.

It has been said that there is no indication that the couple parted acrimoniously, but even if there were not bitter words, there was certainly much distress on Margaret's part.[4] Perhaps she accepted that it would be awkward for her husband to turn up at the court of Henry VIII as a fugitive from Scottish justice, landless and dependent on her brother's goodwill, but she certainly seems to have greatly regretted that Angus put his own interest before that of their marriage. Margaret was 'in great heaviness' and it is easy to understand that the parting made her emotional.[5] The pattern of Angus's behaviour and his willingness to desert her in moments of crisis was already apparent. That he would move to damage her interests proactively was not yet evident. Yet, as has been noted, 'The desertion by Angus of his wife at this crucial moment was to have far-reaching consequences which were to change the course of Scottish history.'[6] As for the queen herself, Angus's departure, her own slow but steady recovery of her health and Dacre's continued manoeuvrings now combined to determine her on a course of action. She would go south to London, to the English court. The day after Angus's restitution in Scotland, Margaret Tudor set out from Morpeth with her daughter to visit the brother she had not seen for thirteen years.

Dacre rode with her as far as Newcastle but his responsibilities as warden of the northern marches meant that he did not go farther. He felt that by then he had fully discharged his obligations to Henry VIII and Margaret. Never entirely certain of his influence over her, he was probably relieved to see her procession disappear south. So he handed her over to Sir Thomas Parr, the courtier the king had sent to conduct his sister to London. Parr, like Dacre, came from a northern family whose lands were originally based in Kendal in Westmoreland. There was, in fact, some tension between the Parrs and the Dacres about an inheritance in which both had a share but the Dacres, claiming seniority, had prevailed. If there was any residue from this disagreement, Parr was far too adroit in courtly skills to let it be seen by Queen Margaret. His interests, and those of his wife, Maud Green, one of Katherine of Aragon's ladies, now lay firmly in the south of England. Acting as an escort to the Queen of Scots was an honour and an opportunity that he knew better than to complicate by any appearance of resentment against Dacre. In fact Margaret, who was susceptible to charming men, found Parr delightful. His attentions and the care with which he ensured her comfort and the honour due to her were a balm for Margaret's bruised ego and aching body.

THE THISTLE AND THE ROSE

Parr helped her rediscover some of the joys, as well as the hardships, of being a queen.

Margaret left Morpeth on 8 April and moved slowly towards London. She wrote to Henry VIII from Stony Stratford in Buckinghamshire on 27 April to:

> let you know that yesternight I came hither, so being comforted of you in my journey in many and sundry ways that, loving be to our Lord God, I am in right good health and as joyous of my said journey towards you as any woman may be in coming to her brother.[7]

Yet she had to wait nearly another week, until 3 May, before she was finally reunited with her brother, at the home of Sir William Compton in Tottenham, on the northern outskirts of the capital. The choice of Compton's house for the meeting between Henry and his sister is interesting. Compton was a long-standing, close friend of the king, having served him since Henry was duke of York. He was the true boon companion, a keen jouster, roisterer – and enormously greedy and acquisitive. Not greatly interested in politics, he would do his master's bidding in all things, especially if it made him richer. Sir Thomas Parr had been viewed as a safe pair of hands for Margaret's journey, but Henry chose the home of someone with whom he was far more intimate as the most comfortable place for this long-anticipated reunion.

Neither brother nor sister recorded on paper their reactions to meeting again after thirteen years and if they did confide any reflections to members of their immediate circle there was no gossip that has survived. They did not wish to acknowledge the unspoken rivalry between them, although it had been present since Margaret's proxy marriage in 1502. Henry was more interested in continental Europe than Scotland but he had resented James IV passionately and he knew that France would cause him trouble through his northern neighbour if it possibly could. With the casual contempt for the Scots that was endemic in the English monarchy, he seems never to have grasped fully that Scotland had strong links with Europe that went beyond the Auld Alliance and that these could not be waved aside as if they were of no relevance. Beyond this political miscalculation, there was a fair degree of misogyny towards Margaret herself. She had been a queen before he became a king, though he always believed that, as a mere woman and his sister, she should do his bidding. Margaret had been through a great deal, her sufferings intensified by the contrast between her stable life as James IV's wife (despite the loss of so many children in infancy) and the nightmare of uncertainty over the past three years as she tried to hold on to power in Scotland.

Now, after months of ill health and the grief of losing her younger son, Margaret, at the age of twenty-six, found herself in the presence of the man she had last seen when he was a twelve-year-old boy. Presumably he had taken a formal leave of his sister when Margaret and Henry VII left Richmond in the summer of 1503, but there is no reference to this in surviving sources. At the home of Sir William Compton she would have knelt before receiving any kind of personal embrace as his sister. The impression of him as she raised her eyes must have been startling. Henry VIII, at twenty-five, was in the full bloom of his strength and vigour, a handsome, red-headed man bursting with energy. The birth of Princess Mary in February 1516 had added to his air of unstoppable confidence. At last, it seemed that Katherine of Aragon had produced a baby that would live. Of course there would be other children, he told ambassadors making slightly half-hearted congratulations. Yet Margaret knew only too well how brutally such hopes could be dashed.

As Henry surveyed his sister, he saw a woman who bore

little resemblance to the dignified, slight girl who had left everything she knew behind at the age of just thirteen. She was only in her mid-twenties but continuous pregnancies had caused her to put on weight. His own wife had followed exactly the same path and, like Margaret, she sought solace in jewels, as if the shimmering stones could somehow make up the sparkle they had both lost. Henry was not a tender man and only sentimental when it came to his own problems. But he was not entirely unwilling to display affection and he wished to see his sister given her due now he had taken on responsibility for her. Margaret would be appropriately lodged and entertained while she was in England. Though unspoken at this stage, both of them knew that her stay would not be indefinite.

Margaret, regally attired and mounted on a white palfrey given to her by Queen Katherine, rode in procession up Cheapside with the king and her attendants. Her party was more likely to have evoked curiosity from passers-by than to have attracted large crowds. It was not a state entry. She went first to Baynard's Castle, a splendid riverside mansion in the City of London, which was the London residence of all the Tudor queens consort. From there she moved to Scotland Yard, the traditional London residence of visiting Scottish envoys, north of York Place on Whitehall. As a child she had only spent time in London for state occasions, most notably the marriage of Prince Arthur to Katherine of Aragon, and she did not know it well. The year she spent there in 1516–17 would have given her a much better appreciation of her brother's capital.

London in 1516 was still a late-medieval city, with a resident population of between 40,000 and 50,000 people. As such, it was a vast metropolis compared to Edinburgh (about four times as large), defined by the River Thames, its main source of transportation and trade. There was a significant, if transient, population of foreign merchants and workers, not always popular with the local inhabitants, but giving it the air of an international hub. The skyline of the city, when approached from the south, was one of many graceful church steeples. Far less appealing were the rotting heads of executed traitors displayed on poles on London Bridge and the bodies dangling from gibbets at Wapping. A contemporary poet lavished praise on London, calling it 'the flower of cities all'. This praise came, somewhat ironically, from a Scot who was part of the diplomatic delegation for the negotiations surrounding Margaret's marriage in 1501. He called London the new Troy and described it as 'the princess of towns, of pleasure and of joy'.[8] However, the size of London paled in comparison with many other European cities; it was dwarfed by Paris, which had a population at least three times larger. Nor, despite the great impression it made on its Scottish visitor, was it an attractive destination for European diplomats. No one leapt at the chance of a posting to England. The people were viewed as quarrelsome and greedy, the ruling class venal and unreliable, and the country still emerging from the harm wrought by five decades of civil war in the previous century. Few people outside England spoke the language, though Henry VIII and his courtiers were fluent in Latin and French, and competence in foreign languages was considered the mark of an educated gentleman in Tudor England. It is worth stressing these points in order to give an accurate depiction of the reality of the times. England in the early sixteenth century was not the leader of Europe, or even close.

For Margaret, however, her homecoming had other pleasures than time spent in a city whose size and activity brought home to her the hardships and limitations of her life in Scotland. She could spend time at Greenwich with her sister-in-law, Katherine of Aragon, and her own younger sister, Mary, now duchess of Suffolk but still known as the French Queen. Mary's remarriage had caused much more of a scandal in England than Margaret's decision to wed Angus. Henry's ire at his younger sister's temerity in marrying Brandon so precipitately had dissipated but there was an ever-present reminder of it in the financial obligation for the couple to pay the king reparation for their rash action. The sum demanded, £100,000 as recognizance, was so huge that it left Mary virtually nothing from her French lands, though it certainly prompted her husband to pay very close attention to the management of his estates in Suffolk. Mary had also just given birth to her first child, a son, on 11 March 1516 and was only recently back at court when Margaret arrived in London. Even so, the idea that the three royal ladies spent their time together with heads bent over embroidery chatting about babies and their husbands is surely rather patronizing. We have no idea what passed between them or how frequently they met.[9] They could just as well, since all were devout and well-informed ladies, have discussed religion and international politics. And Margaret was increasingly involved in discussions with Henry VIII about her position in Scotland, especially the management of her rents and dower properties and the terms on which she might, eventually, return.

We do, however, have a revealing insight into the great tournament and celebration on 19 and 20 May 1516 which was given by Henry VIII at Greenwich in honour of Margaret. On these two spring days were held jousts, a great banquet and an unidentified play. The records show the enormous amounts spent by the king on apparel and accoutrements for the joust. These are some of the few surviving accounts that reveal how lavish were the jousts in the first decade of Henry VIII's reign; this one cost £972.2s.2d (over £500,000 today). For this sum, it can easily be imagined that the clothing of the king, the duke of Suffolk and other leading lords were of the richest materials. The athleticism demonstrated by Henry, Suffolk, the earl of Essex and Nicholas Carew when they challenged all comers in the joust was no doubt impressive, but so were the striking outfits they sported, of blue and black velvet, superbly embroidered with branches of honeysuckle vine, whose leaves were made of flat gold of damask. The knights on horseback, who included the marquess of Dorset and the earl of Surrey (son of the man who had so irritated Margaret on her progress to Edinburgh in 1503), wore blue velvet, fringed with cloth of gold. Various other gentlemen, echoing the colour theme of the tournament, wore blue satin and blue damask, with blue bonnets and hose. Amid this visual spectacular, the prowess of the participants was far from an afterthought. All acquitted themselves well, according to Hall's *Chronicle*, but, perhaps predictably, the overall honours went to Henry himself. As evening approached, Henry and his entourage went to the queen's chamber, 'where was a great banquet for the Queen of Scots'.[10]

Interestingly, one of the recipients of payment for the silks and gold of damask was a woman, Mistress Philip, a dealer in luxury materials, who supplied such items regularly to the king in the first part of his reign. Beyond her name, we know nothing about this lady, though her involvement gives us a tantalizing glimpse of the role of female merchants in London at the time. We do, however, know more about the producer of the play, William Cornish, though there are few details of what the content of this theatrical entertainment actually was. Cornish's father produced three pageants for the marriage of Margaret's brother Arthur to Katherine of Aragon. The son was master of the Children of the Chapel Royal at the start of Henry VIII's reign and by 1516 he was in charge of devising all courtly entertainments. These theatricals can best be characterized as a cross between a pageant and a masque, and though none of the text survives it has been suggested that Cornish, who also wrote entertainments for the Christmas season, used the Children of the Chapel as actors. There is no indication that either of the three queens present was involved. As has been pointed out, Henry VIII spent far more on these types of revels than James VI and I a century later.[11]

All of this was a fitting tribute to mark Margaret's arrival in London and, for that summer, it may have sufficed to keep her content. Yet it did nothing to solve the problems of authority, her financial situation and access to her son that had caused her to flee Scotland. Unless there was a satisfactory resolution to the complex issues surrounding Margaret's position as Queen of Scots, she could not be tranquil. Margaret was far too determined to recover what she had lost to remain in London forever. Neither did Henry VIII want her there as a permanent exile. Earlier writers have claimed that she was reluctant to return but this is not the case. Margaret was an inveterate letter-writer and could plead her own cause with vehemence. She continued to do so throughout her time in London. Thomas Wolsey knew well how eloquent and persistent she could be. The Queen of Scots also had a good grasp of the legal complexities and political considerations that she knew would need to be addressed before all of the parties concerned – herself, her brother, Albany and the Scottish lords and Francis I – could agree.

The diplomatic game was already afoot before Margaret made her entry into London. The Scottish ambassadors, the bishop of Galloway, Sir William Scott and James Ogilvy, accompanied by the French ambassador, de Plains, who had been consistently thwarted in his attempts to appeal directly to Margaret herself, arrived two weeks before the queen. Henry refused to see them before he had consulted with his sister, so they were left to cool their heels for nearly two weeks as Margaret made her more leisurely progress south.

Initial attempts at diplomacy foundered on the absolute insistence of the English that Albany must be removed from the regency and leave Scotland. It has been suggested that Henry VIII played on his sister's concerns about the welfare of young James V, continuing to cast Albany in the role of sinister heir-presumptive, just waiting for one of the convenient illnesses that stalked children at the time to carry off Margaret's son. And, if such were to happen, who could say what direct hand the wicked duke might have had in hastening the demise of his helpless little relative? These, and the grievances drawn up in her name by Dacre, were what Margaret laid before a meeting of Henry's council in late May. De Plains did eventually see the queen, but could not convince her of Albany's genuinely good intentions. So the opportunity for an early resolution of Margaret's problems was lost. They were inextricably caught up in the wider questions of how Scotland would be governed and England's relations with France that all that came out of this embassy was a prolongation of the truce between England and Scotland into the autumn.

Pageants and jousts were all very well, but it soon became apparent to Margaret that her time in London could have the unfortunate effect of further damaging her interests in Scotland unless she took the lead in moving matters forward. She must press her claims, especially those that would safeguard her Scottish finances, at every opportunity. For a woman often dismissed as shallow and only interested in the trappings of royalty, she was absolutely single-minded in her determination to make headway in this respect. Without financial security she could not expect even to live comfortably, let alone wield any kind of influence. Hoping to reassure the queen that he was not simply appropriating her possessions, Albany agreed that an inventory be taken of all the jewels and clothing she had been forced to abandon at Tantallon as she fled from Scotland the previous year. This revealed that, on paper at least, Margaret was still a wealthy woman in right of these items alone, even before the disputed rents from her dower lands were taken into consideration. There were nearly two pages of items listed. They included everything from gold collars and chains, 'the great diamond sent by the King of France' and a 'great balast ruby with three pearls', sleeves of cloth of gold, silk and satin, partlets set with pearls and rubies, a 'target' – a golden medallion – with an image of the Virgin Mary (Margaret was a collector of religious items), beds and bed linen and a number of books.[12] Several of these items, including more portable ones such as various pairs of sleeves, were, it was noted, sent to the queen in England.

Happy as Margaret was to receive a few pieces of jewellery and some of her wardrobe, her right to all of the jewels was unclear. As in England, the jewels of a queen consort were the property of the crown in the first instance and it could be hard to prove which ones were personal gifts (in this case, from James IV to his wife) and which should revert to James V. He was far too young to appreciate them or have any use for them himself but a future wife might be expected to enjoy them, and even at this stage thought was being given to a bride for the five-year-old king among the daughters of Francis I. This would form part of the text of the Treaty of Rouen in 1517 and it would not be forgotten when, twenty years later, the adult James V went to France in search of a consort to sit beside him on the Scottish throne.

The question of Margaret's lands was even more contentious. Albany agreed to the arrival in Scotland of three English commissioners to assess the monies owed to the queen from her dower properties and to enquire why these were not being properly administered. The commissioners did not like what they found, especially as a number of the Scottish lords, including Margaret's own husband, his Drummond relatives and the earl of Argyll, appeared to be 'interfering' with her lands. Simply put, this meant they were helping themselves to Margaret's rents. Without oversight and the introduction of legally based financial penalties, the commissioners could remonstrate all they wanted. Margaret was well aware of this, as was the ubiquitous and self-serving Dacre, but he would, when it came to the final arrangements for Margaret's return to Scotland, in which his advice was key, agree to the removal of some of the clauses of the Anglo–Scots treaty intended to safeguard Margaret's position. He let her down, as he always did, and her brother, never a man for detail, failed to grasp the implications of Dacre's advice. Henry VIII was tiring of supporting his sister out of his own revenues. He would, of course, do so while she remained in London but by the beginning of 1517 both brother and sister were looking for her return to Scotland.

Albany was more open to the terms that the English demanded, as part of an overall peace treaty with Scotland, than the Scottish lords themselves were. In time, Margaret would come to realize that his intentions towards her and James V had always been honourable, within the obvious limitations imposed on him by the suspicious and often hostile Scottish nobility and the machinations of his own master, Francis I, and Margaret's brother, Henry VIII. For the immediate future, Albany's withdrawal from Scotland, for an undisclosed period of time, was one of the conditions Henry VIII insisted on for his sister's return. He did not want her to come under the influence of Albany, preferring instead to leave her at the mercy of Angus, who had already proved himself unreliable, and the new regent, the earl of Arran, whose intentions for Scotland were unknown but who had his own track record of shifting with the political wind. Much that was to befall Margaret Tudor on her return to Scotland can be attributed to Dacre and Henry's failure to protect her interests or to have any kind of alternative strategy for helping her if things became difficult.

Margaret set out from London with her daughter on 18 May 1517 to begin a much more low-key progress north than the one she had undertaken as a thirteen-year-old. There were, of course, processions and official entries to cities like York, but she was no longer the golden Tudor child of 1503. She departed shortly after the 'Evil May-Day riots', an outburst of xenophobia directed at foreign merchants by London's apprentices, put down swiftly by Henry VIII.[13] It was not a good omen. Her brother would have strenuously denied the accusation that he was setting her up to fail. Yet he certainly did not want Scotland, as a country, to succeed. This conundrum would plague Margaret Tudor for the rest of her life.

18

A Change of Heart

'I am sore troubled with my lord of Angus.'
Queen Margaret to Henry VIII, October 1518

Margaret left London on 18 May 1517. Her brother accompanied her for four days as they rode into the Midlands. He left her at Doncaster, evidently disinclined to go further. Henry seldom ventured outside south-east England and would continue this indifference to other parts of his realm for the rest of his life.[1] Margaret already had much more experience of her native land than the king did.

Henry delivered his sister into the care of the earl of Shrewsbury, who was in charge of her itinerary and arranging receptions with local dignitaries along the way. The king had made sure that his sister would be treated with the deference appropriate to a queen wherever she halted, and greeted with display, albeit not on the scale of the entertainments she enjoyed in 1503. This was not the triumphant progress of a Tudor princess, merely the muted return of an exiled queen to a land riven by political faction and personal rivalries. Margaret was already well aware of how she would be drawn into this maelstrom and, indeed, she expected, perhaps even wanted, to be. The queen was no shrinking violet when it came to participation in Scottish politics. She knew she would be the focus for anti-English sentiment. But she was also aware that this feeling, though strong, was not universal. Her references in 1514 to 'my party' were not just wishful thinking. She undoubtedly wanted to exercise power and influence because this would enable her to strengthen her son's perilous position as a small child otherwise at the mercy of ambitious men who sought only to exploit his vulnerability.

The journey back to Scotland was far from easy. Margaret does not appear to have been a good traveller. Shrewsbury wrote to Wolsey on 28 May that she had been ill for several days after Henry left her, but was now recovered.[2] He also reported that the 'lords and gentlemen of the shires have done their duty towards her'. If this hints that Margaret's reception was not as fulsome as on her previous progress, there is further evidence of the reluctance of some of the northern dignitaries to expend time and money on the Queen of Scots. Henry Percy, earl of Northumberland, told Shrewsbury that his wife would not be able to accompany the queen from York to Newborough, as requested, and he clearly resented the expense he would incur in riding with Margaret's party himself.[3]

Margaret arrived in York on 3 June and went on from there to Durham, waiting in the north of England until she received assurance that Albany had, indeed, left Scotland. So it was not until 15 June that she crossed the border once again at Lamberton Kirk, as she had done fourteen years earlier. She was no longer a nervous bride awaiting the first meeting with her royal spouse, but a wary, though determined, queen. She was also a wife with considerable cause to wonder about the commitment of her second husband. Angus had been instructed by the Scottish council to meet her. He did not go of his own volition, though Margaret would not have known this at the time. She discovered the reasons for his reluctance soon enough. At this reunion, there appears to have been a polite cordiality rather than the ecstasy fancifully described by an earlier biographer: 'Seeing him once more, thrilling to the sight of his handsome countenance and warmed by his embrace, Margaret forgot the doubts that had been nagging her.' We have no idea what Margaret's private thoughts at this time were but the import of Angus's refusal to come and visit her during her year in London, despite having been given permission, was certainly not lost on Albany and it is unlikely that it was lost on the queen either.[4] Angus was accompanied by his kinsman George Douglas, earl of Morton, and by the Frenchman Antoine de la Bastie, nominated by Albany as deputy-governor when he took ship from Dumbarton back to France. A force of 3,000 Borderers completed the reception party.

Margaret was permitted to return under letters patent issued in the name of her son, 'with the counsel and assent of Albany and the three estates'. It was stated that the queen was to:

enjoy all profits and rights of her dowry in Scotland as it justly pertains to her and with such assistance in exaction as is given in the case of crown property. Her jewels and goods are to be restored at once and entire, on condition that she restores what she detains of crown property. She and her company are to be free from arrest, injury, or impediment. It is provided that neither she nor any of her company shall do or devise anything prejudicial to the king, governor or realm.[5]

Margaret had spent much of her time in England trying to ensure that her financial position was secure when she went back to Scotland. Henry, who had every reason to encourage his sister to her English affinity, was generous in terms of supporting her day-to-day living requirements. She had, however, little cash she could call her own and was still requesting what amounted to handouts for small expenses and rewards for her servants from Wolsey, even while on her journey back to Scotland. Precisely how she would be able to enjoy her dowry and what the assistance in obtaining this would actually be was alarmingly lacking in specifics.

There were also stringent restrictions on her access to James V, agreed by the Lords of the Council on 24 May 1517: 'because the queen's grace is now to come in this realm and will desire to see and visit her son … in what manner she shall be received in the castle of Edinburgh' (where the king was then living, in the part of the castle known as David's Tower).[6] Margaret was hardly encouraged to be a frequent visitor. She could bring only four of her attendants with her and was expressly forbidden from any overnight stays. The Lords of the Council who still supported Albany feared that her influence over her son could grow quickly beyond their control if she was allowed to spend too much time with him. They were alive to the possibility that the mixture of Margaret's natural maternal affection and her strong personality could easily undermine the council's position. The queen took up residence at Holyrood while she considered her next moves and familiarized herself with the changed landscape of Scottish politics.

The country to which Margaret returned was without strong leadership or direction now Albany had gone. The duke left a complex arrangement of 'regents' among the leading magnates of Scotland who were given responsibility for James V's welfare and education, such as it was. No doubt Albany hoped that his arrangements would balance the conflicting interests and personal animosities of the most powerful Scottish lords, but the reality that ensued in the four years that followed his first tenure as lord governor are the most confusing in the long and convoluted minority of Margaret

Tudor's son. The Scottish government was thrown into crisis within months of Margaret's return by the assassination of de la Bastie by David Home of Wedderburn on 17 September 1517. As deputy governor in Albany's absence, de la Bastie had taken his duties seriously, attending council meetings throughout the summer. This and the fact that he was French might have been irritant enough, but the Homes, a family every bit as extensive and self-serving as their neighbours the Douglases, were infuriated by de la Bastie's appointment as royal lieutenant in the Merse and Lothian, the very centre of their own lands. The family's hatred of de la Bastie and the French influence that he represented had been growing since October 1516, when Lord Home and his brother William were executed for treason. Across the border, Lord Dacre had continued his efforts to draw the Homes into conspiracy and the constantly reiterated schemes for kidnapping James V. By the autumn of 1516, Albany's patience had worn thin. The Homes were too untrustworthy to go unchallenged any longer. Their luck had run out.

The execution of the Homes confirmed Albany's authority. It also sent a sobering message to the earl of Angus, once an ally of the Homes, that he needed to be careful how he was perceived. Margaret's husband took note and fell into line, at least while Albany remained in Scotland. Once Albany left, the fate of his conscientious and by all accounts charming and handsome deputy, de la Bastie, was sealed. The Homes were not likely to forget the grievous injury to their family honour, though there were other, more local, concerns and resentments, including an ongoing dispute with the Blackadder family, that may have prompted the revenge they plotted. Accounts of the precise circumstances surrounding de la Bastie's death vary. The traditional ballad gives a colourful account and may contain more than a grain of truth. It claims that de la Bastie heard of a dispute about Langton Tower, near Duns, and was attempting to negotiate an amicable outcome with David Home of Wedderburn when reasonable words deteriorated into a violent disagreement. De la Bastie is said to have tried to escape (perhaps feeling he had been lured into a dangerous trap) but, in the words of the ballad:

Sir David Home that stern old carle
Came up and in a trice
As Beautie and his horse were bogged
Did stab him twice or thrice
Tam Trotter then cut off his head
And tied it by the hair
Upon Sir David's saddle bow
To Dunse they did repair

There, to general approbation, de la Bastie's head was displayed at the market cross and subsequently fixed to the wall of Castle Home, while his corpse was buried without ceremony in the grounds.[7]

The deputy governor's death left a vacuum at the heart of Scottish government, though not one that Margaret, however much she might have wanted, was in a position to fill. Nor did the lords, her own husband included, turn to the queen as a natural choice to take over again as regent for her son. Instead, the role was given to James Hamilton, earl of Arran, the next in line to the throne after Albany himself. It was not to be a role that the earl, a major landowner in south-western Scotland, would ultimately be able to fill convincingly. His family had acquired the status of nobility only within the last forty years, as the result of the first Lord Hamilton's marriage to Princess Mary Stewart, the eldest daughter of King James II and Mary of Guelders. James IV had favoured him and given him a prominent role in the command of the burgeoning

Scottish navy. Arran sailed to France with James's ships in 1513, ready to support Louis XII in his quarrel with the Habsburgs and Henry VIII, so he was out of the country when James IV fell at Flodden. Initially, he did not get on with Albany, but by the time of the duke's departure in 1517, the two were reconciled.

Arran managed tolerably well initially, while he was still viewed as a kind of extension of Albany's power. Yet by 1519 it was obvious that Albany would not come back to Scotland as long as the truce remained between England and France. Arran's attempts to establish his own direction firmly were, as Lord Dacre had remarked, doomed to failure. 'The Scottish lords cannot agree to be governed by one of themselves', he wrote in July 1519. A year later, Margaret voiced her own despair at the state of her son's kingdom, saying that 'Scotland was never like to be so evil ruled'.[8] One of the major causes of this quarrelsome stalemate was the underlying animosity between Angus and Arran: the Douglases and the Hamiltons hated each other. Their adherents fought themselves to a standstill in Edinburgh in the street-fight known as 'Cleanse the Causeway', which took place on Edinburgh High Street on 30 April 1520. By that time, Margaret's despair was not just for Scotland, but for the irretrievable breakdown of her marriage to Angus, and its implications for her future.

Although it is often asserted that one of the major factors in the bitterness that ensued between Margaret and her second husband was Angus's infidelity – a charge repeated by the queen's recent biographers – there is no evidence for such an affair, or the existence of an illegitimate daughter as the result. 'The alleged mistress of Angus was a creation of the fertile imagination of David Hume of Godscroft' writes

Michael G. Kelley in his doctoral thesis on the Douglas earls of Angus, reminding us of the danger in putting too much confidence in the chroniclers of this period of Scottish history.[9] Nor is there any evidence that Margaret publicly or privately accused Angus of adultery. The quarrel between Margaret and the earl grew out of her discovery, which was not long in coming after her return to Scotland, that he was mismanaging her estates and creaming off the rents due to the queen for his own use.

The management of her finances was Margaret's overriding concern before she left London. She was not convinced by the vague assurances made to her by the Scottish council and was dismayed that she would have to take legal action to recover what she believed to be her rights. This she did with a tenacity that has been sneered at by male commentators, pursuing fourteen separate cases at the beginning of 1518 as the full extent of what was being withheld became apparent. The rents in dispute were mostly in Ettrick Forest, where Margaret's dower manor of Newark Castle was situated. It was over the possession of Newark that the first serious breaches in the queen's marriage became public knowledge. Angus believed he had every right to it as Margaret's spouse and made it clear that he intended to live there. Margaret was furious. She demanded that he leave, which he eventually did, but only under threat of forfeiture. He was ordered to deliver Newark 'for the good public weal of the realm'.[10]

Angus's reluctance indicated a level of hostility towards his wife which added to her alarm. His underlying argument, which he was eventually to make crystal clear, was based on his rights as Margaret's husband. This amounted quite simply to a belief that what was hers was also his. As his wife she had no legal right to cut him out of her estates. He should be responsible for their management and the rents due were monies that were owed to him in the first place. Admittedly, he does not seem to have been very competent in their collection, since Margaret's main contention was that her tenants were not paying up at all. When they did, Angus pocketed the receipts. Gavin Douglas, the bishop of Dunkeld and Angus's uncle, appeared before the council in February 1519 to plead his nephew's case, saying that the earl had rights to dispose of her dower lands as he wished, because he was her husband. This conveniently overlooked the fact that Angus had signed an agreement two years earlier renouncing his rights. Even then Margaret, far from being the love-struck wife so often depicted, had been clear in her own mind that she must retain independent control of her dower properties.

The Lords of the Council gave the queen their official backing in her quest to stabilize her finances but did not put in place sufficient measures to ensure that she actually received what was due to her. There may well have been some anxiety that if too clear a precedent was established to facilitate the queen's claims, this could encourage any dissatisfied wife to pursue legal redress against her husband, an unwelcome possibility to many Scottish lords. So each of the queen's cases was regarded separately, putting great pressure on Margaret and depriving her of any security or peace of mind. She was not to be discouraged, however, appearing in person for wearying sessions with the council as each one of her cases was heard separately. In these circumstances, her determination is surely to be admired rather than condemned. Margaret was not the person to give in easily and, besides, she had little choice.

The picture of a greedy, whining woman relentlessly pursuing her cause merely because this was part of her nature is unjustified. It is true that complaints of poverty were common among the upper classes in the sixteenth century; few people readily admitted that they were rich or had money to spare. Those who were wealthy were happy to demonstrate it but far more coy about discussing it. Describing one's abode as 'humble' and oneself as 'poor' were social conventions. Was Margaret really living in hardship? On paper, she was a wealthy woman, with lands and jewels, luxurious possessions and a glamorous wardrobe. In reality, she had little income she could call her own. In modern terms she was cash-poor. Of course, she was not a beggar, even if her letters to her brother, to Wolsey and to Dacre come close to pleading penury. As early as October 1517 Margaret was writing to Dacre about the extent of her financial embarrassment. 'I stand in a sore case', she wrote:

> an I get not the king's grace my brother's help, and my
> lord cardinal's; for such jewels as his grace gave me at
> my departing from him, I am so constrained that I must
> put it away for money; and hath put away all my servants,
> because I have nought to give them ... And had [it] not
> been Robin Barton, comptroller, that hath laid out of his
> own purse five hundred pounds Scots, I had been fain to
> have lived a poor gentlewoman, and not like the woman
> that I am: for I am not answered of no part of my living,
> except Stirling and Linlithgow, and you know, my lord,
> what that is.

She went on to reveal how distressed she was at being kept away from her son, James V. 'I am holden from him like a stranger, and not like his mother, which doth me great displeasure in my heart, considering I have no comfort here but him.' In these first, unhappy few months of her return to Scotland she was already pleading to go back to England permanently, ready to hand over all her Scottish revenues to her brother, who would, she contended with a note of bitterness, be more successful than she, a mere woman, in getting redress. She fiercely criticized the Scottish lords, saying there was 'neither kindness nor truth with them'.[11] Her animosity towards Angus increased. She seldom saw him and first mentioned divorce as the inevitable and, from her perspective, desirable outcome in 1518, telling her brother that she was 'minded to part' from Angus. Henry VIII was appalled. He sent one of his religious advisers, Friar Chadworth, to dissuade his sister from such an unfortunate course. For a while, the friar's intervention seemed to be working. There was a brief reconciliation in the troubled marriage of Margaret Tudor and the earl of Angus, as they tried to pursue several aims that would be of mutual benefit. But in this, as in every other aspect of their relationship, failure would come, sooner rather than later.

Both Margaret and her husband hoped to profit from the weakness of Arran's government. Angus's priority was to establish himself in Edinburgh, believing that whoever controlled the capital would be in a strong position to dominate the whole of Scotland. Given the nature of Scottish lordship and the importance of men like the earl of Argyll in the north and the earl of Lennox in the west, this was only partly true. In one of the mini coups d'état that characterized the shifting patterns of power in the period between 1517 and 1521, Angus had managed to establish himself and his supporters in Edinburgh by manipulating the friction between the city council and Arran to his own advantage. Arran then tried to rule Scotland from Stirling but by November 1519 it was obvious that his hold on government, never strong, was seriously weakening. Arran's faction attempted to get Margaret on their side, warning that she would lose their support if she once more sided with her husband.

Initially, Margaret chose to ignore this threat. Perhaps she genuinely wanted to overcome the difficulties in her marriage to Angus, especially as Henry VIII had made his opposition to such an outcome very clear. Certainly, it seemed that the reconciliation was working when the queen and Angus rode into Edinburgh together in October 1520, to be greeted by gun salutes and pipers. This show of marital unity hid a deeper rift that could not be so easily mended by spectacle, gratified as Margaret no doubt was by her reception. She was wounded by her brother's energetic defence of Angus and by the realization that Henry was only willing to countenance her restoration to the regency if she was allied to the Douglases and the Homes, who would safeguard English interests in Scotland. Margaret knew from experience that Angus would not respect her role or allow her any influence. There was nothing in Angus's past behaviour towards her that encouraged confidence. A spouse willing to cream off her revenues for his own use, when he had expressly undertaken not to, could hardly be expected to agree to Margaret once again assuming the reins of power.

In fact, the queen was moving to an entirely different view of what might constitute her best interests. No fool in such matters, Margaret had not completely severed her ties with Arran or with the French. She knew how concerned the new French ambassador, Lafayette, had been about the disarray in Scottish government when he arrived in the late autumn of 1519. At the request of the Scottish council Margaret had written to Francis I before the famous meeting between the French king and Henry VIII at the Field of Cloth of Gold outside Calais in June 1520. In this letter, she suggested that Albany should return to Scotland to restore good government. Although Margaret could represent herself to Dacre as having been constrained to write by pressure from the Scottish lords, her later actions suggest that she was already moving towards the view that her own interests would be best served in a Scotland that was no longer at the mercy of constant faction-fighting and changes of power. She knew from bitter experience that it was fruitless to rely on English help; her brother's assistance came with strings attached that were unacceptable and were likely to compromise her effectiveness in Scottish politics while also damaging her financial interests. Family loyalty was all very well, but not when it meant consigning her to a nominal role and depriving her of the ability to live as befitted a queen.

One can only imagine Henry VIII's reaction when Francis, so often depicted with a smirk on his face in portraits, informed him of the letter he had received from the Queen of Scots. Henry always believed that Margaret should do his bidding and the realization that she was taking any initiative, let alone one that might diminish him in the eyes of the French king, was profoundly irritating. For his part, Francis was not inclined, at this stage, to enter into hostilities with England. He was, however, increasingly disturbed by reports of the decline of effective order in Scottish government and the inability of the Scottish lords to work together for the good of their country. Scotland, he knew, might have a key role to play in safeguarding the European balance of power. A memorandum was prepared for him before the Field of Cloth of Gold which covered all of what the French perceived as the key points regarding James V, Margaret and Albany.

Before going, it would be well to find out what England will do for Scotland, telling them that Albany has authority to treat, if they think fit. If they agree to that, to propose an alliance for mutual defence between the three kingdoms, without in any way infringing the previous treaties between France and Scotland. If they do not wish Albany to return to Scotland, alleging that the King would be in danger and that the Queen would be probably ill-treated, he is to reply that she would be more glad than anyone else to have him back.

As well as the rotating guardianship of James V, under the 'three great personages' appointed by the Scottish government it was proposed that the pope and Denmark, as well as England and France, should send resident ambassadors to Scotland 'to watch over the safety of the king'. Clearly the French were still concerned about the possibility of Margaret's son being kidnapped and taken to England, just as the English were equally anxious about the purity of Albany's motives, given that he was next in line to the Scottish throne. As for Margaret herself, 'the Queen's property [is] to be restored to her according to the conjunct feoffment'. This was a grant of ownership of freehold property.[12] Margaret had heard all of this before she left London two years ago. It sounded impressive on paper, but she knew too well by this time that making it happen in reality was a much more difficult proposition.

Despite the enforced bonhomie of the Field of Cloth of Gold, one of history's more ostentatious displays of contrived one-upmanship, relations between France and England were much less friendly by the summer of 1521. Cardinal Wolsey negotiated an Anglo–Imperial treaty which bound Henry VIII to enter into war with France by the spring of 1523 if the Valois provoked hostilities with the Habsburgs. Henry VIII was certainly not keen on war with Scotland but he most emphatically did not want Albany to assume the reins of government there again. In this, he was to be disappointed. Francis I, alarmed by the continued wranglings among the Scottish lords and resigned to the fact that Henry VIII would not support France in any European war, authorized Albany's return to Scotland. The duke arrived at Gareloch near Dumbarton on 21 November 1521. From there he rode to Stirling Castle, where he was graciously received by none other than Queen Margaret herself.

Part IV

A Divided Family, 1521–28

19

A New Direction

'I had no help of his grace my brother, nor no love
of my lord of Angus.'

Queen Margaret to Lord Dacre, 1521

Four years back in Scotland had given Margaret a clearer vision of what she wanted for herself and her children. She knew there would always be difficulties in obtaining her desires and she was prepared to change course quickly if necessary and without wasting too much time on the dictates of conscience. The Tudors were a devious bunch and Margaret was just as capable of hedging her bets as any of them. The sixteenth century was an age in which doing the right thing was frequently subservient to personal interest, and moral steadfastness, however laudable in theory, was no recipe for survival in the swift currents of political change. Margaret knew that her own situation was inextricably tied to that of her son, James V. Her security lay in his and although she was never permitted to spend as much time with him as she would have liked, theirs was a close bond and she undoubtedly had influence over him. To James, a child cooped up for most of his time in Stirling Castle, his upbringing supervised by distant, if well-meaning, lords, his mother represented a glimpse of the more exciting world that beckoned as he grew older. Margaret's attention to her dress and jewels, for which she has been so unfairly derided, demonstrated to her son the power and glamour of royalty. She had been brought up as the first princess of the House of Tudor and trained by his own father to fulfil the role of queen consort with aplomb. Although his day-to-day affections were given to his loyal and adoring household staff, most notably to Sir David Lyndsay of the Mount, an accomplished poet who was his master usher, there is no doubt that James V loved and respected his mother. And Margaret, for her part, was committed to ensuring that he attained his majority – the time when he could rule in his own right – by remaining as much a part of the young king's life as the complex struggle for power in Scotland would allow.

Lady Margaret Douglas, her daughter by Angus, was then six years old. We know little of her life at this time, though as the daughter of the Queen of Scots she was likely to have been treated as a princess in all but name. She was probably cared for by her own staff in the houses that were part of Margaret's dower, but nothing is known of her movements in her very early childhood, or how often she saw her mother. The presumption is that young Margaret's life was uneventful in these early years. That, as we shall see, would change dramatically soon enough.

Meanwhile, Queen Margaret believed that her best hope of ensuring her financial stability and improving her personal influence would come from supporting the duke of Albany. Their aims were far from identical and, in an ideal world, neither would have wished to have to deal with the other, but Margaret had come a long way from the suspicion and antipathy she had exhibited towards John Stewart in 1514–15. Her husband and brother had both let her down badly, leaving her to struggle for everything that she believed was rightfully hers. Albany, who had never demonstrated any personal animosity towards the queen, was relieved to find that, far from standing in his way, she was now willing to present herself to the world as his ally. Both of them knew that, as far as Anglo–Scottish relations were concerned, they stood, in the eyes of the Scottish lords and the English government, for different interests. Albany could not escape being regarded as a stooge of Francis I of France by Henry VIII and Wolsey, while Margaret was equally hampered by the mere fact of being the king of England's sister. She distanced herself from the unpopular Douglas family of her husband as it became obvious that her marriage to Angus really was beyond repair, but more than one Scottish lord might have been forgiven for believing that the queen was changeable. She could ride into Edinburgh in triumph with Angus in 1519 and with Albany in 1521. We can understand Margaret's actions in the wider context of her aims for personal and familial survival but the queen did not always appreciate how her behaviour could be seized on and used against her, as further proof that women were emotional creatures unfit to govern. Angus, however, was not going to hang around at this point to challenge Albany or his estranged wife. He had initially accepted Albany's authority but was forced to leave Scotland in March 1522. By that time, his embittered uncle, Gavin Douglas, the bishop of Dunkeld, who owed his preferment to Margaret's committed support of his appointment, had fled to England. There he declaimed against his nephew's pusillanimity and encouraged the scurrilous rumours about Margaret's relationship with Albany that originated with the ever-inventive Dacre. But Dunkeld's days were numbered. He never returned to Scotland, dying of plague in London in the summer of 1522. The queen was shaken by his denunciation. She knew that Henry VIII would be displeased by her acceptance of Albany's return but she had not expected the degree of vituperation and the aspersions on her character that followed. Being Margaret, she was, of course, more than able to speak up for herself.

'I know the false information of the bishop of Dunkeld … for I think never to take part with them that is contrary to the king my son and his weal.' She then went on to reprimand Henry for his neglectful attitude towards her and the continued pressure that was being put on her to reconcile with Angus.

> As to my entreating [treatment]in this realm, I have often times advertised your grace, trusting to have gotten remedy, but I got it not; wherefore I was constrained to make me friends, through my good bearing to my lord governor of Scotland, wherein I have found me more kindness than I have in any other in these parts. Although your grace may be displeased that I say this, I may say as I find cause hitherto … but your grace may do to me, your sister, as ye please, but I shall make no evil cause, but it does me great displeasure in my heart of your unkindness.[1]

Margaret's reproof cut little ice with Henry VIII. He was inflexible when it came to anything involving Albany. The duke was his bugbear, a sore that he would worry away at for as long as John Stewart, a reasonable and conscientious man, remained in Scotland. Though the policy of Henry and Wolsey towards Scotland could, in the short term, be adapted to suit circumstances, on this point the king of England was not to be moved. Whatever he might have publicly claimed to the contrary, strong government in Scotland was not in his interest unless it was totally under his control.

Henry already knew that his sister was a woman of independent mind and spirit and his natural suspicion of these attributes in a female fuelled the sibling rivalry that had long simmered under the surface of his relationship with Margaret. Henry VIII's insecurities as regards women are often overlooked but they are evident in his dealings with his sister and, in different ways, with each of his six wives. Margaret stood up to him well before Katherine of Aragon opposed Henry's attempts to cast her aside or Anne Boleyn made her dignified rebuttal of the ludicrous charges brought against her when he had had enough of their marriage. Henry was ruthless with those who opposed him, with the notable exception of his daughter, the future Mary I of England, though his treatment of her did profound psychological damage. Margaret at least had the good fortune to be living in a separate country, though at the time she did not see her situation that way and even, in her lowest moments, felt like running back to London.

Such depression did not last for long. Still driven by a great deal of mental energy and an ambition to succeed, Margaret used Albany's return to develop the role of mediator in Anglo–Scottish affairs, whether her brother liked it or not. This had been one of her key aims since James IV fell at Flodden. It promised influence, putting her at the heart of Scottish politics and making her a player in the wider European scene. She would never openly acknowledge herself as her brother's rival, but she had, in fact, been so since that wet day in September 1513 when her first husband was cut down on a Northumbrian hillside. Nearly ten years had passed. Margaret was older, perhaps not always wiser, but certainly brave and much more experienced, able to withstand the vicious calumnies that her brother seemed so willing to believe. As mediator she also had a fine grasp of the tools that were available to her in her quest to ensure peace between the country of her birth and the country of which she had long been queen.

Recent research on Margaret's letters from this period has presented a radically different picture from the querulous, selfish whinger who appears in the pages of the works of Agnes and Elizabeth Strickland. Their prissy character assassination tells the reader a lot more about prevailing Victorian attitudes than it does about Margaret Tudor.[2] Dr Helen Newsome's groundbreaking thesis has revealed, in a forensic approach to Margaret's correspondence, a wealth of information about the queen's attitude to mediation, her understanding of the conventions of diplomacy and the different communication methods she used in pursuit of her goals.

It is particularly instructive to look at Margaret's correspondence with Henry VIII in the winter of 1521–22 and her correspondence with Thomas Howard, earl of Surrey, in the autumn of the following year. The contrast between the documents in question reveals much about Margaret's approach to the role of mediator (or mediatrice, as she described herself), in contrasting circumstances, since in the eighteen months that separate these sets of communications, much had changed. We also learn a great deal about the networks that Margaret used and the messengers she employed, men whom she had to trust implicitly. Initially, the task she set herself, at Albany's behest, must have seemed straightforward, though its success could not be by any means guaranteed. Albany wanted an extension of the peace between England and Scotland. He was never a bellicose man. He had not come to Scotland to make war on England, despite the neurotic misgivings of Henry and Wolsey, and the duke saw Margaret as a natural conduit to the king of England. This was, after all, one of the permissible – even expected – roles of a foreign-born consort. A little over two weeks after his return to Scotland, Margaret sent on 9 December 1521 a holograph letter (in other words, a letter written in her own hand and not dictated to a scribe) to her brother, requesting a continuation of the Anglo–Scottish peace. This method of correspondence between royals was intended to underline intimacy and respect as well as demonstrating authenticity. Margaret was showing affection for her brother in approaching him this way, hoping to appeal to a sibling bond.

The importance of what she was writing was emphasized by the messenger chosen to deliver her letter to Henry. This was Ross Herald, who accompanied the Scottish delegation to the English court in December 1521 as part of a wider strategy to discuss peace between the two countries in person with Henry VIII. The king would have known him, since he had delivered Margaret's letters before. To reinforce the seriousness of the Scottish desire for peace, even though this was an unofficial delegation, Albany sent his own secretary, the abbot of Glenluce. Every effort was being made to convince the English that the Scots' desire for a continuation of peace was genuine. Margaret's letter was a key component of this strategy.

Margaret chose her words carefully, mindful, perhaps, of her brother's paranoid nature and what was at stake. She could not afford to offend him or suggest, however obliquely, that he might be in the wrong. 'I am assured', she wrote:

> that the said duke of Albany, [the] governor, desires greatly your grace's favours and good will as he that will make you the best cause he can for he desires greatly the amity and peace betwixt the said realms, beseeching your grace to hold your hand to the same, that the peace betwixt your said realm and this may be prolonged.

The extension she mentioned was up till St John's Day, 24 June. Carefully presenting Albany as subservient to Henry's will in this wording, the Queen of Scots went on to remind her brother gently but firmly of his family obligations to her and to her son. There would be personal difficulties for them if Henry did not accede positively to this overture.

> Otherwise it will be right heavy to me and troubling, considering that one of them is my brother and the other is my son and therefore I beseech your grace to pardon me that I write so plainly for it touches me right near and be there not kindness betwixt your grace and the said duke of Albany it will be great occasion to him to treat me the worse, which I trust ye will never do to me your sister.

She went on to flatter Henry, assuring him that while peace was the most natural course in Anglo–Scottish relations, it would be 'both for your honour and the pleasure of God'.[3] Invoking the Almighty in this way was more than just an early-sixteenth-century throwaway line. Its significance would not have been lost on Henry VIII. The question was, how would he react to his sister's overtures? Alas, for all her efforts to persuade, to play to Henry's vanity while reminding him of his obligations as her brother, answer came there none. Undaunted, Margaret tried again, in a different type of correspondence, at the very beginning of 1522.

Christmas festivities would scarcely have been over when the queen busied herself with a more comprehensive strategy to gain her brother's attention and to reinforce her role as the Scots' chosen mediator. This time she would construct a memorial, to be delivered in person by her messenger. This type of communication is only now beginning to be properly appreciated. It could, in propitious circumstances and with an expert deliverer, be a most powerful tool. Perhaps the best way of understanding the early-modern memorial is to describe it as being more informal than the mannered delivery of a heraldic message, which seldom gave room for manoeuvre on the part of the herald or his regal audience. The memorial was clearly also more personal in tone than a scribal letter and could not be ignored in the dismissive way that Henry VIII had failed to respond to his sister's holograph letter.[4]

The key aspect of the memorial is that it is a performance requiring skill beyond that of mere acting, since an important part of its success hinged on the speaker picking up cues from the 'audience', in this case, Henry VIII himself. Though the queen and her chosen messenger would have discussed the contents of the memorial and how it was to be delivered in detail, even down to accompanying physical gestures and changes of tone or emphasis, the messenger would have been very much on his own during the interview with the king. Diplomacy and a keen ear for nuance were vital to his success, ensuring that the gist of what Margaret wanted to get across was adapted to the unpredictable reactions of her brother. Where necessary, her representative could rephrase, curtail or even omit a line of argument or exposition if it was evidently irritating the king. The skill involved is not to be underestimated. Nor is Margaret's commitment to this type of approach to her testy sibling, since she wrote out the memorial in full in her own hand so that Henry would have a 'hard copy' to study.

The identity of the man entrusted by Margaret to deliver this memorial is not known. Her most frequently used messengers were Patrick Sinclair and the wonderfully named Jammy Dogge, but there could well have been others. It is highly unlikely that the queen would have given this delicate mission to someone she had not worked with for a long time. And she also knew that no amount of preparation, careful wording and rehearsal before her messenger departed for London could actually ensure that he would be granted an audience in which he could deliver the memorial. The signs were not promising, as Henry had already ignored her first attempt to elicit a response about extending the peace treaty between England and Scotland. At the end of the memorial, Margaret addressed the best method of gaining Henry's ear and suggested an alternative if he simply refused to listen to her messenger. The tactic then would be for her representative to present the queen's written copy of the memorial to Henry 'and say to his grace that ye have to show him on my behalf matters as I trust he will be contented of and to his honour, beseeching him to assign a time to you that ye may show the same and give his grace pleasure'. She added that she wanted Cardinal Wolsey to be present at this meeting but if her messenger was refused any contact with the king then he should 'pass to my lord cardinal ... and pray him, on my name, to cause you to have audience and that the matters that ye come for are pleasant and agreeable to the king's grace my brother and him'.[5] A two-pronged approach would, Margaret thought, maximize the chances of her intervention being given serious consideration.

It remains unclear whether Margaret's unnamed messenger actually performed his memorial in front of a quizzical Henry VIII or merely left the written document with Wolsey, but we do know that this second attempt to get her brother's attention worked. Unfortunately for the queen, the outcome could scarcely have been more humiliating. Her request that the peace treaty be extended into the summer was roundly rejected and, even worse, Henry VIII, perhaps encouraged by the denunciations of Gavin Douglas, seriously impugned Margaret's morals while belittling her involvement as being unseemly for a queen and the mother of the King of Scots. His prejudices against a woman ruler, his deep-seated resentment of his elder sister and his disapproval of Margaret's personal behaviour were evidently in full flow. Sadly his letter to the queen does not survive, but her answer does. Deeply upset but, as ever, unbowed, Margaret did not collapse into meek submission on the receipt of what must have been an offensive excoriation by Henry. She would give as good as she got and without loss of time or humble acknowledgement of the criticisms aimed at her. Henry's 'sharp and unkindly writing' was unacceptable. She rejected her brother's accusation that she had been deceived by Albany and was outraged by his belief that she was having an affair with the duke, especially his claim that this would cause 'danger and peril' to her own son, James V. This time, she sent a scribal letter, signalling to Henry VIII her displeasure at his treatment of her and his lack of respect. This series of vicious, inaccurate depictions of herself as a queen and a mother required a cold, legalistic response, for which the scribal letter, with only its signature in her own hand, was the perfect response. 'It had been your part, dearest brother', she told him,

> to have been my defender in all evil reports and not to have alleged undeservedly dishonour to me, which shall prove of the self false and contrary. And where that your grace alleges plainly in your writing that my mind is to marry the duke of Albany and desires divorce to that intent, that was never my intent nor his, as it will be well known.

This is revealing of Henry's alarm at a time when he was gearing up for war with France.

She went on to claim that Henry was indebted to her, as mediator, for her pursuit of peace, an activity that she had performed selflessly on his behalf and at his behest. And she attacked the credence he had given to evil reports of her as being irrational and unnatural and to suggest that Henry's behaviour towards her would, if he was not careful, damage his international reputation. 'For my part, God and the world will know the verity of the untrue report that is made of me.' As his 'humble sister', she pleaded with him to 'look well and discretely upon these matters and refuse not reasonable ways. For if ye do the contrary it will be thought among all Christian princes, suppose ye write never so well, that ye desire the destruction of my son and his realm and thereupon make an unjust quarrel.'[6] This spirited and remarkably forthright defence was typical of a woman who, when it came to defending her own interests, was every bit her brother's equal. Margaret Tudor knew Henry VIII only too well. She had demonstrated, in her creative and multi-layered approach to the language and practice of diplomacy, that she was a force to be reckoned with in Anglo–Scottish relations and someone who understood the wider international implications of a sibling rivalry that she must now fight overtly on her terms, not those of an obstructive brother who cared nothing for her reputation.

However much Margaret wanted to be heard, Henry was not listening. In the day-to-day world of Anglo–Scottish relations, reality had a way of intruding on Margaret's carefully crafted missives. Henry's refusal to recognize Albany's role or engage with him in any way proved a powerful stumbling-block. Nor was it just his sister that the English king was willing to offend. In mid-January, possibly as an indirect riposte to Margaret's 9 December letter, he had pompously upbraided the Scottish estates for their support of Albany. He accused the duke of removing James V from 'rightful custody' into the care of a low-born foreigner and of encouraging a divorce between Margaret and the earl of Angus so that Albany could marry the queen himself. He then went on to claim that Albany had left France without the knowledge or consent of Francis

I himself, thus simultaneously belittling and insulting the French king whose friendship he had so ostentatiously sought just eighteen months ago. The Scots were exhorted to disown Albany and abandon all support for him if they wanted peace to continue. Bluster towards Scotland was ingrained in Henry VIII but he certainly did not want war on two fronts. His threats were dismissed by the Scottish parliament but they concerned Albany, who twice wrote to Francis I asking for aid in case of war with England.[7] In the early spring of 1522 Albany was apparently ill and no firm decisions were taken, but by the summer it was obvious that relations between England and Scotland were reaching a critical juncture. Though neither side wanted war, both were preparing. Indeed, Albany kept pressure on the Scottish parliament to be ready with men and arms. The situation became even more serious when the English invaded northern France in August 1522. Scotland and France were still allied by the Treaty of Rouen and though this had always benefitted the French much more than the Scots, Albany, 'the Scot who was a Frenchman', believed that Scotland must respond. He assembled the Scottish host, intending to attack the western borders and to take the city of Carlisle. He might have succeeded, since Dacre and the other northern lords were ill-prepared, but the Scots under Albany's command lost their nerve and refused to cross the border. The memory of Flodden was raw and there was a collective failure of will. James V was still a child and another defeat at the hands of the English was something that even Albany's closest allies did not want to contemplate.

Disheartened but still determined to leave his mark on Scotland, Albany went back to France at the end of October 1522. His plan was to gather enough French soldiers who would be more reliable than the unpredictable Scottish host. He appointed another council of regency, headed by the chancellor, James Beaton, and the earls of Arran, Huntly and Argyll, all experienced in government and committed to following Albany's instructions. He promised to return by August of the following year, or forfeit his role as governor. Despite his failure on the western border, Albany's second period in Scotland had largely removed those who opposed him, notably the Douglases, and re-established the rule of law. When he did come back, in September 1523, it was with a fleet of eighty-seven vessels and a substantial military force. The duke had finally got the army he wanted but he still did not have the unequivocal support of the Scots for a war with England. All these preparations and continued border raids by the English alarmed Margaret greatly. She began to question her continuing commitment to Albany. Fearful for her future and that of her son, she was about to play a very dangerous game.

For Margaret, the decision to try to thwart Albany's plans for a war with England needed to be handled with extreme care. Passing information on his military strength to Thomas Howard, the earl of Surrey and later duke of Norfolk, the English commander in the north, was treason, no matter how it might be dressed up as an attempt to avoid hostilities by someone who was still keen to portray herself as an effective mediator. Maintaining these two different – and, her enemies would have said, duplicitous – approaches risked everything that the queen had struggled so long for. She was compromising her freedom and opening the probability, if she was discovered, that she would never be allowed to see James V again. So why did she decide on this course of action and how did she protect herself in the secret negotiations she undertook with Howard in the summer of 1523?

There are various factors explaining Margaret's behaviour,

beyond the overlooked aspects that, however consistent her determination to survive was throughout her life, she was a born intriguer and risk-taker. Another, seldom given suffi-cient weight, is the fact she caught smallpox just before the end of 1522. The queen was seriously ill: 'My hands and all my body are so full of the smallpox that I might neither write, nor sit, nor scarcely speak', she told Wolsey on 26 December, apologizing for sending a scribal letter and not writing to him personally.[8] There is no indication that Margaret's life was threatened, but smallpox was a deadly disease, one that seems to have spread like wildfire in early-modern royal courts, and survival was by no means guaranteed. At the very least, some degree of scarring was almost inevitable. However spirited Margaret was – and one has to smile at her scathing criticisms of Lord Dacre, who had failed to pass on letters that she wrote to Wolsey, and her contemptuous dismissal of dip-lomatic attempts by the French and English over the vexed question of her finances – she must have feared the outcome of her illness. A doughty lady, Margaret did pull through, but the illness and the fact that she could still not live as she believed was her right caused her to reconsider her backing of Albany. It was a conundrum. He was no longer there in Scotland in person to lend her his support and when he did return it would be with the intention of fighting her brother. She needed to tread very carefully. The manner in which she did so is highly revealing, not just of Margaret's resource-fulness but also for what it tells us of the communications networks at the disposal of an early-modern queen.

Margaret's underlying aim at this time was to return to England. Continued denial by the Scottish government of what she considered to be her rights had worn her down. This explains why she was willing to pass state secrets to Thomas Howard. Yet she could not afford to burn all her bridges. To safeguard herself in Scotland, she needed still to be seen as a mediator, someone with enough influence and diplomatic skill to keep the peace between England and Scotland. There was no guarantee that Henry VIII would let her come back for a second time. His financial support ran to sending the occasional jewel, as if palming his sister off with a diamond here and there was sufficient. She was, after all, a mere woman and diamonds were, in the language of political messaging, an encouragement to constancy. But this woman wanted to be more than a recipient of his occasional largesse. While publicly acting as a mouthpiece for the Scottish government, she was also establishing a sophisticated secret communications network with Howard. Using spies and secret messages delivered verbally by trusted agents including her priest and the keeper of her wardrobe, Margaret was able to play a double game. While she did not resort to ciphers or invisible ink, both used liberally in later-sixteenth-century espionage networks, her approach was still a high-stakes gamble. 'For God's sake', she wrote to Howard in the autumn of 1523, 'keep my writing secret for it is my destruction'.[9] Indeed, it would have been, if discovered by the Scottish lords.

Albany's return on 22 September 1523 did not stop the English from carrying out the most destructive of all their border raids of this period, the attack on Jedburgh, just a day later. The Scottish regency council had ample time to muster men in support of Albany's French troops but sat back on their haunches awaiting his return. The price they paid for this indecision was the sack of one of their most important border towns. Frustrated as he had always been throughout his off-and-on presence in Scotland by the divisions and hesitance among the country's leading men, Albany was nevertheless committed to pulling his Franco–Scottish forces together for a push across the border. It was late in the season for campaigning and the autumn of 1523 was wetter than usual. As the eleven-year-old James V fretted under renewed restrictions and was sent back to Stirling Castle for his own safety, Albany took his forces to besiege one of the of the major English border fortresses, the castle of Wark. He arrived outside its defences on 1 November and, despite having launched a heavy bombardment, was unable to take what would have been a considerable prize. He withdrew after three days. The attack had been undertaken entirely by his French soldiers. The Scots, ever mindful of Flodden, once again refused to cross the River Tweed.

Albany's withdrawal from Wark was not quite the complete humiliation that English propaganda, deriding the duke's failure, ridiculed at the time. Recent research has enhanced our understanding of this affair and pointed out that Albany still had the confidence of a majority of the Scottish lords. His own confidence, however – or, at least, his own patience with the Scots – was nearly exhausted. Yet he stayed on for another six months, still trying to bring good government and good order to Scotland and trying to thwart the English interest. If he could not defeat them on the battlefield he could, at least, try to ensure that their influence in Scotland was never going to be detrimental to French interests. Albany wanted to return to France at the end of January 1524, when he wrote to Louise of Savoy, the French queen mother, that he had 'reduced the kingdom to excellent order and could leave it without danger'. But Louise and her son, Francis I, were not quite ready for him to quit Scotland and the Lords of the Council were reluctant, as always, to let him go. He finally departed on the last day of May 1524, leaving behind his only surviving child, his illegitimate daughter, Eleanor, whose mother was Jean Abernathy.[10]

While an important part of his diplomatic and military career still lay ahead for Albany, his achievement in bringing stability to Scotland is little known except to specialists in the complicated minority of Margaret's son, James V. He could probably have achieved much more if his tenure of office there had not been interrupted. In 1524, however, there was one person who had most to gain from his departure: Margaret herself. At last, after ten long years of frustration, there was a real prospect that she could exercise power again. James V was now twelve years old and considered to be of an age to rule in his own right. He would, of course, need his mother's support and guidance and she would be at his side to advise him as he left his childhood behind.

20

Margaret and Her Family

'I shall treat her grace at my power, so long as we are
undivorced, as law, conscience and honesty of her grace
requires ... and to give her occasion to adhere to me as her
husband, for the weal of both our consciences.'

Angus to the Lords of the Scottish Council, July 1525

By the spring of 1524, Archibald Douglas, earl of
Angus, had been living discontentedly in France
for two years. Dacre told Wolsey in March 1522
that Angus and his brother William had accompanied Lord
Fleming and Lord Hay, James V's secretary, who were on an
official mission to France at that time. It has been claimed
that this made Angus 'an emissary from the Scottish crown'
but it seems unlikely that the French viewed him in quite so
generous a light, since the earl and his brother were taken
into custody on arrival in France.[1] More plausible is that
they were put on the same boat as Fleming and Hay, both
experienced diplomats, for convenience and because it was
easier for their compatriots to keep an eye on them once
they arrived. Angus's stay in France began in these dubious
circumstances and little is known of his time there. In May
1524 he wrote to Henry VIII a rambling letter in French, with

such poor spelling, even given that there was no standard-
ization at the time, that some of it is hard to decipher. The
choice of language is interesting. Like most educated Scots
Angus could evidently read and write French, perhaps better
than he could actually write English. He may have felt that,
if his correspondence was intercepted by his French hosts, it
would look less suspicious if they could read it freely. On the
other hand, using a mixture of Scots and English might not
have been well received in London. The letter hints that he
could have had other correspondence with the English court
while in France. Certainly he began by thanking Henry for
his goodwill and acknowledged the English monarch's apparent desire for Angus to escape from France. This assertion
may, of course, have been wishful thinking on the earl's part.
He could not resist a dig at Albany, whose peace overtures
towards England he derided, claiming that they were just a
front to buy the duke further time for a war which he could
not win and for which there was no real support in France.
Angus's main concern seems to have been for his brother
George, left behind in Scotland, and he expressed the hope
that Henry would protect George if Albany moved against
him. This all became irrelevant when Albany left Scotland for
the final time a few weeks later.[2]

Manoeuvres concerning the eventual departure of the earl
of Angus are equally unclear but he had definitely left, with
or without the permission of Francis I, by June 1524, when
he turned up in London. Angus at first denied that he had
been given official permission to leave France, aware that the
charge that he had, in effect, become a French agent would
not sit well with Henry VIII. Several months later, however,
it was widely believed among the diplomatic community in
London that his departure from France was agreed with
Francis I and that Angus had actually acknowledged this.
The Venetian ambassador poured scorn on the claim that

Angus had 'escaped', remarking how unlikely it was that 'the brother-in-law of the king of England arrives in Scotland pretending to have escaped from France. The whole thing was a fiction devised by the Cardinal [Wolsey].'[3]

Why, though, had Angus been permitted to leave France if, indeed, his departure was countenanced by Francis I? We know that Angus could be charming and persuasive, with a remarkable ability to pull the wool over people's eyes. It had been, and would remain, one of the hallmarks of his adult life. He was very far from the 'witless young fool' decried by an elderly relative. Wolsey acknowledged an important shift in English confidence in Angus when he wrote to Dacre at the beginning of July 1524 that he and the king had met the Douglas brothers (William had managed to flee as well) on several occasions,

> and though, from what the king heard in times past, it seemed that the earl was a young man not of the best knowledge and experience, it appears that since he has been in France, he has greatly amended, and has now good understanding in matters of wisdom and policy.[4]

But Francis I was not so easily persuaded and he had ample reason to be suspicious of this Scottish aristocrat who had caused the duke of Albany so much trouble. However, Francis was heavily involved once more in the Italian Wars, an extension of his ongoing rivalry with the Emperor Charles V, and it may be that his wider European objectives were much more important to him than paying close attention to an unreliable Scot whom he had barely tolerated for more than two years. For Francis, like his predecessors, was primarily interested in Scotland only when the alliance between the two countries could be of immediate advantage. Perhaps he genuinely believed that Angus would use his considerable influence in Scotland to the advantage of France. By September 1524

Francis was completely disabused, writing to James V that Angus had fled 'without the knowledge of Francis or Albany. No faith is to be put in him, as he has been declared a partisan of England and rebel to the king and the duke.'[5] Yet the person who had most cause to be dismayed by Angus's departure from France and his apparent support from her own brother and the English government was Queen Margaret, who knew only too well that Archibald Douglas was completely untrustworthy. Were he to return to Scotland, she feared that he would use all his power and influence to thwart her ambitions for her son and diminish the power of the Scottish crown. It was in vain that her brother tried to reassure her about her husband's character and intentions. Henry VIII might tell her that he was pleased to find Angus to be 'her loving and faithful servant and husband', who had 'secretly conveyed first his brother and next himself out of France, intending first to reconcile himself to her, and then to assist in procuring peace'.[6] Margaret had every reason to believe that Angus wished, above all else, to further his own interests. How Henry's letter must have jangled her nerves. But she was determined to oppose her husband implacably.

Margaret's handling of her second regency has been, as is so much with her, roundly criticized as a further demonstration of her inadequacy as a politician and her weakness of character, allowing her animosity towards Angus to get in the way of balanced judgement. In this analysis, she still lacks, more than ten years after Flodden, a grasp of Scottish politics, failing to understand the inevitable tensions of being caught between the French interest and the English interest. She is just a power-hungry woman out of her depth and doomed to fail. I would suggest, however, that there are other ways of looking at Margaret's second regency and, in particular, at the disastrous failure of Henry VIII in deciding to support his brother-in-law, a man he scarcely knew but who had given scant evidence of reliability, over his more clear-sighted sister. For the choice of Angus over Margaret was compounded by an ignorance of Scottish affairs encouraged by the interfering, overbearing Lord Dacre and the deep-seated hostility to the idea of a woman ruler that was so soon to show itself in Henry VIII's obsessive desire for a divorce from Katherine of Aragon. His only legitimate heir was a daughter, Princess Mary, then aged eight, while Margaret's son was twelve years old and itching to exercise power in his own right. If Henry had given Margaret his support in her aims, he would have won over his nephew as well. James V was growing weary of French interference, as he saw it, in Scotland and might well have listened to his uncle if Henry had shown any sign of supporting Margaret. What happened between 1524 and 1528 turned James V permanently against his uncle.

Margaret began her campaign to regain power from a position of reasonable strength within Scotland. Her first step was to ensure that she had the support of the southern Scottish lords in her project to declare James V of age to govern himself. This was accomplished during a visit to the shrine of St Ninian in Galloway. It had been one of James IV's favourite pilgrimages and Margaret had learned much from her first husband's exuberant love of connecting with his subjects in this way. She also seems to have been a woman of genuine religious faith herself, so there is no need to be overly cynical about her motives in undertaking this journey. James V was left behind in Stirling, growing more anxious by the day to begin the exercise of the power that beckoned.

The queen now looked to shore up her strength. She was thirty-six years old and knew that she must take this opportunity. Her main allies were the Hamiltons, in the person of the earl of Arran and his son, and the Maxwells. Both families detested Angus and the Douglases as much as Margaret did. In Scotland it was very difficult to rely on the unqualified and permanent support of any of the great families but Margaret and Arran were united in their determination to keep Angus out of Scotland. Arran, second in line to the throne after Albany, was very conscious of the significance of his family in the Scottish succession. However much power and wealth the numerous Douglases possessed in southern Scotland, they had no dynastic claim to play a role in government. Also supporting the queen were nearly a dozen other great lords: the earl of Moray (illegitimate son of James IV), the earl of Lennox and the lords of Eglinton, Cassillis, Avondale, Glamis, Semple, Somerville and Ross of Hawkhead. They signed a bond to serve the queen at the end of August 1524. This and the removal of James V from his many years of being cloistered at Stirling seemed to indicate that Margaret's strategy was working. On 25 July, in Edinburgh, James V was formally invested by Arran with the crown, sceptre and sword of state, the 'honours of Scotland'. His mother, who now took up residence with him in Edinburgh Castle, was very proud. Yet she knew that stability was always no more than an aspiration in Scotland, at least when a king was youthful, and she was rightly suspicious and anxious about the extent of her brother's support for her. Was it just a matter of time before Henry gave in to Angus's persistent demands and sent her estranged husband back to Scotland with his blessing?

Henry VIII offered his sister an encouraging picture of Angus's supposed devotion to her and to the cause of good government in Scotland, which would help ensure peace between the Scots and the English. He never grasped

– perhaps because he did not want to – the depth of Margaret's antipathy towards her husband. The king seems always to have pictured it as an embarrassing marital dispute which could easily be overcome with a little goodwill on both sides, though more especially on Margaret's. So he would cajole her by assurances that Angus was 'intending and minding none other but first to reconcile himself unto your grace and favour'. Beyond this vision of Angus as the perfect spouse was the conviction that he was a responsible politician, desirous only of the welfare of Scotland. The earl wanted, Henry affirmed, 'to interpose his help, study, travail and authority, to the conducting of such good peace between us and that realm as may be for the weal and surety of the same'. His next few sentences would have made the queen's blood run cold, for in them her brother made it clear that Angus would be on his way back to Scotland, with Henry's backing, before much longer. 'Perceiving this his commendable mind and intent', Henry wrote,

> not only have [we] lovingly received him unto our said presence but also intend, with all convenient diligence, to dispatch him, in such wise as he may take his journey towards that realm; there to execute and do further to the advancement of his honourable desire, as you shall think good and convenient.

Henry finished this unwelcome epistle with the assurance that he desired to see nothing more than 'our dearest nephew once more brought out of the danger wherein he is, by reason of the suspect governance, and is likely to be more, if the duke of Albany may, before some good way taken, return into Scotland'. He did not think this an imminent threat, however, noting that Albany was not in good standing with the king of France and his formidable mother, Louise of Savoy, because he was suspected of having supported the uprising of the duke of Bourbon.[7]

To say that Margaret was dismayed by her brother's apparent warm regard for the husband she loathed, and to note that he trusted Angus despite her own repeated denunciations and the opposition of leading Scottish nobles, is an understatement. Yet she needed to tread carefully in July 1524, since she could not afford to offend Henry so much that he withdrew all support for her. She was also well aware of his hostility towards Albany. In this, he remained entirely implacable. Margaret had reaped the rewards of a much more pragmatic policy towards France and the duke and she needed to maintain a positive relationship with Scotland's old ally and, on a personal level, with the man whose support for her divorce from Angus might help sway the pope. She and Albany had parted on cordial terms only a couple of months before this exchange of letters with her brother and she was just as mindful as Henry VIII that the duke could return, with the blessing of Francis I, once the current difficulties in France blew over.

The queen chose her words carefully, hopeful that they might have some impact on Henry. She addressed both her own situation and that of Scotland. Of Angus, she noted that her brother had 'written … right specially … saying many good words of him, and praying for me to bear him good favour, and to let all displeasure pass; – my lord, I did him no displeasure, but did for him as far as I might'. It was well known all over Scotland, she continued, that Angus had spread all kinds of falsehoods about her to Henry 'but that I lay apart as now'. She must, however, speak her mind about her brother's intention to send Angus back to Scotland:

as to his coming here, I trust it will not be thankfully taken with the lords of this realm, and specially with the greatest; for it is not unknown to you, my lord, the great displeasure that was done betwixt him and the lords of this realm; wherefore I think his coming here will rather hinder the king my son in his matters than further it, as I understand by them.

She exhorted Henry not to do anything 'that may bring hurt to the king my son and me' and made clear her despair at the likely outcome – nay, almost the inevitability – of Henry's ill-judged support for Angus: 'I being so well as I am now, having the king my son at my rule, and breaketh the lords to my ways and then to *tine* [an old Scots word meaning 'fail'] for this, for pleasure of my lord of Angus.'[8] She saw, only too clearly, what would happen. She would lose the advantage she had worked for over so many years, just as it seemed that she could finally exercise power with the consent of a majority of the Scottish nobility. She knew that their loyalty could disappear quickly once Angus set foot again in Scotland. He was identified too strongly with the English interest, whereas she had striven, since her return to Scotland in 1517, to present herself as pursuing the interests of the Scottish crown. Now she had almost succeeded and her brother's actions were threatening to undermine everything she had so painstakingly achieved.

Henry VIII ignored her concerns. He found Angus to be a plausible fellow. After all, Margaret was a mere woman. Neither he nor Wolsey had complete confidence in her. For a while they played her along, noting that she liked to think she was in charge. She could, after all be 'a most propitious and convenient instrument ... pretending that nothing shall be wrought but only by her means'. But there was never a serious intention to follow her advice where it might diverge from English interests: 'Nevertheless', wrote Wolsey, 'so to be used that all shall depend upon her proceeding and doing, it were perilous and dangerous ... For it is no folly for a good archer to have two strings to his bow, specially where one is made of threads wrought by woman's fingers!'[9] Wolsey was sixteenth-century misogyny personified. Nor could Henry VIII rise above the sibling rivalry that prevented him from backing his sister when she most needed him. He did not really care if she *tined.*

Angus returned to Scotland in October 1524, having given Wolsey his bond that he would support English interests in Scotland before he left. The delay does not signify that Henry and Wolsey were paying serious attention to Margaret's concerns, but rather that they were waiting to see how events in Scotland would develop after the declaration that James V had come of age. On 30 July the Scottish lords signed a bond assuring the young king of their fidelity. Margaret worked with Dacre to bring about peace in the Borders and the parliament which met in August laid out the expectations of the new government. These formally ended Albany's regency and transferred executive power to 'the King, with consent of his mother and the lords of his council'. The programme was weighted towards the provision of better justice in the realm. Margaret also had a bold vision for an enduring peace with England, based on a proposed marriage between her son and Princess Mary, the king's only legitimate child and heiress to the English throne. The queen also wanted the English to recognize James V as second person in the English realm – an overt acknowledgement, in other words, that he was Henry's heir. Her son was to be given lands appropriate to this new status. Should Henry subsequently produce a legitimate male heir of his own (which he did, but not for another thirteen years), then Berwick was to be handed back to the Scots as recompense. It was a bold series of requests and one which, as has been noted, 'would have assured her a principal and unassailable place in the government of both England and Scotland'. For Margaret Tudor, so often criticized for an apparent absorption with her wardrobe and jewellery, was nothing if not the complete Tudor dynast. Henry VIII was never going to agree to such sweeping demands and he certainly was not willing to share power in this way with his elder sister. Neither was Margaret's position in Scotland, even without the immediate return of Angus, as secure as she would have liked. Her uncompromising attitude to government was already causing offence and she was laying herself open to criticisms of precisely the sort that Wolsey had so patronizingly characterized. In her eagerness to dispense patronage to her nearest supporters, there was one name that began to attract attention and unfavourable comment. Just who was this Henry Stewart and why was Queen Margaret plying him with a string of lucrative grants?

The younger brother of Lord Avondale was probably about six years younger than the queen. This was not a significant age gap and writers who have made fun of Margaret for becoming entranced by a 'toy boy' have merely added to the general assumption that the queen was, once again, prey to her passions. There seems little doubt, however, that she did fall in love, perhaps for the only time in her life. The marriage to Angus was primarily a political gamble that had gone badly wrong. It deprived her of her first regency and tied her to a man whom she came to loathe on a personal level. Henry Stewart could not offer any specific political advantage but the loyalty of his family to the crown counted for a good deal. He offered stability and unquestioning support, qualities that were frequently in short supply in Margaret's life after the death of James IV. One of Margaret's biographers has described Henry Stewart variously as 'brash', 'weak and amiable' and 'a handsome youth'.[10] The truth is that we know almost nothing about him at this stage of his life, that no likeness of him survives and that reports mostly come from English diplomats who were themselves reliant on second-hand information. Someone in his late twenties was hardly a youth and we have no way of knowing whether he was brash or not. But we know that Margaret did bestow favours on him during her second regency, which certainly caused unease among some of her supporters and led to an unfortunate cooling of relations between the queen and Patrick Sinclair, who had been her loyal servant and chief messenger in her dealings with Dacre and the duke of Norfolk. Henry Stewart was given Sinclair's role as lieutenant of the king's bodyguard and there were rumours about his relationship with Margaret which opponents of the queen were delighted to disseminate. Henry VIII, always willing to believe ill of his sister, found that he had further ammunition to use in his often wounding criticisms of her private life.

The queen's relationship with Henry Stewart deepened over the next three years, surviving political turmoil and English disapproval. Once Margaret's divorce from Angus was allowed by Pope Clement VII (himself a survivor of momentous events in Europe far greater than any faced by Queen Margaret in faraway Scotland), the couple married in the spring of 1528. During those intervening years Margaret saw power slip away from her once again. Even as she attempted to consolidate her power in the autumn of 1524, her worst fears were realized. Her husband, the earl of Angus, that arch-disruptor, was finally given permission by his brother-in-law, Henry VIII, to leave England and return to Scotland. By early November he was at one of his properties in Roxburghshire, from where he wrote a courteous and con-ciliatory letter to Margaret. It was delivered to her while she was in discussions with the two English ambassadors, Roger Radcliff and Thomas Magnus, who had been sent by Henry

VIII to negotiate the final terms of the peace with England that Margaret so earnestly desired. Apprehensive, as well they might have been, about the queen's reaction to the news that her much-detested spouse was once again on Scottish soil, they were thoroughly dismayed when Margaret contemptuously threw the epistle away unopened. When she saw the English diplomats again the next day, her position had, in fact, hardened. She would, she told them, 'make friends for herself and trusted her son would be able to protect her against Angus'. This not very subtle reference to the possibility of reopening links with France dismayed Ratcliff and Magnus. In just a few weeks, they would have further cause for alarm when Margaret demonstrated her determination to restrict Angus's power in a display of force that they found shocking.

In order to reinforce her position, Margaret and her advisers had called a parliament for mid-November. There were doubts about the legitimacy of the parliament that met in August 1524 and the queen had, meanwhile, fallen out with Chancellor Beaton and with Archbishop Gavin Dunbar, both of whom were temporarily imprisoned for failing to give unqualified support to the assumption of full power by the young James V, or, more crucially, the exercise of government on his behalf by his mother. Neither the English nor Margaret fully trusted Arran, a pragmatic politician who remained unsure, at this stage, whether Albany might not return to Scotland at some point in the near future. He had sworn allegiance to the man who was just above him in the line of succession and wondered what might happen if he appeared to abjure this. Given that many nobles in Scotland seem to have been as unpredictable as the weather in their ability to take oaths and speedily discard them, Arran's conscience on this point might raise an eyebrow. Margaret was never entirely certain of Arran's motivation either, and with just cause. For though she and the Hamiltons had worked closely to bring about their coup in the summer, and she knew how much ill-feeling there was between Arran and Angus, Arran's constancy was not his strong point. Even now, the English were suggesting to him that a reconciliation with Angus might be worth considering. Arran began to wonder whether he could swallow his reservations about his rival in return for securing a prominent role in government. None of this was known to Margaret at the time, but she might well have had her suspicions. It is instructive that she refused to let the English ambassadors see Arran alone. If Henry Stewart and her feelings for him were a distraction, she did not let this throw her off-course. The parliamentary session opened on 14 November, by which time both Beaton and Dunbar had been released. Its composition favoured Margaret and its legislation ignored Angus. His reaction to this slight and his capacity to cause dissension speedily became apparent.

Angus was never going to live peaceably on his estates in southern Scotland like some contented country gentleman. Forbidden from attending the parliament, or coming too close to the king, he took action just over a week later. On 23 November he arrived in Edinburgh, supported by three key lords, the earl of Lennox, the Master of Glencairn and Scott of Buccleuch. At his back was a force said to number about 400 men. This, despite their proclamation at the market cross in the city that they came as loyal subjects merely to serve the king, was obviously an insurrection. James V now saw his mother take direct action, rather in the manner she had done when Albany besieged her at Stirling nearly ten years earlier, though this time with no attempt at compromise. She ordered the guns of the castle to be trained on her husband

and gave the order to fire. There were a small number of casualties among local bystanders but Angus had the sense to stay well out of range and was unharmed. The timid Magnus, sending a message counselling restraint, was appalled by this unwifely gesture, but Margaret took no notice of his witterings, forbidding him to interfere or come into her presence.

Her husband retired to his seaside fortress at Tantallon, writing letters to Henry VIII and Wolsey in an attempt to exonerate his conduct, and despairing of any reconciliation with his wife. 'The queen', he lamented, 'stands extreme in my contrary, and casts all ways [that] can be devised for the destruction of me and mine; and she will no way of concord with me, and I have offered her grace all the offers that I and my friends can devise'.[11] He also, with that air of shrewd nastiness that belied his protestations of wishing to be on good terms with his wife, suggested that no more English money be sent to Margaret while she remained intransigent. This was rich coming from a man who had helped himself to Margaret's rents for many years in a sustained plundering of her finances and who had himself been kept afloat by an English pension during his years of exile in France. Margaret pointed out to her brother that she was fully justified in her misgivings about Angus. His behaviour on return to Scotland, so predictable, was merely a foretaste of the havoc he could wreak and as strong an earnest of his true intentions as could have been given. She told Henry VIII that she 'must do her best to keep herself from her unfriends; and if they get assistance against her, she must make friends of her foes'.[12] This oblique threat that she could, once again, turn to France and Albany for support was, alas, hollow. On 25 February 1525 Francis I suffered a crushing defeat at the Battle of Pavia on the plains of northern Italy. Imprisoned for a time by the Emperor Charles V, he was in no position to help her. Louise of Savoy, regent in her son's absence, promised financial support, but that would not, in itself, have done much to strengthen Margaret's position. As the New Year of 1525 dawned, the queen was still in control of her son and, at least nominally, in charge of the government of Scotland. Yet she knew, as did the entire polity of Scotland, that no way forward could be regarded as certain until the bitter enmity between herself and Angus was played out.

Margaret's loss of power was not sudden, but it was inexorable and, in retrospect, unavoidable once Angus had returned to Scotland. While both husband and wife were viewed as pro-English (which indeed they were, though with different visions of what this might mean for Scotland), the pro-French outlook which had characterized most of the Scottish lords in the previous decade was being replaced by the reluctant recognition that little had been gained by Scottish support of their traditional ally. Here was an opportunity to reshape Scottish politics, but it could not be achieved while Queen Margaret remained at war with the earl of Angus. Disliked as he was by many, and mistrusted by even more, Angus had learned a great deal about the art of political survival during his time in France. He recognized, as did his adversaries, that control of James V was the key to power. Margaret had spent her entire life since Flodden fighting to achieve this aim and wresting the power she still had from her would not be easy. Men who still held strong reservations about him played into his hands by opposing Margaret and questioning her guidance of the king. Beaton, Dunbar, Angus, Lennox, Patrick Hepburn and Argyll all now wrote to Henry VIII on 26 January 1525 requesting him to support them against the queen, his own sister. As more and more support slipped from her towards Angus, Margaret fought desperately, but by

February it was evident that she would have to give ground. She even accepted a nominal reconciliation with Angus but her opponents wanted something more concrete than what was viewed as an insincere gesture of goodwill. On paper, the terms she was offered seemed reasonable, given the weakness of her position. She would retain control of her son, but with the advice of others on a council that included Angus. She must, though, bring James V out of Edinburgh Castle. So long as the boy remained within its stout defences, Margaret was felt to have the upper hand. The queen was also reluctant to give up her patronage of religious benefices and other offices, as well as her direction of foreign affairs. Angus had also agreed not to interfere in the management of her estates, albeit only for a short time, until Whitsun. This was a small victory, but it could not compensate for the loss of overall authority. In accepting that she could no longer exercise power in her own right, Margaret had forfeited her regency. The form of conciliar government, in which she hoped to play an important part, was untested but offered some hope of a workable compromise. Such optimism was short-lived. There was no treaty with England for a lasting peace and the Borders remained as lawless as ever. Scottish finances were chaotic and the Treasury depleted. By the time of the July parliament of 1525, the achievement of real stability in Scottish government seemed as elusive as ever.

The decision was taken at this parliament to introduce the idea of a rotating council consisting of twenty-four lords, six of whom would have sole charge of the king (and, by extension, the chief role in government) for a period of three months each. Though this scheme has been characterized as 'sensible' by a recent writer on James V's minority, it is hard to agree with such a judgement.[13] Even in an ideal scenario, where each of the six lords was competent, well-intentioned and enjoyed a positive relationship with his fellow councillors, it would still, at best, have been awkward. In the cauldron of suspicion, ambition and resentment which characterized Scottish politics at the time, it was never going to work. And it is a telling indication of the continued rise of the Douglas interest that Angus was appointed as the first of the king's 'guardians'. His term in this office was meant to finish on 31 October 1525. None of the other lords challenged his appointment, though some must surely have had their reservations about it. They already knew that the earl was intent on resurrecting his claim to Margaret's dower lands now that the Whitsun deadline had passed. Realizing that all pretence that she might retain an influential role in Scotland was now being abandoned, Margaret rode out of Edinburgh and retired to Stirling. She felt safter there, even if it did mean leaving her son to this strange game of pass-the-parcel that had been agreed for his future governance.

Angus affected to be aggrieved. After all, he was merely asserting his conjugal rights, as he told the council. They were all men and husbands. Surely they would understand? So long as the pope delayed the granting of Margaret's divorce, the law was firmly on Angus's side. He had never, he said, intended to do bodily harm to his wife and she should therefore 'adhere to me as to her husband ... as she is bounden and obliged by the law of God and the holy kirk'. He wrote to Henry VIII along the same lines, saying that Margaret had shut herself up in Stirling with her son, where she was 'governed by evil counsel, against the law of God and the Church'. He assured his brother-in-law that he had 'not meddled with her lands or goods'.[14] Margaret remained unmoved by these protestations and the threat of damage to her immortal soul. Henry VIII thundered at her often enough along these lines for Angus's moralizing to sound tame in comparison. All she wanted, regardless of any infatuation with Henry Stewart, was to be free of her husband.

In her absence, the queen was deprived of the powers given to her at the beginning of the year, when it had still seemed possible that she might retain some patronage and the control of James V. Arran was now unable, or unwilling, to make any move to help her. He preferred to make accommodation with a man he disliked intensely rather than lose the possibility of proximity to the king. Beaton wanted to keep the office of chancellor and his dubious adherence to the queen was now gone completely. Margaret's most loyal supporter, the earl of Moray, remained true, but he chose, perhaps wisely, to stay away from the parliament and from Edinburgh. Now he offered succour to his stepmother on his lands in northern Scotland. Margaret was so depressed and so convinced that she must put as much distance between herself and Angus that she readily accepted Moray's hospitality. In Edinburgh, only the young James V, indignant at his mother's treatment, spoke out firmly for her. He did not agree that she should be deprived of all authority and face financial hardship once again. 'He trusted the queen his mother had not so highly offended.'[15]

For Margaret and especially her son, who had enjoyed his brief taste of freedom, much worse was to follow. Aware that he needed to tighten his grip on government, having failed to achieve any notable success that would bind the other Scottish lords to him, Angus staged a coup d'état in October 1525. When it came time to hand James V over to the next lord in the rotating council, he forced the king to accompany him to the west of Scotland, where his Lennox allies were well-nigh impregnable. He knew that having control of the person of the king was his trump card. James V returned to his capital at the beginning of November but he was, to all intents and purposes, the captive of his stepfather. A prolonged agony awaited James V, as the ascendancy of the earl of Angus solidified. The young king came to hate the entire Douglas family with a passion that exceeded that of his mother. Nor did he have much time for his half-sister, Lady Margaret Douglas, about whose legitimacy he was often scathing after the divorce of her parents. Though she seems never to have felt for her daughter the deep affection she did for her sons, Queen Margaret was to suffer further family loss during these dismal years. Some time between 1525 and 1528, probably towards the end of this three-year period, Margaret Douglas was removed from her mother's control by the earl of Angus and brought up in his household. Angus was perfectly within his rights to do this and his objection may well have been that the queen was living openly with Henry Stewart even before the news that her divorce had been granted. He did not want his daughter, now entering her teens, to continue any longer under her mother's dubious influence. How wounded Queen Margaret was by the removal of her only daughter is hard to assess. As far as we know, they never saw each other again. Margaret Douglas became close to her father and was, by 1530, living at the court of Henry VIII, her uncle, in London. For much of the rest of the sixteenth century, she would play a considerable part in Anglo–Scottish politics.

Part V

Twilight, 1528–41

21

The Queen Mother

*'For the weal of your soul and to avoid the inevitable
damnation threatened against adulterers ... reconcile
yourself with Angus as your true husband.'*

Wolsey to Queen Margaret, April 1528

Margaret was, by this time, used to being lectured
and browbeaten by her brother and his servants.
It is astonishing how Henry VIII could have had
the gall to instruct his chief minister to inveigh against her
at this time, when he had already started to look for ways to
annul his marriage with Katherine of Aragon, who had then
been his wife for nearly twenty years. But self-awareness was a
quality utterly lacking in the second Tudor king of England.
At the same time that he was advising Margaret on how she
needed to avoid the fires of hell, he was reproving Wolsey, his
chief minister, for his unwise support of a religious appointment that displeased the king and for irregularities in the
construction of a college that Wolsey wished to endow. 'As a
master and friend', he wrote, 'I must desire you to take what
I say in good part; for I do it upon no other ground than
the weal of your soul and mine'.[1] He was never that gentle
with Margaret, but the principle that others were in the

wrong and he alone in the right was second nature to Henry VIII. He did, of course, worry about his own soul, or so he said. It was a convenient excuse to discover belatedly that the marriage to Katherine, his brother's widow, was displeasing in the eyes of God. He was appalled to discover that he had lived in sin for all those years. It was greatly distressing and he would earnestly seek a way out of it. As, indeed, Margaret had herself been seeking papal approval for her divorce from Angus, though she had been unable to discover such useful scriptural justification and had, at one point, been reduced to claiming that she had married Angus while her first husband was still alive. This resort to a tradition that had crept in after Flodden, of James IV staggering from the field wounded and then wandering in Europe, speaks to Margaret's growing desperation to be rid of Angus. Neither did it address the interesting question of what might have happened to James subsequently if this romantic tale were true.

When Pope Clement VII eventually granted the divorce, it was on the firmer ground of a pre-contract with Lady Jane Stewart of Traquair. This ruling had the merit of allowing Lady Margaret Douglas, the child of the Angus marriage, to avoid the taint of bastardy, as it was argued that Queen Margaret had been unaware of her second husband's existing obligation when they married. This did not persuade the girl's half-brother, James V, to soften his opinion of what he continued to regard as the dubious circumstances of her birth. Queen Margaret's divorce had actually been granted in February 1527 but the subsequent Sack of Rome three months later and the general state of uncertainty and warfare in Europe meant that Margaret did not learn of it till 2 April 1528, over a year later. Even given the chaos on the continent it seems extraordinary that so much time passed before Queen Margaret knew that she was free of the husband she hated. As can be seen from Wolsey's correspondence, it took longer still for the news to filter into the consciousness of the English government. By spring 1528, Wolsey's attention was increasingly consumed by his sovereign's own marital troubles. Henry VIII was still five years away from ending his own marriage and when he did, it would be without papal approval. Margaret had won a victory of sorts over him and could argue that papal approval meant that her mortal soul was safe at last. Her relief was great and she marked it by marrying Henry Stewart as soon as she was assured that she was free. Her personal situation at last promised happiness. It would soon get even better. For the downfall of Angus was at hand.

Angus's power was never unquestioned and lasted barely two years, during which time Margaret, with the consistent support of the faithful Moray and changes of heart along the way from the unpredictable Arran and Beaton, attempted to rescue her son from the earl's clutches. She had left the Scottish capital when Angus's ascendancy seemed insurmountable but she never gave up on the idea of getting her son back. Margaret knew that James V loved her and she was greatly troubled by the private letters she received from the young king imploring her to rescue him from the domination of his stepfather.[2] Angus kept a close watch on James V, replacing the king's household staff, and, most notably, the affronted Sir David Lyndsay of the Mount, with his own hand-picked followers, many of whom were relatives from the extensive Douglas family. Whatever he might have wanted the world, and particularly his English backers, especially the naïve Magnus, to think, the truth was that Angus held sway.

Who with his prince was more familiar,

Nor, of his grace, had more authority?
Was he not great warden and chancellor?

But Lyndsay, through the mouthpiece of James V's pet parrot, went on, in the next two lines, to show how short-lived this supreme power was.

Yet when he stood upon the highest gre [step or tier]
Trusting nothing but perpetuity,
Was suddenly deposed from his place
Forfeit and flemit [exiled], he got none other grace.[3]

These lines were written in 1530, so are a contemporary judgement, admittedly from someone hostile to Angus, but there is an undeniable authenticity to them.

Nevertheless, James V, anxious and depressed by his lack of freedom, had no idea how long his captivity, as he felt it, would last. In hindsight, it is easy enough to see how Angus's power-base, dependent almost entirely on his own family, could not last. There were many factors against him. The continuing problems on the Borders, which his English backers came to realize soon enough were beyond the earl's capacity to handle effectively, bedevilled Anglo–Scots relations for another seventy years. Albany may not have been physically in Scotland, but he maintained an interest in the country and the possibility of his return had not entirely gone away. The duke's support of Margaret's divorce, which included not just appeals to the pope but the actual financing of the process, merely added to the enmity Angus felt for him, while leaving open the possibility that his wife could still out-manoeuvre Angus, no matter how many relatives he appointed to high office. The justice system in Scotland was unreliable and a cause of national embarrassment. The state of the country's finances was even more parlous. James V had been declared of age (yet again) by the June parliament of 1526, but while this hollow gesture apparently shifted financial and political control to his stepfather, its success was reliant on consistent support from England and stability in Scotland. Neither was likely. And, in the end, despite putting down a conspiracy to free the king headed by his erstwhile ally the earl of Lennox, who was murdered during a skirmish at Linlithgow, Angus was regarded with too much suspicion and resentment by his fellow Scottish nobles. He had failed to learn the lessons of 1514, when, so soon after his marriage to Margaret Tudor, he saw his wife deprived of the regency. Perhaps he thought his grip on power was much stronger now but he failed to take into account one crucial factor: the king was now a young man with a mind of his own. Despite Angus's attempts to distract James V with a sumptuous wardrobe, an arsenal of kingly weapons to feed the teenager's love of martial arts and the company of nubile young women, the king had suffered constraint and marginalization long enough.

Easter Sunday in 1528 fell on 15 April, just five days after James V's sixteenth birthday. The Scottish chroniclers, writing years after the momentous events of that spring, claimed that the king was at his palace at Falkland in Fife, to the east of Edinburgh. While there, it is said, he planned and executed a daring escape from the Douglas stranglehold. With both Angus and his brother, George Douglas, absent temporarily, James was under the supervision of James Douglas of Parkhead, who held the office of master of the larder. Such an appointment sounds as though it might suit someone who was more interested in his stomach than the exercise of government but these sorts of posts were attractive to Douglas kin for their prestige and remuneration. If Douglas of Parkhead was in a responsible position as regards the security of the king at Falkland then what happened that Easter, according to the chroniclers, suggests that he had, indeed, been paying too much attention to the contents of the royal larder than to keeping a firm grip on the discontented boy under his control.

James announced that he intended to go out hunting early the next morning. Like all members of the ruling class, and certainly all Tudor and Stewart monarchs, hunting was one of his major pastimes. His mother was very competent with a bow and arrow in her youth and was clearly a proficient horsewoman. James V had hunting and equestrian skills in his blood. His request, even involving an early start at seven o'clock in the morning, must not have seemed remarkable to James Douglas. As the story goes, the king plied him with wine and advised him to get an early night; the unsuspecting Douglas complied. When he eventually awoke, it was to find James gone. The king had escaped under cover of darkness, donning the clothes of a yeoman of the stable, and ridden hard for Stirling Castle with just two servants. His arrival was warmly greeted by Margaret and her new husband, who promptly raised the drawbridge to keep out anyone who might demand James's return. When Angus and his brother and kinsmen approached Stirling to try to retrieve the king, they were greeted by a herald bearing a proclamation forbidding them to come within seven miles of James V's person. This they might have ignored if they had sufficient political backing but it soon became obvious they did not. Almost all the lords of Scotland who were not directly related to them had gone over to the king and his mother. Moray, of course, was chief among them but now he was joined by a formidable array of men who had vacillated since Margaret lost her second regency. Arran was among their number, as were Argyll, Eglinton, Bothwell, Rothes and Montrose. Maxwell had been brought back into the fold, as had the Douglases' great rivals in the Borders, the ever-watchful Homes. Faced

with such overwhelming opposition, Angus and his supporters retreated to Tantallon Castle, whose impregnable position
made it all but impossible to be taken by attacking forces.
Free at last, James V named Gavin Dunbar as his chancellor
and elevated Henry Stewart, his new stepfather, to the title of
Lord Methven.

As told by the chroniclers and seventeenth-century historians of Scotland, this is a rousing tale, but it has gained a lot
in the telling. The sequence of events, in particular, is unclear
and may well have happened differently from this swashbuck-
ling narrative. Historians now believe that the outcome was
the result of a more protracted series of events as much as
any detailed planning. However, what does seem indisput-
able is that James V started to plan his escape at Easter 1528,
around the time of his sixteenth birthday. His mother's
divorce was known, her remarriage public and the possibility of any reconciliation with Angus or his Douglas affinity
completely gone. James needed his mother's support if he
was going to escape once and for all from Angus and it was
clear to him that possession of Stirling Castle would be vital
to his success. James witnessed a Great Seal Charter at Stirling
on 9 May, and though it is not certain that Angus was with
him at this time, it seems unlikely that he would have allowed
the boy to carry out one of the key functions of monarchy at
Margaret's dower castle without his presence. Margaret's own
whereabouts at the time are unclear.[4] Nor can we be certain
of precisely when she agreed to hand over control of Stirling
to her son, a price she was willing to pay to ensure that this
time he would succeed in throwing off the Douglas yoke and
which was balanced by the ennoblement of her new husband.
In an undated missive which she entrusted a messenger to
pass on to the earl of Northumberland for transmission to her
brother, Margaret wrote that her son had ridden 'privily' with

five or six horsemen from Edinburgh (not, one should note, Falkland) to Stirling, where he had consulted with a number of lords, including Arran and Argyll. She ends with the cryptic note that 'a change is expected'. The most probable dates for James V's escape from Angus's control are that it took place between 31 May and 19 June, when a proclamation was issued commanding the Douglases not to come within seven miles of the king's person and to stay away from Stirling altogether. But though the Douglases were able to raise a force with the intention of removing James from Stirling, this enterprise did not succeed. James had definitely returned to Edinburgh by 6 July, when he revealed the names of his new councillors, who were 'to remain ever with the king's grace ... for the direction of all matters that shall happen to occur concerning his grace's realm'.[5] There was, however, one significant omission from the list: Margaret was not among them.

This does not mean that James V's relationship with his mother had suffered a sudden collapse, or that she was to play no further political role. Yet a change had definitely taken place. The assumption of authority by the sixteen-year-old king was something he evidently felt passionately about. Free at last, though obviously still advised by an influential and experienced group of men, he was determined that the world should see him as his own man, a king who ruled with good counsel but was not the darling of his mother or the puppet of an ambitious stepfather. His freedom from Angus also meant distancing himself from Margaret. Though it may be an exaggeration to say that the price of the king's acceptance of Margaret's third marriage and the elevation of her husband was the diminution of her role in public life, she had to accept that her relationship with her son was changing. James

V's priority in 1528 was to be rid permanently of Angus and the Douglases while pursuing the long-awaited peace treaty with England. This was finally achieved in December 1528, a positive note at the end of a momentous year for James V and Margaret. The timid Magnus, almost a permanent fixture in Scotland now, had changed his tune during the autumn. He came round to the view that the English government's support of Angus had perhaps not been such a good idea after all and Angus was forced into exile just before the treaty was signed. He had not gone quietly, remaining in Tantallon for as long as possible and causing trouble in the Borders even after he had crossed into England, which displeased James V greatly and clearly embarrassed Magnus when he conveyed an account of Angus's misdeeds to London in February 1529.[6] The earl was still too close to Scotland for comfort and James complained vehemently about his activities. Magnus was forced to acknowledge to Henry VIII that his own journey south from Edinburgh had been perilous because of unrest and violence in the Borders. He certainly came round to the belief that his masters had backed the wrong horse, even if they were unwilling to acknowledge this truth themselves.

James wrote to his uncle about the troublesome earl, noting that he had offered him a pardon but this had been refused. He was, he said, convinced that Angus intended to cause a rupture between the two realms.[7] He assured his uncle that he would never follow such a course himself, since this would be to his own destruction. Yet he began almost at once to restore Scotland's relations with France, a move that displeased his mother and was further evidence that he was determined to direct affairs of state himself.

Margaret was relieved by Angus's ignominious departure but concerned for the fate of her daughter. Lady Margaret Douglas remained in Berwick-upon-Tweed for a year in a state of uncertainty, in the household of Sir Thomas

Strangeways, where Angus had lodged her for safe-keeping. He failed to provide much financial support for his daughter and Strangeways ran up considerable debts in keeping the girl in the manner to which she was accustomed. There are hints that Queen Margaret might have tried to get her daughter back, as the English reports at the time refer to Angus's concern for Margaret Douglas's security.[8] The girl remained in Berwick for a year until she received the long-awaited summons to travel south to the court of her uncle in London. She may, however, have stayed initially with her aunt, Mary Tudor Brandon, duchess of Suffolk, at Westhorpe, before being summoned to join the household of her cousin Princess Mary, as chief lady of the princess's privy chamber, at the end of 1530.

If letters passed occasionally between Queen Margaret and her daughter at this time, none have survived. It seems reasonable to suppose that the queen was relieved that her daughter was finally settled and out of the clutches of Angus. Margaret knew that her former husband had been welcomed by her brother and given a pension. Knowing Henry VIII as she did, this could not have come as a surprise. Her own financial situation, the managing of her estates and rents, had again been assured in the 1528 treaty between England and Scotland. As before, it sounded fine on paper but worked far less well in practice. Despite the musings of earlier writers that Margaret was 'supremely happy' for the next few years, details of their relationship at this time remain elusive. It no doubt began well enough, and Margaret made over to her third husband some of her lands. If this was an impulsive act born of deep affection at the time, the queen had ample cause to regret it. She had clearly not learned from past experience, because Methven began to help himself to her rents just as Angus had done. By the mid-1530s the marriage had foundered on

Methven's infidelity and his appropriation of her finances. Margaret was humiliated when he set up household with Lady Janet Stewart, the daughter of Lord Atholl. This blotted out the memory of the brief happiness Margaret had enjoyed with him. She was weary of marriage and began a new set of divorce proceedings. Whatever the strength of her case, this time her son stepped in to prevent any further action. He did not want to be humiliated by his mother's marital difficulties just as he was beginning the search for his own bride in France. Yet though they might have disagreed on this highly personal matter, James was always well aware that Margaret still had a part to play in Anglo–Scottish relations. He could call upon her for more than advice about building work on his palaces and other domestic issues.[9] Her role in the politics of the British Isles was no longer so intense, but it had by no means faded altogether.

So we see her, in 1531, offering to mediate anew, at a time of considerable tension between London and Edinburgh. Yet again, she received a stern rebuff from Henry VIII. While he thanked her for her 'gentle letters' he had not responded directly because she was 'the mother of our enemy' and it would be dishonourable to listen to her entreaties.[10] Margaret's resilience in the face of this kind of response, which she endured so often in matters of state as well as on a personal level, is an eloquent testimony to her perseverance and genuine commitment to follow a course that she always believed would benefit both England and Scotland. There can be no doubt that Henry's pompous belittling of her offer to mediate must have hurt badly. Not everyone was so dismissive. The earl of Northumberland, left in charge of northern England following the death of the interfering Dacre in 1525, held the Queen of Scots in higher esteem than her brother evidently did. In the spring of 1533 he was writing to Margaret, seeking her help. He knew, he said, 'the favourable mediation [she] always made between her brother and son' and he trusted that she would 'consider the humble requests and desires which will be made to him [Henry VIII] ... to be set forth by her good mediation'.[11]

These letters prove that Margaret did not suddenly burst again onto the diplomatic scene in the mid-1530s and that she still retained some influence. This improved her standing at home (where she remained anxious about her finances for much of the decade) and also allowed a more constructive relationship with Henry at a time when he had finally cast off Katherine of Aragon and married Anne Boleyn. Though dismayed by the disavowal of all papal authority over England that was the fallout from this second marriage, she was careful not to show disapproval of Henry's new queen consort. Indeed, there seems to have been a positive relationship, at least at the level of politely following protocol, between the two women. Shortly before Christmas 1534, Margaret wrote to Thomas Cromwell, saying that she had 'received our dearest brother's most loving letters' – something of a rarity in itself – 'with sundry other honourable tokens of remembrance ... and also a goodly letter with a loving token from our dearest sister the queen'.[12] Margaret had a long memory and her acceptance of Anne Boleyn may have had something to do with the resentment she felt against Katherine of Aragon over Flodden. She perhaps also had positive recollections of the services rendered to her by Anne's father, Sir Thomas Boleyn, one of the courtiers who had accompanied her to Scotland in 1503 and who had also been assigned to her service for part of her year in London in 1516–17.[13] Boleyn was an able and experienced courtier with the kind of manners that Margaret liked.

She did not share the disapproval of her sister, Mary, who fell out with Henry VIII over Anne Boleyn in the last year of her life. Margaret's attitude may, of course, have been dictated by an element of pragmatism. Despite Henry's dismissiveness of her role in Scotland, she was mindful of the fact that she might still need her brother's support. When Mary died in 1533, having been ill for a long time, probably with tuberculosis, Margaret and Henry were the only children of Henry VII and Elizabeth of York left alive. The Queen of Scots was then forty-four years old. The death of the sister she had not seen for sixteen years no doubt touched Margaret deeply, though no letters of hers on the subject survive. Neither are her thoughts on Henry VIII's Reformation known. Margaret would have kept them to herself, realizing that challenging Henry on matters of religion was not a course likely to endear her at a time when she was still hoping to play a part in Anglo–Scots diplomacy. She and her first husband had both been dutifully observant followers of the old faith and their son followed the same path. Although there was support for new religious ideas in Scotland at this time, it took much longer to gain momentum. James V himself, without issuing an outright challenge on doctrinal matters to his uncle, demonstrated his own commitment to traditional piety in more subtle ways, such as ordering a copy of a book by the anti-Lutheran French scholar Johannes Cochleus (Jean Cochlée) in 1534. We do not know how much James paid for the book, but he gave the messenger who brought it to him £50 (about £7,500 today) for his pains, a most generous reward.[14] It seems likely that Margaret would have found this new acquisition by her son, a man not noted for his interest in literature, something that she herself would like to peruse.

The following autumn, however, as Henry VIII's break with Rome and his assumption of the title of head of the church in England reverberated through Europe, there was an interesting diplomatic exchange between the courts of London and Edinburgh which involved Margaret, for the final time, as a mediator between England and Scotland.

The divorce and its fallout had placed James V in a potentially awkward situation in respect of Scotland's wider European diplomacy. He was put under pressure in the autumn of 1534 by the Emperor Charles V to state unequivocally his position as regarded Katherine of Aragon and Princess Mary, her daughter, now declared illegitimate and cast out of her rightful place in the succession to the English throne. The emperor's envoy, Gotschalk Eriksson, was 'to deplore before James the cruel wrong inflicted by Henry on the queen and their daughter'. There were also dire warnings of the consequences of Henry's alienating England from obedience to the Church of Rome and his toleration of Lutheran heretics. Not that Charles V was optimistic. He felt that nothing would move Henry (a sound judgement) but he reminded James V of the implications of what was happening in England, which 'lies in a sea of peril and anxiety' for his own situation, for what was happening 'is to preclude the rightful heir and James himself as next in succession'. While promising the utmost secrecy, the emperor wanted the King of Scots's 'frank opinion as to what James thinks feasible, and what line of remedial action he has resolved to take himself, so that Charles may communicate his own plans'.[15] In his additional instructions to his envoy, the emperor made clear what these were: 'to put the matter plainly', he wrote,

> providence offers an opportunity if James was prepared to ask for the emperor's niece Mary in marriage. No more splendid or more auspicious union seems possible for James. The old strife between England and Scotland would come to an end, and, as the princess is the true heir to the throne, the nations would be united for good.[16]

THE QUEEN MOTHER

All of this put James V in something of a quandary. He was already pursuing a marriage with Princess Madeleine of France, the daughter of Francis I, and had written warmly to that effect two months earlier. Indeed, in respect of what he might offer Madeleine in the way of income, he was already helping himself to Queen Margaret's lands, although, in fairness, these would only come Madeleine's way after Margaret's demise. Clearly, he did not want to offend Charles V, who had been instrumental in facilitating the prestigious imperial award of the Golden Fleece to the Scottish king in 1532. James also knew that his mother would heartily approve of an English marriage alliance. She had been pushing for it since both he and Mary were children. But it was not what he wanted now. Naturally Francophile in policy and taste, James was never going to oblige either Charles V or his mother by marrying his cousin, especially since she was now illegitimate. The daughter of the king of France was a far greater prize. A month passed before Charles V received an answer, sent from Linlithgow at the end of October 1534. It was very carefully worded. James was, he said, 'distressed at the misfortunes of the queen and princess'. He noted that peace between England and France had been concluded before he actually received the imperial envoy and there was nothing in it prejudicial to Charles V's interests. It had been his desire to find a wife from what he termed 'the imperial stock' but it would not, alas, be his English cousin. For, as he could not refrain from pointing out, 'attractive as the English princess is, she is not at present at the emperor's disposal, and the enterprise would mean serious commotion. The vital matter of the Scottish succession forbids the inevitable delay.' Naturally, there was no mention of any French princess, though Charles V must have known that James was inclining in that direction. Instead the Scottish king, in a manner worthy of both his uncle and father, decided to obfuscate matters by claiming

311

that his real desire was 'the emperor's niece of Denmark'. Such a solid family union (James V was a quarter Danish) would benefit both the Stewarts and the Habsburgs. On a personal level, such an outcome was not James V's preference, though he was never going to tell the emperor that. The Danish princess might, however, be a reasonable choice if the French marriage did not proceed.

Charles V was not the only monarch keen to get James V on his side in the autumn of 1534. At the same time that the imperial envoy was in Scotland, Henry VIII sent Lord William Howard, the duke of Norfolk's half-brother, north to pursue the idea of a meeting with his nephew. The facilitator of such a conference, which was to include the king of France as well, was to be Queen Margaret. Lord William's letters of credence informed James V that his uncle was 'greatly desirous, and nothing more covetous, than to see his person and especially to have conference and communication with him'.[17] The proposal was for James and Henry to meet in England and travel on to Calais to meet Francis I. It would, in other words, be an even more important event than the Field of Cloth of Gold, now a glorious memory of some fourteen summers ago.

There were, however, certain curious aspects to this approach from the English king – and, indeed, to the manner of James V's response. Henry never wrote directly to his nephew, preferring to set the matter before his sister in the first place, and James, evidently because he considered his mother still useful to him in matters of Anglo–Scottish diplomacy, chose to have Margaret respond on his behalf. It had been Margaret who, in James V's absence in northern Scotland, received Lord William Howard. His instructions from Henry told him to wait upon the queen and to thank her heartily for the goodwill she had always shown towards England and her long-standing efforts to preserve peace between England and Scotland. Margaret was delighted to

receive personal letters and gifts from her brother and from
Anne Boleyn. She naturally warmed to the proposal of a
meeting, assuring her brother 'that there could be no more
pleasant sight in this earth, of wordly thing, as we to see our
most dearest brother and our most dearest son, in proper
personages together, and of one loving mind: which now, we
doubt not, will hastily be, with God's grace'.[18] Her enthusiasm, characteristically overstated, is touching. Sadly, this final
flourish ended, as had many of her earlier interventions,
without the success she so craved. Her distress was deepened
by the realization that her constant encouragement of the
meeting, over the next eighteen months, had caused a rift
with James V. It was the most serious and long-lasting of any
difference of opinion between Margaret and her son. Lord
William Howard wrote to Henry:

> the queen's grace your sister hath taken as much pains to
> bring to pass the meeting betwixt your highness and the
> king's grace, your nephew, as ever any woman did in any
> matter; and her grace hath been so plain with him in it,
> that he is very angry with her. Your highness hath cause to
> give her great thanks.[19]

Henry did not demonstrate any tangible gratitude at this
time. He rebuffed Margaret's plea to be allowed to come to
England. Relations might be strained with her son, but only
James V could properly make such a request. Alas, worse was
to follow. Margaret had, with boundless enthusiasm rather
than sober judgement, spent a great deal more than was wise
on preparations for her participation in this much-vaunted
meeting. Depredations on her estates in earlier Border raids
deprived her of a vital source of income when she was compelled to remit rents for three years, adding to her severe
financial embarrassment at a time when her marriage to the

slippery-fingered Methven was damaged beyond repair. She wrote several times pleading for help from Henry VIII, even suggesting that the violence in the Borders that had cost her so dear was England's fault, and, as such, she was justified in seeking redress from her brother.

This was a provocation too far for Henry VIII, coming at a difficult time in the year 1536, soon after the execution of Anne Boleyn and with unrest against his religious reforms festering in the north of England. Not normally a man given to writing long letters, he left his sister in no doubt of his disapproval. He reminded Margaret that James IV had 'right nobly endowed you with rents and possessions to live in your honour and estate'. Her pleas caused him to 'much marvel that ye should be so far behind the hand, as that ye should make such allegations for an appearance of the same, as though the cause thereof had sprung from us and our realm'. He would not, he said, 'disburse upon so light a ground, any such notable sum of money'.[20] Rebuffed on all fronts, Margaret was forced to accept that there would be no meeting between her son and brother in the immediate future. Nor was this the only cause of her distress, or of Henry VIII's disfavour. Her daughter, Margaret Douglas, for six years one of the great ladies of the English court, was now incarcerated in disgrace in the Tower of London.

Lady Margaret Douglas was then an attractive and vivacious young woman of twenty-one. As Henry VIII's niece she was very close to the English throne. By the summer of 1536 Henry found himself in the curious – some would say highly unenviable – position of being the parent of two daughters, both of whom he had declared illegitimate. His only son, Henry FitzRoy, the duke of Richmond, was born to the king's mistress, Elizabeth Blount, in 1519 and if Henry ever entertained the idea of naming him as his successor, such a possibility was snuffed out by Richmond's death in July 1536. This left Margaret Douglas as the only heir without the taint of illegitimacy. She had been born in England, unlike her half-brother, James V, whose possibility of succession was sometimes acknowledged by Henry VIII, though eventually the fact that he had been born in Scotland was used as a reason to bar him.[21] This may well have been a cause of irritation to James V and might perhaps explain some of the ill-will he seems to have demonstrated towards Margaret Douglas. But, as events unfolded in the summer of 1536, it became apparent that the young lady was equally capable of bringing her uncle's wrath down on her, with far more serious implications for her future than her brother's lofty censoriousness.

Margaret Douglas inherited characteristics from both her parents. Her mother's determination and passionate nature were evident throughout her long life and she also possessed a fair measure of her father's charm and instinct for survival. The courts of both England and Scotland, with all their danger, intrigue and ambition, were in her blood. Brought up in the Catholic faith, she would remain true to it despite all the upheavals of her uncle's reign, never wavering throughout the tumultuous years that followed. She was close to her cousin Mary, yet would become a thorn in the side of her other cousin, Elizabeth. She knew how to be both a courtier and a confidante and seems to have been popular with the other ladies who served Henry's queens. In Margaret, her father's scheming seemed like artless guile when she smoothly transferred her loyalty from Katherine of Aragon and Mary to Anne Boleyn. She formed a literary circle with two other ladies of Anne Boleyn's chamber, Mary Shelton and Mary Howard, and wrote poems which were collected in a bound edition some time during the 1530s or 1540s.[22]

Perhaps if she had kept her versifying to collaboration with these other women who served Anne Boleyn she might have avoided the near-disaster that overtook her in 1536. Alas for Margaret Douglas, she had fallen deeply in love, exchanging more than poems with the gentleman who consumed her thoughts. In fact, without her uncle's knowledge, she had entered into a pre-contract – an official betrothal, in other words – undertaken in the presence of witnesses, with Lord Thomas Howard.

Lord Thomas, the son of the old earl of Surrey's second marriage, to Agnes Tilney, who would later acquire notoriety herself in the Catherine Howard affair, was half-brother to the duke of Norfolk and therefore half-uncle to Anne Boleyn. The complexities of this extended family can seem confusing but the Howards were one of the most important of all sixteenth-century noble families, their influence far more long-lasting than that of the Boleyns. Margaret Tudor herself did not have fond memories of them after the way she was treated by Surrey (who went on to become the second duke of Norfolk) on her journey to marry James IV. She was also well aware of the role of both Surrey and his son (now the third duke) in the Battle of Flodden. So concern for her daughter's fate no doubt mingled with unhappy memories from long ago when she learned, to her great discomfiture, that Margaret Douglas had so rashly plighted herself to a Howard. Queen Margaret's disapproval was, however, as nothing in comparison to the fury of her brother when Henry VIII learned of his niece's behaviour.

The king was said to be 'much incensed in conceiving that one so joined in blood to him and his nephew, the Scottish king, should not be given or taken without his consent, especially when she lived so near him'.[23] Infuriated as Henry was with Margaret Douglas herself, it then entered his mind that the young lady's mother must be implicated in the affair. He suspected that the other Howard half-brother, Lord William, his diplomatic emissary to Scotland in the matter of the projected meeting between Henry VIII and James V, had concocted this mesalliance with Queen Margaret during his visits to Edinburgh. He saw this as a plot to put Margaret Douglas and her paramour on the throne of England, with Queen Margaret's blessing. Given the unprecedented confusion over the English succession in the summer of 1536, it is not hard to understand his paranoia. He also felt deeply insulted on a personal level by such reckless deception from a young woman to whom he had shown affection and indulgence. Having been betrayed, as he claimed, by Anne Boleyn, he now believed that those near to her were still plotting against him. And the sister who was long such a thorn in his side, importuning him for money constantly, bombarding him with querulous epistles, might even be the driving force behind this latest disaster. The king struck back by impugning Margaret Douglas's birth, describing her in the indictment against Thomas Howard as 'the natural daughter to the Queen of Scots'. His indignation against his sister had reached its height. Yet Margaret, as aghast as her brother when she found out, and naturally fearful for her daughter, knew nothing at all about what had been going on in London.

Thomas Howard, himself a poet of some ability and three years or so older than Margaret Douglas, was committed to the Tower of London on 8 July 1536. Margaret was also taken there, probably on the same day. Two weeks later, following a hasty change of the law (at the time of their pre-contract it was not actually illegal to enter into such an undertaking with the niece of a king), Thomas Howard was condemned to death for 'contemptuously and traitorously contracting himself, by crafty, fair and flattering words to and with the lady Margaret Douglas'. The new Act on royal marriages also spelled out, in frightening clarity, that no one close to the king could marry without his written permission. The implications for Margaret herself when it stated that 'any woman so offending shall incur like danger and penalty' could not have been graver.

By the end of the month, Henry VIII had relented. Neither Howard nor Margaret was executed. Perhaps the king had always intended to frighten and then show mercy, as he was to do with his last wife, Katherine Parr, in 1546. Queen Margaret, however, was not immediately aware of this, probably because she was then at Perth and not in Edinburgh, which was the centre of affairs in Scotland. When she learned of the disgrace of her daughter and the peril Margaret Douglas now stood in, she wrote in desperation to Henry VIII. The tone was intended to pull on Henry's heart-strings, for she clearly believed that this was still a tactic that might work with him. Her phraseology sounds wheedling to modern ears, but there can be no doubt that she was scared for her daughter's life. Had her brother not recently executed Anne Boleyn and several of those who had served him faithfully, as well as meting out the full, ghastly punishments of the time on religious opponents? While appealing to their closeness in blood, Margaret had good reason herself to know just what this meant to Henry VIII, whose unpredictability was increasing as he grew older. There was no point in holding back with the hyperbole now, so she appealed to him in her most fulsome language, begging him to send her daughter back to Scotland, to be under her own care. 'Dearest Brother', she began,

> we are informed lately that our daughter, Margaret Douglas, should, by your grace's advice [information] promise to marry Lord Thomas Howard, and that your grace is displeased that she should promise or desire such thing and that your grace is delivered [decided] to punish

my daughter, and your near cousin, to extreme vigour; which we no way can believe, considering she is our natural daughter, your nepotes [near relation] and natural sister unto the king our dearest son and your nephew; we will not believe that your grace will do such extremity upon your own, ours, and his, being so tender to us all as our natural daughter is. Dearest brother, we beseech your grace, of sisterly kindness, to have compassion and pity of us your sister and of our natural daughter and sister to the king our only son and your dearest nephew and to grant our said daughter Margaret your grace's pardon, grace and favour and remit of such as your grace has put to her charge. And if it please your grace ...

she went on, after this rambling exhortation:

to be content she come into Scotland, so that in time coming she shall never come into your grace's presence. And this, dearest brother, we in our most heartily affectionate, tender manner most specially and most humbly beseech your grace to do, as we doubt not your wisdom will think to your honour, since this our request is dear and tender to us, the gentlewoman's natural mother, and we your natural sister, that makes this pitious and humble request ... we, in our most hearty, affectionate, tender manner, most specially and most humbly beseech your grace to do.[24]

This letter was written on 12 August, by which time, unknown to the queen, any likelihood of the young lovers suffering the death penalty had evaporated. Henry VIII was never going to agree to his sister's request that Margaret Douglas be sent back to Scotland. One querulous Margaret north of the border was quite enough for him. He wanted his niece where it was easiest to keep an eye on her, something which he now realized he and those around him had failed to do with sufficient diligence. Margaret Douglas's marriage was still a great prize and there was no way he would relinquish control of such a headstrong young lady to her mother. Margaret Douglas was kept in the Tower of London for more than a year. As a woman of noble blood she was not thrown into a dungeon, but had a small apartment with servants and a chaplain to attend on her. Her liberty came in the autumn of 1537 and its price was, indirectly, the life of Jane Seymour. The third wife of Henry VIII gave birth to the long-awaited heir in October but died of complications ten days later. The child, the future Edward VI, seemed likely to survive. This meant that Margaret Douglas was no longer Henry's heir-presumptive and she gained her freedom as a result, greatly to her mother's relief. Yet Queen Jane's was not the only death that October. One touched Margaret Douglas even more closely. In the Tower, both she and her lover, Lord Thomas Howard, were very ill, perhaps with typhoid. The king paid for medicines worth thousands of pounds in today's money for both prisoners and sent his own doctors to administer them. Margaret Douglas rallied and eventually recovered, though her recuperation, often mistakenly characterized as some sort of house arrest at Sion Abbey on the banks of the Thames, was slow. Howard was not so fortunate. On the last day of October 1537, he died. Margaret Douglas had assured Thomas Cromwell a year earlier that she was no longer in love with Thomas Howard, but she took the news of his death very badly. Later she remembered that 'his death with my tears I did often lament'.[25] She would go on to find happiness with another man, but not for another seven years. And she would remain close to the English throne, with all the reverberations of favour and suspicion that went with this proximity, for the rest of her life.

Relieved that her daughter had survived this scandal, Queen Margaret could now concentrate on the continuing desperate state of her finances and her relationship with her son. The question of his marriage was becoming more urgent. In 1536, the year he set off for France in search of a bride, James V was twenty-four. It was high time that he married. He had by then enjoyed liaisons with at least nine ladies of the court and his tally of illegitimate children, or, at least, ones that he acknowledged, may well have been greater than that of his father, James IV. Dynastic instincts told him that he should marry a European princess but there was something of the romantic in the man his subjects called 'the Red Fox' because of his colouring – and perhaps, also, because of a trait of deviousness that had helped him survive a difficult childhood. In the mid-1530s his favourite mistress, Margaret Erskine, harboured the belief that the king might marry her. She was the mother of James Stewart, later earl of Moray, a man destined to play a significant part in Scottish history. But the lady was deluded. Most of the nobility and Queen Margaret herself opposed this match. It would be unseemly and bring no advantage to the Scottish crown. The queen counselled her son against it strongly. Margaret Erskine, despite the considerable drawback of already having a husband, felt spurned when James V eventually heeded the advice of almost everyone around him. She never forgave James V personally or the Stewarts collectively for the slight and was a far-from-sympathetic guardian to her erstwhile lover's daughter, Mary, Queen of Scots, during the captive queen's imprisonment on Lochleven. Once he made the decision to abandon her, the King of Scots was eager to conclude the French marriage that he had toyed with for so long. In 1536, while her daughter still languished in the Tower, Queen

Margaret was writing to her brother that her son had already set off by sea on his quest for a bride. She still hoped James V might meet her brother; indeed, there were indications that he would stop off in England to discuss his marriage with his uncle and take his advice.

Margaret was, alas, deceived. James V had no intention of following such a course. In fact, his itinerary made sure that he came nowhere near England. So determined was he to avoid Henry VIII that he set off north around the Scottish coast and down the Irish Sea. Fierce storms forced his little fleet to put in at Whithorn in Galloway, thus bringing the first attempt to an end. The king was not daunted; he returned briefly to Edinburgh and started again. This time he sailed down the English coast without incident and landed at Dieppe in Normandy in September 1537. It would be nine months before he returned as the son-in-law of Francis I of France, bringing his bride, Princess Madeleine, the first French queen consort of Scotland since Yolande de Dreux in the mid-thirteenth century, with him. In his absence, a regency council ruled Scotland. Margaret was not a part of it. Her situation was growing, at least in her own eyes, ever more precarious. Sir Ralph Sadler was sent up to Scotland by Henry VIII to find out more, if he could, and report his own judgement on the queen's financial and political difficulties. Sir Ralph confirmed that Margaret was being deprived of income from her lands by her third husband. He found her sad and impoverished, resentful of what she perceived as abandonment by her third husband, her son and her brother. Henry VIII was sufficiently moved by Sadler's detailed report of Margaret's privations that he sent him off to France to make personal representations of the parlous state to which she was reduced to James V. At Rouen and preparing to depart with his bride, who was already far from well, James at last took steps to remedy his mother's plight. He affected to be astonished and dismayed by what he heard, though one wonders if he had merely grown tired over the years of his mother's constant complaints, no matter whether they were justified or not. Henry VIII had made it clear in congratulating his nephew on the French marriage that he must pay attention to his sister, now dowager queen, who desperately needed his support. James wrote stern letters to the Scottish council and affectionate ones to his mother. It seemed, at last, that Margaret would have some redress. Yet she was still writing to Henry VIII asking for money to buy a new wardrobe to greet Madeleine. This time, Henry agreed, and Margaret was able to receive her daughter-in-law resplendent in a cloth-of-gold gown.

The money could have been better spent, though Margaret was not to know. Madeleine had for some time been suffering from tuberculosis. It was several months after her marriage to James V that she was well enough to travel and then the voyage was protracted and difficult. The new Queen of Scots lived for just seven weeks in her new country before her illness consumed her. It brought James V and his country great international prestige but at the cost of an already sick girl's life. He still had no legitimate heir and would need, speedily, to look again for a wife. His mother never got to know Madeleine. Nor did James V's return bring security or happiness to Margaret. At forty-eight she still considered herself an unhappy, neglected woman.

22

Methven Castle

*'Though I be forgot in England, shall I never forget England.
It had been but a small matter ... to have spent a little
paper and ink upon me.'*

Queen Margaret to the English diplomat
Ralph Sadler, 1540

In these bitter words, Margaret Tudor summed up the resentment and rivalry between herself and her brother, Henry VIII, which had characterized their relationship since he was eleven and she thirteen years old. He had used her occasionally, when he believed she could be of help, grudgingly and without ever really acknowledging her place in the politics of the British Isles. The Queen of Scots was not impressed by Sadler's opening gambit, that Henry had given him 'special charge to visit and see her and also to know how she was used and how all things went there'.[1] Margaret had, though, never given up on him, despite his careless, sometimes insulting, treatment and infuriating support for her hated second husband, the earl of Angus. If she had hoped, during the period between the death of Queen Jane Seymour in 1537 and his fourth marriage, to Anne of Cleves in 1540, that Henry might mellow towards her, by the time of her conversation with Ralph Sadler she was thoroughly disabused. And perhaps a part of her recognized that, however hurtful her brother's neglect was, the quest for a suitable spouse could be all-consuming for a king. Certainly, her own son had not wasted any time looking for a new bride after the death of the delicate Queen Madeleine.

James viewed his wife's demise as a setback rather than a tragedy. Their relationship was once viewed as a romantic love-match, the final scene of which was played out with the young queen dying in her husband's arms. This makes great historical fiction but has no basis in fact. There was, of course, official mourning and Sir David Lyndsay of the Mount wrote a poem of twenty-nine verses lamenting Madeleine's untimely death.

> Oh death! Though thou the body may devour
> Of every man, yet have thee no puissance
> Of their virtue for to destroy the glory:
> As shall be seen of Magdalene of France,
> Somewhile our queen, whom poets shall praise
> And put her in perpetual memory:
> So shall her fame of thee have victory.[2]

Perpetual memory has not, alas, given Madeleine the victory. Her very brief time as Queen of Scots is almost forgotten now.

James's immediate reaction was one of spiteful cruelty rather than personal sorrow, at least as regards the terrible fate of another woman. Convinced that he must demonstrate to Francis I that he was firmly in control in Scotland before he approached the French king to find a replacement for Madeleine, he executed one of the leading Scottish nobles, Sir James Hamilton of Finnart, the bastard son of the first earl of Arran, whose loyalty he had long doubted. Yet this was not enough for a man whose memory stretched back to the bitter restrictions imposed on him by the Douglas family. His resentment led to the most vicious act of his life in the death sentence by burning which he imposed on Janet Douglas, Lady Glamis, the sister of Angus. Lady Glamis, who had stayed in Scotland while her brothers went into exile, was a convenient target for all of James V's simmering hatred. She was accused of treason on the trumped-up charge of attempting to poison the king. James refused to commute her sentence and she went to the stake on Castle Hill in Edinburgh on 17 July 1537. James's ruthlessness reminds us that he was half a Tudor, a fact that is often overlooked. Margaret's thoughts on her erstwhile sister-in-law's fate are unknown.

Yet despite the chagrin that Margaret could not refrain from demonstrating to Sadler, there was, in these closing years of her life, recompense. She was often at court and acknowledged that 'she was well treated and made much of'. She also spoke highly, Sadler reported, 'of the new queen' and, he added dismissively, 'with such other things of light importance'.[3] Her comforts and treatment at court were not of light importance to Margaret and neither, indeed, was the new queen, Mary of Guise.

The eldest daughter of a family whose power and influence with the French crown was growing, Mary was the widowed wife of the duke of Longueville, with whom she had two sons. Despite the unpopularity of her family with the French princes of the blood – that extended family of cousins and more distant relatives that provided an almost unending prospect of heirs for the French monarchy – it was undeniable that the Guises were on the rise. No one questioned their ambition but many were doubtful of their loyalty to France. Their estates in eastern France had once been part of the Holy Roman Empire and it suited their enemies to portray them as Germanic upstarts, more Habsburg than French.

The Guise were thick-skinned and determined to succeed. Disapprobation only made them stronger.

Mary's marriage to Longueville seems to have been happy. She lived mostly at her husband's castle in the town of Châteaudun, north-west of Orléans, on the River Loir.[4] But in the early summer of 1537 the duke was taken ill while visiting his estates in western France and died unexpectedly. His wife gave birth to a posthumous son two months later, but the child died before Christmas. It was while she was recovering from this double loss that Mary learned that her marriage to James V had been negotiated without her knowledge and that Francis I would brook no opposition. As a female member of the aristocracy, Mary knew that her future lay in the hands of others. It was, though, still a shock. While struggling to find the dowry that James V demanded, Francis I had also to fend off the interest of none other than Henry VIII himself, who had heard good reports of Mary of Guise's appearance and wit. The duchess had cause subsequently to be thankful that the king of France, not wanting to raise a Guise to be queen consort of England, rebuffed Henry's enquiries into her availability.

Eventually, after the protracted financial arrangements were concluded, Mary set sail for Scotland with her sister Louise and father, Claude, having taken a tearful farewell of her surviving son, Francis, the new duke of Longueville. She feared she might never see him again but had the satisfaction of knowing that he would be brought up by her own mother on the Guises estates on the banks of the River Marne. It had been a happy childhood and she hoped his would be the same. Mary set sail from Le Havre and landed at Crail, on the coast of Fife, six days later, on 16 June 1538. There, at Balcomie Castle, James V and the leading noblemen of Scotland waited to greet her. The welcome was warm: 'The whole lords, both spiritual and temporal, many barons, lairds and gentlemen ... received the Queen's grace with great honours and merriness, with great triumph and blitheness.'[5] These sentiments may not have been entirely shared by Mary herself, but she was gracious enough to conceal any misgivings. After her marriage to James at the cathedral of St Andrews, Mary went on the traditional tour of her Scottish lands, as her mother-in-law, the dowager Queen Margaret, had done thirty-five years earlier.

The marriage between James V and his second wife was not one of great passion. She was handsome rather than beautiful but dignified and with presence. Though not raised to be a queen, she knew how to act like one. Like Margaret with James IV, Mary would soon have discovered, if she had not already been apprised of the fact before leaving France, that her husband had a sizeable family of children by various women. The king may not have given up his womanizing after their marriage, though there is no evidence that he had further illegitimate children. Like Margaret, Mary was required to tolerate his dalliances and turn a blind eye. In fact, the two women had more in common than either might have supposed on first meeting. They both loved Linlithgow Palace and understood the need to be visible to the Scottish people. They were conscious of the importance of appearance, of the impression of majesty that was created by a splendid wardrobe and jewels. Both found that marriage cast them adrift in a foreign land and if this might have been harder initially for the thirteen-year-old Margaret than the twenty-three-year-old Mary, Margaret had not left behind a young child and the memory of a husband she had loved. In fact, the two women got on well and Margaret was grateful for her daughter-in-law's company and support. She was happy to play the role of queen mother. And in the spring of 1541 Margaret was able, in some part, to repay Mary when tragedy struck the Scottish royal couple.

Mary of Guise had given James V two sons, Prince James and Prince Robert, one born at St Andrews, the other at Stirling. The queen had recovered well from both births and the security of two male heirs was something that Henry VIII, whose fourth and fifth marriages were to prove so disastrous, could not match. Yet if Queen Margaret, godmother to the elder son, took pleasure in this realization she knew better than to crow over it to her brother. Then, in May 1541, there came to London tragic news from Scotland. Both boys had died within days of each other and James and Mary were beside themselves with grief. Prince James had been not quite a year old and the details of his luxurious garments and the furnishings of his bedchamber are hauntingly reminiscent of those supplied to Margaret's long-dead first son, another Prince James, who had succumbed at very nearly the same age. The children were buried together at the Abbey of Holyroodhouse, leaving their parents reeling. 'The death of both the King of Scots' sons ... doth much perplex the said king and divers other nobles and councillors there', wrote an English visitor to the Scottish court.[6] Even allowing for a change of emphasis over the centuries, this was something of an understatement.

Margaret wrote to her brother with the sad news, explaining how she was trying to support her son and daughter-in-law in their distress. There had been, she said, 'great displeasure for the death of the Prince and his brother' and she was constantly with the king and queen to give them comfort. The letter is also interesting for the light it throws on her continued correspondence with Henry VIII. It indicates that Henry had been writing to her after her outburst to Ralph Sadler and that she was still not entirely happy about her situation. Whether this was in respect of her finances, her marital problems with Henry Stewart or her desire to see England again is not clear, but she did ask Henry not to raise anything with her son without first discussing matters with her. She was afraid a direct approach might do more harm than good.[7]

The consolation she was able to offer was Margaret's last service to the son she had tried so hard to protect throughout his life. By the autumn of 1541 she was no longer at court, having returned to Methven Castle near Perth. Her third husband may have been its lord but they had not lived together for many years. And it was here, in the peaceful countryside of central Scotland, that Margaret Tudor fell ill, in mid-October, a month short of her fifty-second birthday. There is no indication that there were concerns about her health until she suffered a stroke. At first, her illness, described as 'a palsy', did not seem too serious and so she did not send immediately for James V. But her condition deteriorated rapidly and the king, who was at Falkland Palace in Fife, could not get to his mother in time.

On her deathbed, Margaret, perhaps confused by the effects of her illness, asked her confessor to convey to her son a plea that he show mercy to the earl of Angus and that Margaret Douglas, her daughter, might have her goods. The queen noted poignantly of young Margaret that 'she never had nothing of her before'. James ignored both these requests, though he took care to lock up what possessions his mother had in the castle. Among the items that had long since left Queen Margaret's possession was the beautiful Book of Hours that James IV had commissioned for their wedding. It would appear that in the year after Flodden, Margaret gave this to her sister, Mary, perhaps on the occasion of her own marriage to Louis XII of France. It appears still to have been in England in 1538, by which time all references to the pope had been erased from it. How it subsequently found its way into the hands of the Holy Roman Emperor Leopold in the mid-seventeenth century is not known. A keen bibliophile, Leopold noted in the flyleaf that it had once belonged to

James IV and his consort, Margaret. From his private library it passed into the Imperial Library in Vienna and can still be seen there.

This and so much of the sumptuous lifestyle Margaret had known as James IV's consort was now long gone. The Berwick Herald, Henry Ray, sent by Henry VIII to discover whether this sister had left a written will (she had not), noted somewhat disparagingly at the end of his report that Queen Margaret had left as 'ready money' only 2,500 Scottish marks, about £337,000 today. He clearly did not consider this a princely sum.[8]

It used to be thought that Margaret's funeral was an under-stated affair, but though there is no surviving evidence of how the queen's funeral was paid for, it is clear that James V and Mary of Guise, scarcely recovered from the deaths of their sons, did observe all the proprieties of royal mourning. James may have appointed his companion and servant, John Tennent, to be in charge of the funeral arrangements. Tennent had been in the king's service since at least 1529 and had accompanied James V to France in 1536. As well as being a close confidant, Tennent would have been well placed, as pursemaster and master of the wardrobe, to organize a fitting funeral for Margaret. Both of his roles gave him access to the initial sums of money that would have been needed for the funeral trappings, the coffin and hangings. Suppliers of such goods could well have provided them on the promise of eventual payment. The Stewarts, like the Tudors, seldom settled outstanding bills quickly. It may also be that James was able to recover his mother's 'unready money', her past and due rents, from her feudal tenants more quickly than the cash-strapped Margaret had ever done. James now had more motive to do so than he had exhibited in the queen's lifetime and while Margaret's tenants and husbands had been brazen in their disregard for what was rightfully owed to her, ignoring the demands of a king would have been a different matter.

The exact date of Margaret's funeral is not known, but it must have been in early November 1541 because invitations to the queen's 'tyrement' were sent on 1 November and to local lairds in the Perth area on 5 November. The ladies of the royal household came from Falkland, dressed in black cloaks made by Thomas Hannay, who had trained with the king's tailor, Thomas Arthur. Mourning certainly continued in Holyrood into December, when the chapel there was draped with black cloth for what may have been a second, more formal type of state funeral.[9] The king and queen continued to wear black mourning clothing until at least Christmas. Mary of Guise and her ladies were also provided with black harnesses and riding equipment, which suggests that they may have taken part in Margaret's funeral procession. Pieced together, the surviving evidence, even if indirect, strongly indicates that the rituals surrounding the queen's death were properly observed and that James V did, indeed, honour his mother appropriately as a Queen of Scots and the daughter of a king in her death. Given Margaret's lifelong concern with the importance of display and ceremony it was surely what she would have wished.

The English court does not appear to have observed any mourning for Margaret's death. Berwick Herald's letter, though undated, indicates that he was sent into Scotland by Henry VIII before the end of October. A period of a week to ten days would have been ample time for the news to reach Henry VIII, then returning from his progress to the north of England with Queen Catherine Howard, his fifth wife. Henry's temper, already affected by ill health, had not been improved by waiting around in York for a meeting with James V that never took place. Anglo–Scottish relations, enflamed by continued border raiding and religious tensions, were worsening rapidly, and shortly after Henry got back to London he was completely thrown by the revelation, made by a nervous Archbishop Cranmer, that his young wife had a very murky past and had been unfaithful to him. Deeply disturbed, Henry was far too preoccupied to give any consideration to a proper commemoration of his sister's death. They had been rivals in life. Her death prompted a mercenary interest in her financial affairs, but nothing more. Henry had, as historian Gareth Russell noted, ordered eleven days of mourning for Queen Isabella of Spain, a woman he never met, when she died in 1538. 'For the sister he had exploited and ignored, who had been the daughter, niece and granddaughter of kings of England, the English court cannot have expressed anything but the most perfunctory mourning.'[10]

Margaret Tudor was buried in St John's Abbey in Perth, to lie among other Scottish monarchs. Her rest did not last long. The abbey was desecrated by Calvinists only twenty years after her death and Margaret's skeleton removed from her coffin and burned. Her ashes were contemptuously scattered around as if they were so much sawdust. So, like her first husband, James IV, Margaret has no resting place and no monument. A pathetic, disturbing end for the young Tudor princess who had arrived in Scotland in such magnificence. But time would give her memory a greater prize.

Epilogue

Linlithgow Palace, 8 December 1542

Winter came early to Scotland that year. Mary of Guise had retired to Linlithgow in the final weeks of her third pregnancy as Queen of Scots. Inside were warmth and comfort, crackling fires and the company of her ladies. Outside, the snow began to fall and did not stop. The rider bearing the news that Mary had given birth to a daughter on 8 December took six days to plough through the drifts before he reached Berwick-upon-Tweed. The arrival of a princess, named for her mother, would have been, in any case, greeted with polite enthusiasm but not the unrestrained joy that would have followed the announcement of a male heir. Perhaps it was too much to hope for that the queen could manage to produce another boy, after the heart-breaking deaths of the two princes the previous year. Yet much worse was soon to follow. For the king himself, the handsome, philandering but capable James V, was dying at Falkland Palace.

He had suffered a humiliating defeat by his uncle's English forces at the Battle of Solway Moss, fought on 24 November 1542 amid the swirling waters and bogs of the River Esk. This was not a disaster on the scale of Flodden, or so it did not seem at the time. Despite the fact that a considerable number of Scottish lords were taken prisoner, while common soldiers died in the river while trying to escape, the king, who watched the debacle from a nearby hillside, had survived. He returned to his capital to deal with matters of government and also went to Linlithgow to visit his wife. It was fortunate for Mary of Guise and her unborn child that he did not pass on the disease that was to end his life a mere six days after his daughter's birth. Romantic accounts of his demise used to claim that he died after a nervous collapse, lamenting with his final breath that he had no son to succeed him. 'It cam wi' a lass and it'll gang wi' a lass' were the words attributed to him, recalling the ill-fated Maid of Norway in the early fourteenth century. The Scottish chroniclers had a flair for this sort of epithet but the truth was much more prosaic. James had almost certainly picked up cholera or dysentery, diseases so common among armies at that time. They flourished in the cramped, wet conditions of a campaign that started very late in the year. James's ever-loyal half-brother, the earl of Moray, was also seriously ill, but did not succumb.

Early on the morning of 14 December James, aware that the end was approaching fast, signed a notarial instrument that decreed the arrangements for government during his daughter's minority.[1] He appointed Cardinal David Beaton, the earls of Huntly, Argyll and Moray, as well as his wife, to act as governors for Mary. The king died later the same day, having survived his mother, Queen Margaret, by just fourteen months.

It was more than a little ironic that the news of James's death was conveyed to Lord Lisle in Northumberland by Sir George Douglas, who had apparently been informed by one of James V's servants. With typical Douglas concern for his own family as opposed to the fate of his country, Sir George made it clear that he and his brother, the earl of Angus, hoped that this unexpected piece of good fortune would facilitate their return to Scotland. It is not clear when the news reached London, but minutes of the Privy Council from 26 December refer to Henry VIII being 'much occupied' with the affairs of Scotland on hearing about his nephew's fate.[2]

That preoccupation was to dog Anglo–Scottish affairs for the rest of Henry VIII's lifetime and into the reign of his son, Edward VI. The 'Rough Wooings' were a period of destructive warfare in the Borders and up the east coast, with hectoring threats from the English that they would destroy Edinburgh and all Scots men, women and children who opposed them. The difficulty of occupying Scotland and the bravery and determination of the minority government of Mary, Queen of Scots thwarted the ambitions of the English. In 1548 the five-year-old queen was sent to France for her own safety and because, once more, most of the Scottish nobility believed that her eventual marriage to the French dauphin was a more propitious outcome than a marriage with her English cousin.

That the little queen's future now seemed safe was in no small part down to her resourceful mother. If Mary of Guise had learned anything from the experience of Margaret Tudor in the early years of the sixteenth century, it was that she should not remarry and must remain in physical control of her child in these crucial early years. She did not demand to be regent or to assume the reins of power in Scotland. Instead, she stayed resolutely put, charmingly batting away the suggestions for remarriage, and then remaining to safe-guard Mary's interests in Scotland, even though parting from her was hard.

The other actors in this story had mixed fortunes. Henry VIII died in January 1547 after a long illness, leaving his throne to the nine-year-old Edward VI. He had never devised a winning formula when it came to his relations with Scotland, always regarding his northern neighbour with a mixture of arrogance, disdain and incomprehension. His three children would not do noticeably better. The fraught relationship between Elizabeth I and her distant cousin, Mary, Queen of Scots, ended in Mary's beheading in 1587 for plotting the English queen's death.

Archibald Douglas, earl of Angus, lived on till 1557. He married again but left no male heirs. He cut his daughter, Margaret Douglas, out of her inheritance and entailed his lands and title on his nephew. Quite why he had chosen to ignore Margaret and her family remains unclear, especially as there are contemporary accounts that he retained an interest in them, asking messengers from England for news of his grandson, Lord Darnley. In his later years, Angus discovered a Scottish patriotism notably lacking from his early life and fought with distinction against the English during the Rough Wooings. He disliked Mary of Guise – indeed, it is hard to escape the impression that he had little time for women – and resolutely refused to dress appropriately when visiting court. There is still no biography of Angus, yet he was a crucial figure in sixteenth-century Scotland.

Henry Stewart, Lord Methven, Queen Margaret's third husband, was also active in Scottish politics after his wife's death. He was a member of the Scottish Privy Council during the minority of Mary, Queen of Scots and also served as a diplomat and soldier during the late 1540s. By 1545 he had married his long-term mistress, Lady Janet Stewart, daughter of the earl of Atholl. She was twice widowed and their marriage seems to have been based on genuine affection. The couple produced four children, all later legitimized, before their wedding. Methven died between 1553 and 1554. The exact date of his death is not recorded.

Margaret Douglas, the only child of Margaret Tudor and the earl of Angus, had a most eventful life. In 1544, her tragic relationship with Thomas Howard now firmly in the past, she married Matthew Stewart, earl of Lennox, who had himself a claim to the Scottish throne but had chosen to throw in his lot with Henry VIII. Margaret, who was then one of Queen Katherine Parr's ladies, was given a splendid wedding, the greatest social event of the year. Yet by the end of her uncle's life, Margaret Douglas had quarrelled with Henry VIII, apparently over religion, and the rift was not healed. He removed her from the line of succession, despite the fact that she had the strongest legitimate claim of any of his heirs.

The Lennoxes' elder son, Henry Stewart, Lord Darnley, was the second husband of Mary, Queen of Scots. Pampered by his parents, Darnley was a vicious and unstable young man whose marriage to the Scottish queen was a disaster. His murder in the explosion at Kirk o' Field in 1567 remains a mystery – he was, in fact, asphyxiated while trying to escape the burning house – but it effectively finished Mary's rule in Scotland. Darnley's distraught parents harboured suspicions about Mary's involvement in their son's violent end, though these were eventually allayed and better relations between Mary and Margaret restored.

The earl and countess of Lennox had originally set up house in the Catholic heartland of northern England, but were sporadically at the court of Elizabeth I. They both appreciated the value of being visible and, if possible, staying on good terms with the new monarch. But the relationship between the English queen and her first cousin ranged from being cool to icy and Margaret was even imprisoned in the Tower of London for a time. She had long been a figure-head for Catholics in England and regarded herself as having a better claim to the English throne than Elizabeth, whose legitimacy she never accepted. In 1571 Margaret suffered another body-blow when Lennox, briefly regent in Scotland, was assassinated. Theirs had been a close and loving marriage, producing eight children. But by 1576 her younger son, Charles, the only survivor, was very ill with tuberculosis and his death the same year seems to have crushed his mother. She died in 1578, at the age of sixty-three, her dreams still unrealized. As a child she left her homeland for the promise of security at Henry VIII's court but was always conscious of her Scottish roots as well as her proximity to the English throne. Her dramatic life mirrors perfectly the turbulent century in which she lived.

Margaret Douglas had, as she grew older, placed all the hopes for the future of her family on her grandson, James VI of Scotland.[3] The wait was long. Elizabeth I lived for another twenty-five years, refusing to name a successor. Yet as the sun set on her reign, no one seriously doubted that James would be the next English monarch. On 8 May 1603, after a triumphant and leisurely progress south from Edinburgh, James entered London to the acclaim of the capital's citizens, uniting in his person the crowns of England and Scotland. The English had not known a king for half a century and were eager and curious in equal measure to see their new monarch, the first of that name to sit on the English throne. It was a moment of great splendour and celebration.

Perhaps there were others, unseen, who shared in the rejoicing that early spring day. If we indulge ourselves, just for a moment, we can imagine the shades of James IV and Margaret Tudor, regally attired, processing hand in hand through the streets of London, one hundred years after their wedding, its distant promise having been, at last, fulfilled. For, in the sibling rivalry that had poisoned Henry VIII's relationship with his elder sister, it was Margaret who triumphed in the end.

Notes

Prologue

[1] Emma Cavell (ed.), *The Heralds' Memoir, 1486–1490: Court Ceremony, Royal Progress and Rebellion* (Donington, 2009), p. 129.
[2] Ibid., p. 130.
[3] Ibid., pp. 130–31.

Chapter 1

[1] The Order of the Bath had been awarded as part of the appointment to knighthood since medieval times. It was an ancient chivalric ceremony. The order in its current form dates from 1725 and the reign of George I.
[2] Alison Weir, *Elizabeth of York: The First Tudor Queen* (London, 2014), p. 281.
[3] It was said that James III of Scotland had, at least in part, lost the respect of his subjects because of his poor horsemanship.
[4] Quoted in David R. Carlson, 'Royal Tutors in the Reign of Henry VII', *Sixteenth Century Journal*, XXII, No. 2, 1991, p. 265.
[5] Margaret Tudor's letters have been analyzed by Dr Helen Newsome in her groundbreaking dissertation, '"Sche that schuld be medyatryce (mediatrice) in thyr (these) matars": Performances of Mediation in the Letters of Margaret Tudor, Queen of Scots (1489–1541)', unpublished Ph.D. dissertation, University of Sheffield, 2018.
[6] See Michelle L. Beer, *Queenship at the Renaissance Courts of Britain: Catherine of Aragon and Margaret Tudor, 1503–1533* (Woodbridge, 2018) and J. L. Laynesmith, *The Last Medieval Queens* (London, 2004).

[7] The queens of King John and Edward II (both called Isabella) were twelve years old at the time of their marriages, as was Margaret of Denmark, wife of James III of Scotland.

[8] See Nicola Tallis, *Uncrowned Queen: The Fateful Life of Margaret Beaufort, Tudor Matriarch* (London, 2020), pp. 67–8.

[9] Julia Boffey (ed.), *Henry VII's London in the Great Chronicle* (Kalamazoo, 2019), p. 84.

Chapter 2

[1] Gordon Kipling (ed.), *The Receyt of the Ladie Kateryne* (Oxford, 1990), pp. 9–10.

[2] Ibid., p. 32.

[3] The tomb was destroyed in the Great Fire of London in 1666.

[4] Quoted in Alison Weir, *Elizabeth of York: The First Tudor Queen* (London, 2014), p. 358.

Chapter 3

[1] Archbishop Blackadder set out on a pilgrimage to Jerusalem in 1508 but, like many others who made this journey, it proved fatal. He took ship from Venice to Jaffa but died at sea with most of the other pilgrims on board, probably of cholera or dysentery, which could wreak havoc in the confined conditions of a ship.

[2] Quoted in Norman Macdougall, *James IV* (Edinburgh, 1989), p. 250.

[3] Ayala to Ferdinand and Isabella, 25 July 1498, *Cal.SP Spanish*, I, No. 210, (London, 1862–1954).

[4] John Leland, *Antiquarii de Rebus Britannicis Collectanea*, ed. Thomas Hearne, Volume 4 (London, 1774), p. 262.

[5] *The Great Chronicle of London*, p. 108.

[6] See Michelle L. Beer's revealing monograph, *Queenship at the Renaissance Courts of Britain: Catherine of Aragon and Margaret Tudor, 1503–1533* (Woodbridge, 2018). Biographies by Arlene N. Okerlund, *Elizabeth of York* (Basingstoke, 2009) and Alison Weir, *Elizabeth of York: The First Tudor Queen* (London, 2014) give a rounded picture of this hitherto underestimated figure.

[7] The necessity of circumspection on behalf of a queen's ladies when discussing highly personal matters is exemplified in the

careful probing of Anne of Cleves's ladies-in-waiting as to the precise physical details of her relationship with Henry VIII.

Chapter 4

1 Sean Cunningham, *Prince Arthur: The Tudor King Who Never Was* (Stroud, 2017), p. 171.
2 Quoted in ibid., p. 168.
3 Gordon Kipling (ed.), *The Receyt of the Ladie Kateryne* (Oxford, 1990), p. 80.
4 Ibid., p. 81.
5 Ibid., p. 81.
6 For details of Elizabeth of York's 1502 summer progress and further speculation about its origins, see Alison Weir, *Elizabeth of York: The First Tudor Queen* (London, 2014), pp. 390–95.
7 Ibid., p. 402.
8 Linda Porter, *Crown of Thistles: The Fatal Inheritance of Mary Queen of Scots* (London, 2013), p. 138.
9 See Michelle L. Beer, *Queenship at the Renaissance Courts of Britain: Catherine of Aragon and Margaret Tudor, 1503–1533* (Woodbridge, 2018), pp. 41–43.

Chapter 5

1 Nicola Tallis, *Uncrowned Queen: The Fateful Life of Margaret Beaufort, Tudor Matriarch* (London, 2020), p. 233.
2 Sarah Carpenter, '"TO THE XALTACYON OF NOBLESSE", A Herald's Account of the Marriage of Margaret Tudor to James IV', *Medieval English Theatre*, 29, 2007, pp. 104–20.
3 John Leland, *Antiquarii de Rebus Britannicis Collectanea*, ed. Thomas Hearne, Volume 4 (1774), p. 280.
4 See ODNB entry for 'Thomas Howard, second duke of Norfolk' by David M. Head.
5 Somerset Herald's detailed description is in Leland, *Collectanea*, pp. 271–72.
6 Ibid., p. 273.
7 Ibid., p. 276.
8 Ibid., p. 279.

Chapter 6

1 John Leland, *Collectanea*, ed. Thomas Hearne, Volume 4 (1774), p. 282.

2 Today it is the county town of East Lothian and well worth a visit.

3 Ada was herself the mother of two Scottish kings, Malcolm IV and William the Lion. She was a daughter of the earl of Warenne and Surrey, a prominent supporter of the Norman dynasty in England.

4 Princess Margaret, the second daughter of James II of Scotland, resided with the nuns at St Mary's between 1464 and 1477. The notion that the nuns were actively involved in educating girls has been questioned. Perhaps it has been overstated but it seems unlikely that a Scottish king would have consigned his daughter to a nunnery without at least the expectation that she would be given some form of education while she was there.

5 Leland, *Collectanea*, p. 282.

6 Ibid., p. 283.

7 Ibid., p. 283.

8 It has been suggested that this may be a different St George, though the original had no connection with England, having been born in what is now Turkey and certainly never setting foot in England. The Holy Roman Empire also had an Order of St George in Carinthia.

9 Confusingly, James IV's younger brother was also called James, though his title was different. It was not uncommon for siblings to have the same name, but it has been suggested that perhaps James IV was unwell at the time of his brother's birth and having a second son called James was a kind of insurance. The youngest boy, the earl of Mar, was called John.

10 The senior Scottish cleric, Archbishop Scheves of St Andrews, a staunch supporter of James III, was not present, an indication of the divisions in the higher echelons of the church and government, which did not suddenly disappear with James IV's accession.

11 When Anne Boleyn caught the sweating sickness in 1528 and had to retire to her family home at Hever in Kent, Henry VIII demonstrated his devotion by staying well away and sending her his second-best physician. That Anne recovered perhaps

says more for the state of her general health than Henry VIII's devotion.

12 P. Hume Brown (ed.), *Early Travellers in Scotland* (Edinburgh, 1891), pp. 50–54.

13 Ibid., pp. 39–41.

Chapter 7

1 John Leland, *Collectanea*, ed. Thomas Hearne, Volume 4 (1774), p. 284.

2 Ibid., p. 286.

3 Ibid., p. 288.

4 Bishop Gavin Douglas, quoted in J. G. Dunbar, *Scottish Royal Palaces* (East Linton, 1999), p. 56.

5 Ibid., p. 57.

6 Austrian National Library, Vienna, Cod. 1897, Gebetbuch Jakobs IV von Schottland.

7 British Library, BL Ms Facs 581/85.

8 This raises an interesting point about the timing of the production and presentation of the Book of Hours to James and Margaret. If the artist had actually seen Margaret in person the commission is unlikely to have been finished until after the wedding itself. However, it is possible that he had obtained an existing portrait or miniature of her beforehand and worked from that.

9 Leslie Macfarlane, 'The Book of Hours of James IV and Margaret Tudor', *Innes Review*, 11–12, 1960, pp. 3–19.

10 R. L. Mackie, *King James IV of Scotland* (Edinburgh, 1958), p. 110, quoted in Linda Porter, *Crown of Thistles: The Fatal Inheritance of Mary Queen of Scots* (London, 2013), p. 147.

11 Henry's most fully described wedding is his last, to Katherine Parr, in July 1543; the reports mention the guests and the vows that the couple took but say nothing at all about what either Henry or Katherine wore.

12 Leland, *Collectanea*, p. 291.

13 Ibid., p. 294.

14 Ibid., p. 293.

15 Ibid., p. 297.

16 British Library, BL MS Cotton Vespasian FXIII, fol. 61b.

Chapter 8

[1] J. G. Dunbar, *Scottish Royal Palaces* (East Linton, 1999), p. 47.

[2] See Chapter 9, p. 123.

[3] The same seems to have been true in the case of Henry VIII's third wife, Jane Seymour. I am grateful to Dr Nicola Tallis for pointing this out.

[4] Amy Hayes, 'The Late Medieval Scottish Queens, c.1371–c.1513', unpublished Ph.D. dissertation, University of Aberdeen, 2016, pp. 181–82.

[5] Norman Macdougall, *James IV* (Edinburgh, 1989), p. 155.

[6] Quoted in Linda Porter, *Crown of Thistles: The Fatal Inheritance of Mary Queen of Scots* (London, 2013), pp. 154–55.

[7] National Library of Scotland, Seaton Armorial, Acc 9309, f. 18.

[8] The Register of the Privy Seal of Scotland, I, 1471, quoted in Michelle L. Beer, *Queenship at the Renaissance Courts of Britain: Catherine of Aragon and Margaret Tudor, 1503–1533* (Woodbridge, 2018), p. 104.

[9] For more on Elizabeth Barlow and her marriage, see Beer, *Queenship at the Renaissance Courts*, pp. 118–20.

[10] National Records of Scotland, MSS E21/6 f.343, quoted in Beer, *Queenship at the Renaissance Courts*, p. 108 fn. 60.

[11] The probability that Margaret took part in the *pedilavium* is supported by the purchase of four ells of Holland cloth for the queen and her almoner, which would likely have been made into towels for the Maundy foot-washing in 1504. See Beer, *Queenship at the Renaissance Courts*, p. 138.

Chapter 9

[1] T. Dickson and J. Paul (eds.), *Accounts of the Lord High Treasurer of Scotland (Treasurer's Accounts)*, 7 Volumes, (Edinburgh, 1877–1905) Volume 2, p. 238.

[2] Ibid., p. 239.

[3] Margaret Drummond's fate has been the subject of much dramatic speculation, fuelled by the stories surrounding her death in the writings of William Drummond of Hawthornden, a member of the same family. These claim that she was the one true love of James IV and that she and two of her sisters were deliberately

poisoned in 1502 to get her out of the way before the king's marriage to Margaret Tudor. In reality, the affair between Margaret Drummond and James IV seems to have been comparatively short-lived and there is no firm evidence of foul play in her death.

[4] The castle of Darnaway was traditionally the seat of the earls of Moray but the husband of Elizabeth, countess of Moray (the title could pass in the female line) was killed fighting against James II of Scotland in the mid-fifteenth century and the lands passed to the crown. They were eventually given to Mary, Queen of Scots's illegitimate half-brother, James Stewart, and are still held by the earls of Moray.

[5] This earl of Moray, not to be confused with James Stewart, half-brother to Mary, Queen of Scots (though they shared the same name), died childless. Maria Perry, in *Sisters to the King* (London, 1999), p. 45, asserts that James IV legitimized him, but does not give a source. But papers of legitimization might give title to property and inheritance but most certainly did not mean that he had a right to inherit the throne. The Scottish crown, like the English, had no tradition of admitting bastards to the line of succession. It would also have rendered James's marriage to Margaret pointless.

[6] See Helen Newsome, 'Reconsidering the Provenance of the Henry VII and Margaret Tudor Book of Hours', *Notes and Queries*, LXIV, 2017, pp. 233–34. The possibility that Margaret named her younger son, Alexander, duke of Ross, for Alexander Stewart seems less convincing. Alexander was a name frequently chosen by Scottish royalty and especially, in the later medieval period, for second sons.

[7] See Patricia Buchanan, *Margaret Tudor, Queen of Scots* (Edinburgh, 1985), p. 51, where reference is given to payments to a lady known only as 'L of A' in the *Accounts of the Lord High Treasurer of Scotland (Treasurer's Accounts)* (Volume 3) of 1505. I cannot find a page number for this reference.

[8] See *Treasurer's Accounts*, Volume 3, pp. 266–68.

[9] R. K. Hannay, *The Letters of James IV, 1505–1513* (Edinburgh, 1953), pp. 57–8.

[10] Ibid., p. 61.

[11] Ibid., p. 79.

[12] St Ninian is credited with being the first Christian missionary to Scotland and is believed to have been active in Galloway in

the late fourth century, well before St Columba, a better-known
saint, came to the Hebridean island of Iona. He was said to have
been associated with a number of miracles and was particularly
powerful in healing the sick.

[13] Quoted in Buchanan, *Margaret Tudor*, p. 56.

Chapter 10

[1] J. S. Brewer (ed.), *Letters and Papers, Foreign and Domestic, of the
Reign of Henry VIII*, Volume 1 (London, 1862), nos. 670 and 698.

[2] Norman Macdougall, *An Antidote to the English* (East Linton,
2001), p. 3. It is also worth pointing out that General de Gaulle
called the 'Auld Alliance' the oldest alliance in the world.

[3] Quoted in Louise Fradenburg, *City, Marriage, Tournament*
(Madison, WI, 1991), p. 178.

[4] The *Margaret* was later joined by an even larger ship, the *Michael.*

[5] For more on the Scottish navy under James IV, see Norman
Macdougall, *James IV* (Edinburgh, 1989), ch. 9.

[6] While James IV is often cast as a dreamer in this context, it is
worth pointing out that later popes in the 1520s and 1530s,
alarmed at the threat the Turks posed to Austria, did also call for
crusades. James IV may have been more far-sighted than is often
thought. I am grateful to Steven Veerapen for this insight.

[7] Brewer, *Letters and Papers*, Volume 1, no. 2077.

[8] Marguerite Wood (ed.), *Flodden Papers, Diplomatic Correspondence
between the Courts of France and Scotland, 1507–1517* (Edinburgh,
1933).

[9] R. L. Mackie (ed.), *The Letters of James IV* (Edinburgh, 1953)
p. 111.

[10] Jenny Wormald, 'Thorns in the Flesh: English Kings and
Uncooperative Scottish Rulers, 1460–1549', in G. W. Bernard
and S. J. Gunn (eds.), *Authority and Consent in Tudor England*
(London, 2002), p. 70.

[11] John Guy, *Tudor England* (London, 1988), p. 81.

[12] British Library, BL MS Cotton Caligula BVI, f. 74.

[13] Quotations from Mackie, *The Letters of James IV*, appendix II,
pp. 322–24. The original is in the British Library, BL MS Cotton
Caligula BVI, f. 69.

Chapter 11

[1] J. S. Brewer (ed.), *Letters and Papers, Foreign and Domestic, of the Reign of Henry VIII*, Volume 1 (London, 1862), no. 2157.
[2] Over the centuries, estimates of the size of James IV's army have varied wildly. There is no contemporary Scottish account of the Battle of Flodden and the Scottish Treasurer's Accounts for 1513–15 are missing. The English may well have overstated the numbers of the Scots for political reasons. Recent books about Flodden take the view that the Scottish army was around 40,000 men when it crossed into England. Some may have subsequently deserted.
[3] Sir Walter Scott, *Marmion: A Tale of Flodden Field* (London, 1868), pp. 70–71. A colourful account of Lady Heron and James IV's supposed dalliance with her is given by Robert Lindsay of Pitscottie in *The History of Scotland; from 1436 to 1565* (Edinburgh, 1749), pp. 205–207. Pitscottie, who was born at least twenty years after the Battle of Flodden, is an entertaining but highly unreliable source.
[4] Edward Hall, *The Union of the Two Noble and Illustrious Families of Lancaster and York, Hall's Chronicle* (1809) p. 555. Quoted in George Goodwin, *Fatal Rivalry: Flodden 1513* (London, 2013), p. 149.
[5] Hall quoted in Goodwin, *Fatal Rivalry*, p. 150.
[6] Brewer (ed.), *Letters and Papers*, Volume 1 (1862) no. 2026, p. 916.
[7] James believed that Bainbridge had encouraged Pope Julius II to excommunicate him for his support of Louis XII of France. The excommunication deeply hurt James, who always viewed himself as a godly monarch.
[8] Hall, *Chronicle*, pp. 559–60, quoted in Goodwin, *Fatal Rivalry*, p. 177.
[9] Henry Ellis, *Original Letters, Illustrative of English History*, Volume 1 (London, 1846), pp. 86–87.
[10] Joseph Haslewood (ed.), 'The Trewe Encountre or Batayle Lately Don Betwene Englande and Scotlande', *Proceedings of the Society of Antiquaries Scotland*, 7, March 1867, p. 146.
[11] Several books on Flodden state that there was a fifth 'battle', a reserve led by Patrick Hepburn, earl of Bothwell, to James IV's right, which later moved behind him, unintentionally adding to

his difficulties. George Goodwin says that while Hepburn was at Flodden, there was no reserve; see *Fatal Rivalry*, p. 197. Goodwin does not give any further amplification of this assertion.

[12] For a fuller description of the Battle of Flodden, see my earlier book, *Crown of Thistles: The Fatal Inheritance of Mary Queen of Scots* (London, 2013), pp. 175–87 and also Goodwin's *Fatal Rivalry*, pp. 174–214.

[13] British Library, BL Harley MS 2252.

Chapter 12

[1] R. K. Hannay (ed.), *Acts of the Lords of Council in Public Affairs, 1501–1544* (Edinburgh, 1932), p. 1.

[2] I am grateful to Professor Julian Goodare for pointing out to me that, while colourful troublemakers have grabbed popular attention, many of the Scottish nobles were committed to the crown.

[3] Hannay, *Acts of the Lords of Council*, p. 5.

[4] Amy Blakeway, *The Regency in Sixteenth-Century Scotland* (London, 2016), p. 69.

[5] Ibid., p. 25.

[6] J. S. Brewer (cd.), *Letters and Papers, Foreign and Domestic, of the Reign of Henry VIII*, Volume 1 (London, 1920), no. 2268.

[7] Marguerite Wood (ed.), *Flodden Papers, Diplomatic Correspondence between the Courts of France and Scotland, 1507–1517* (Edinburgh, 1933), pp. 87–88.

Chapter 13

[1] J. S. Brewer (ed.), *Letters and Papers, Foreign and Domestic, of the Reign of Henry VIII*, Volume 1 (London, 1862), no. 2793.

[2] It has been suggested that this letter was to be read out at a meeting of the Scottish parliament in Edinburgh but there is no record of any parliament meeting in 1514. This could have been a special meeting, or convention, of key members of the Scottish nobility, but it was not an actual session of a full parliament. See Maria Perry, *Sisters to the King* (London, 1999), p. 75.

[3] Paniter was abbot of Cambuskenneth, the monastery outside Stirling where James III and his wife, Margaret of Denmark, the

parents of James IV, were buried. In the proposed reassignment of church offices, he was supposed to move to Holyrood.

4 Brewer, *Letters and Papers*, Volume 1, part 2, no. 2355. So 'nearly', in fact, when it came to religion, that he hoped to abolish the primacy of St Andrews altogether and bring it under the authority of Durham. This flagrant attempt on Scottish sovereignty through its religious institutions was never endorsed by the papacy.

5 Brewer, *Letters and Papers*, part 2, no. 2973.

6 Quoted in Ken Emond, *The Minority of James V: Scotland in Europe, 1513–1528* (Edinburgh, 2019), p. 19.

7 R. K. Hannay (ed.), *Acts of the Lords of Council in Public Affairs, 1501–1544* (Edinburgh, 1932), p. 18.

8 John Lesley, *The History of Scotland, From the Death of King James I in the Year 1436, To the Year 1561* (Edinburgh, 1830), p. 99.

9 The Black Douglas lands were divided between the Scottish crown and various lords, including, of course, the Red Douglases, who greatly increased their power base in southern Scotland.

10 James Hamilton, earl of Arran was unmarried at the time. The son of Princess Mary Stewart, a daughter of James II of Scotland, he was next in line to the Scottish throne after Albany. This would have made him a strong candidate for marriage with Margaret, but there were doubts about the validity of his divorce from his first wife, Elizabeth Home, and he would have been a very divisive choice himself. He was also about fifteen years older than Margaret.

11 Quoted, without precise source, in Patricia Buchanan, *Margaret Tudor, Queen of Scots* (Edinburgh, 1985), p. 86.

12 Perry, *Sisters to the King*, p. 76.

Chapter 14

1 R. K. Hannay (ed.), *Acts of the Lords of Council in Public Affairs, 1501–1544* (Edinburgh, 1932), p. 22.

2 Margaret was not actually as cash-strapped as she claimed, having been given 18,000 French crowns by James IV just before he departed for Flodden. This was an advance payment from Louis XII for Scottish involvement in the war against England. See Ken Emond, *The Minority of James V: Scotland in Europe, 1513–1528* (Edinburgh, 2019), p. 29.

3 M. A. E. Green (ed.), *Letters of Royal and Illustrious Ladies of Great Britain, from the Commencement of the Twelfth Century to the Close of the Reign of Queen Mary*, Volume 1 (London, 1846), pp. 166–9, quoted in Linda Porter, *Crown of Thistles: The Fatal Inheritance of Mary Queen of Scots* (London, 2013), p. 204.

4 Raphael Holinshed, *Holinshed's Chronicles of England, Scotland and Ireland*, Volume 3 (London, 1808), p. 610, quoted in Erin Sadlack, *The French Queen's Letters: Mary Tudor Brandon and the Politics of Marriage in Sixteenth-Century Europe* (London, 2011), p. 93.

5 Lord Dacre refers to this letter, sent via the papal legate in Scotland, in his report to the Lords of the Council of 14 July 1515. J. S. Brewer (ed.), *Letters and Papers, Foreign and Domestic, of the Reign of Henry VIII*, Volume 2 (London, 1864), no. 705.

Chapter 15

1 Alexandre Teulet (ed.), *Relations Politique de la France et de l'Espagne avec l'Écosse au XVIe siècle*, Volume 1 (Paris, 1862), p. 5, quoted in Ken Emond, *The Minority of James V: Scotland in Europe, 1513–1528* (Edinburgh, 2019), p. 34.

2 She was, confusingly, also called Anne de la Tour and shared her name with Albany's mother.

Chapter 16

1 TNA, SP 49.1, fol. 50, quoted in Helen Newsome, '"Sche that schuld be medyatryce (mediatrice) in thyr (these) matars": Performances of Mediation in the Letters of Margaret Tudor, Queen of Scots (1489–1541)', unpublished Ph.D. dissertation, University of Sheffield, 2018, p. 52.

2 British Library, BL MS Cotton Caligula BVI, fol. 80, quoted in Newsome, ibid.

3 British Library, BL MS Cotton Caligula BVI, fol. 125.

4 Marie Stuart, *The Scot Who Was A Frenchman* (London, 1940), pp. 42–43.

5 R. K. Hannay (ed.), *Acts of the Lords of Council in Public Affairs 1501–1544* (Edinburgh, 1932), 28 September 1515, p. 57.

6 Ibid., p. 58.

[7] J. S. Brewer (ed.), *Letters and Papers, Foreign and Domestic, of the Reign of Henry VIII*, Volume 2 (London, 1864), no. 1350.

[8] The assertion that Margaret was thrilled to see Angus again and that he was 'as fond and proud as any new father' of his daughter is surely fanciful. We have no idea what passed between them at this time and Angus's subsequent treatment of his daughter never showed much affection. See Patricia Buchanan, *Margaret Tudor, Queen of Scots* (Edinburgh, 1985), p. 124.

[9] Ibid.

[10] Ibid.

Chapter 17

[1] R. Brown (ed.), *Calendar of State Papers Relating to English Affairs in the Archives of Venice (CSP Venetian)*, Volume 2, no. 671 (London, 1867).

[2] J. S. Brewer (ed.), *Letters and Papers, Foreign and Domestic, of the Reign of Henry VIII*, Volume 2 (London, 1864), no. 1598; also in M. A. E. Green, *Lives of the Princesses of England, From the Norman Conquest*, Volume 4 (London, 1852), p. 234.

[3] British Library, BL MS Cotton Caligula II, f.211; also in Brewer, *Letters and Papers*, Volume 2, no. 1672.

[4] Ken Emond, *The Minority of James V: Scotland in Europe, 1513–1528* (Edinburgh, 2019), p. 63. See also Dacre to Henry VIII in Brewer, *Letters and Papers*, Volume 2, no. 1759.

[5] There is no truth in Agnes Strickland's claim that Margaret had typhus at the beginning of the year and that Angus deserted her as soon as 17 January 1516. See Strickland, *Lives of the Queens of Scotland and English Princesses Connected with the Regal Succession of Great Britain* (London, 1851), p. 119.

[6] Michael G. Kelley, 'The Douglas Earls of Angus', unpublished Ph.D. thesis, University of Edinburgh, 1973, p. 279.

[7] Brewer (ed.), *Letters and Papers*, Volume 2, no. 1829.

[8] The poem is printed in Julia Boffey (ed.), *Henry VII's London in the Great Chronicle* (Kalamazoo, 2019), pp. 106–07.

[9] Patricia Buchanan, *Margaret Tudor, Queen of Scots* (Edinburgh, 1985), pp. 139–40.

[10] For further details, see W. R. Streiberger, 'Henry VIII's Entertainment for the Queen of Scots, 1516: A New Revels

Account and Cornish's Play', *Medieval and Renaissance Drama in England*, 1, 1984, pp. 29–35.

[11] Ibid., p. 33.

[12] R. K. Hannay (ed.), *Acts of the Lords of Council in Public Affairs, 1501–1544* (Edinburgh, 1932), pp. 68–69.

[13] Margaret had, with her sister, Mary, and Queen Katherine, interceded for the wrongdoers, some of whom were only in their early teens. This was one of the last examples of this rite of medieval queenship and the only time Margaret took a direct role in English public affairs.

Chapter 18

[1] His one major foray into the north of England took place nearly twenty-five years later, during the progress to York with his fifth wife, Catherine Howard, in 1541. Ironically, this was supposed to be the occasion of a meeting with Margaret's son, James V, but James, nervous of his uncle's intentions and fearing a trap, pulled out at the last minute.

[2] J. S. Brewer (ed.), *Letters and Papers, Foreign and Domestic, of the Reign of Henry VIII*, Volume 2 (London, 1864), no. 3294.

[3] Ibid., no. 3278.

[4] Patricia Buchanan, *Margaret Tudor, Queen of Scots* (Edinburgh, 1985), p. 153. Buchanan's biography is full of these flights of romantic fantasy, which seem inappropriate in what purports to be a serious work of biography, published by an academic press.

[5] D. Hay (ed.), *The Letters of James V* (Edinburgh, 1954), p. 40.

[6] R. K. Hannay (ed.), *Acts of the Lords of Council in Public Affairs, 1501–1544* (Edinburgh, 1932), p. 91.

[7] The ballad 'Death of de la Beaute' is reprinted in full on the website of the Duns History Society, www.dunsehistorysociety.co.uk.

[8] Quoted in Ken Emond, *The Minority of James V: Scotland in Europe, 1513–1528* (Edinburgh, 2019), p. 91.

[9] Michael G. Kelley, 'The Douglas Earls of Angus', unpublished Ph.D. thesis, University of Edinburgh, 1973, p. 299. The claim that Angus took Lady Jane Stewart of Traquair as his mistress is still made in the earl's entry in the ODNB. Angus did have an

illegitimate daughter, Joan Douglas, but her mother has never been accurately identified.

[10] Hannay, *Acts of the Lords of Council*, 23 February 1518, p. 134.

[11] Printed in M. A. E. Green, *Lives of the Princesses of England, From the Norman Conquest*, Volume 4 (London, 1852), pp. 268–69.

[12] Brewer, *Letters and Papers*, Volume 3, no. 859.

Chapter 19

[1] British Library, BL MS Cotton Caligula BI, f. 166, quoted in M. A. E. Green, *Lives of the Princesses of England, From the Norman Conquest*, Volume 4 (London, 1852), p. 310. Also calendared in J. S. Brewer (ed.), *Letters and Papers, Foreign and Domestic, of the Reign of Henry VIII*, Volume 2 (London, 1864), no. 2038.

[2] Margaret was far from being their only victim. Mary, Queen of Scots and Anne of Denmark are also castigated. The Stricklands' use of sources is also suspect but the sisters are still widely used and quoted.

[3] For a fuller explanation of Margaret's aims and the methods she used, see Helen Newsome, '"Sche that schuld be medyatryce (mediatrice) in thyr (these) matars": Performances of Mediation in the Letters of Margaret Tudor, Queen of Scots (1489–1541)', unpublished Ph.D. dissertation, University of Sheffield, 2018, ch. 3. The quotations are from pp. 96–98.

[4] It is probable rather than certain that Henry VIII ignored Margaret's 9 December 1521 letter. No answer survives and while this could have been lost, Margaret does not refer to it in subsequent correspondence and her swift move towards another form of communication strongly suggests that she knew she had been snubbed.

[5] Quoted in Newsome, '"Sche that schuld be medyatryce"', p. 105.

[6] Ibid., p. 115.

[7] Alexandre Teulet (ed.), *Relations Politique de la France et de l'Espagne avec l'Écosse au XVIe siècle*, Volume 1 (Paris, 1862), pp. 26–31.

[8] Brewer (ed.), *Letters and Papers*, Volume 3, no. 2725.

[9] Quoted in Newsome, '"Sche that would be medyatryce"', p. 118.

[10] Eleanor had a strong place in her father's affections and later joined him in France, where she married the comte de Choisy in 1547, eleven years after Albany's death.

NOTES

Chapter 20

[1] See Michael G. Kelley, 'The Douglas Earls of Angus', unpublished Ph.D. thesis, University of Edinburgh, 1973, p. 315.

[2] J. S. Brewer (ed.), *Letters and Papers, Foreign and Domestic, of the Reign of Henry VIII*, Volume 4 (London, 1875), no. 315. A fuller version is in M. A. E. Green, *Lives of the Princesses of England, From the Norman Conquest*, Volume 4 (London, 1852), p. 524, but Green's modernization of Angus's chaotic French grammar and spelling is not always reliable.

[3] R. Brown (ed.), *Calendar of State Papers Relating to English Affairs in the Archives of Venice (CSP Venetian)*, Volume 3 (London, 1869), no. 865.

[4] Brewer (ed.), *Letters and Papers*, Volume 4, no. 474.

[5] Brewer (ed.), *Letters and Papers*, Volume. 4, no. 1394.

[6] Brewer (ed.), *Letters and Papers*, Volume 4, no. 473. Written on 6 July 1524, the same day as Wolsey's letter to Dacre, and evidently following a series of meetings between the earl of Angus, Wolsey and Henry VIII.

[7] Quoted in Green, *Lives of the Princesses*, pp. 375–76.

[8] Ibid., pp. 366–67.

[9] Ibid., pp. 380–81.

[10] See Patricia Buchanan, *Margaret Tudor, Queen of Scots* (Edinburgh, 1985), ch. 16, passim.

[11] British Library, BL MS Cotton Caligula BI, f. 96.

[12] Brewer (ed.), *Letters and Papers*, Volume 4, no. 876.

[13] Ken Emond, *The Minority of James V: Scotland in Europe, 1513–1528* (Edinburgh, 2019), p. 222.

[14] *Acts of the Parliament of Scotland*, Volume 2, pp. 293–4.

[15] Quoted in Green, *Lives of the Princesses*, p. 452.

Chapter 21

[1] J. S. Brewer (ed.), *Letters and Papers, Foreign and Domestic, of the Reign of Henry VIII*, Volume 4 (London, 1875), part 4 (London, 1836), no. 4507. A copy of the letter declaring Margaret's marriage to Angus invalid is in National Records of Scotland, GD 220/6/254.

[2] Angus had compelled James V to write a public missive assuring the world that he was happy with his situation under the earl's guidance.

[3] Sir David Lyndsay of the Mount, 'The Testament and Complaint of our Sovereign Lord's Papyngo', in Janet Hadley Williams (ed.), *Sir David Lyndsay: Selected Poems* (Glasgow, 2000).

[4] See Ken Emond, *The Minority of James V: Scotland in Europe, 1513–1528* (Edinburgh, 2019), pp. 260–61. It also seems to me equally unlikely that Margaret would have welcomed her former husband into Stirling Castle if she was present, or that she would have been happy at his coming there at all, with the very real possibility that it might afford him the opportunity to garrison the castle with his own forces.

[5] R. K. Hannay (ed.), *Acts of the Lords of Council in Public Affairs, 1501–1544* (Edinburgh, 1932), p. 277.

[6] Brewer, *Letters and Papers*, Volume 4, no. 5289.

[7] Brewer, *Letters and Papers*, Volume 4, no. 5253.

[8] Alison Weir, *The Lost Tudor Princess* (London, 2015), p. 31.

[9] See ODNB entry for 'Margaret Tudor', by Richard Glen Eaves.

[10] British Library, BL Add MS 19,401, f. 28.

[11] Ibid., f. 29.

[12] *State Papers published under the authority of His Majesty's Commission, King Henry VIII, volume 5, part 1877*, Volume 5, part 4, London, (1836), no. CCLXXIII, 12 December, 1534, p. 12.

[13] Eric Ives, *The Life and Death of Anne Boleyn* (London, 2004), pp. 4, 11.

[14] T. Dickson and J. Paul (eds.), *Accounts of the Lord High Treasurer of Scotland*, Volume 6 (Edinburgh, 1877), p. 85.

[15] R. K. Hannay and D. Hay, eds. *The Letters of James V*, (Edinburgh, 1954), pp. 264–65.

[16] Ibid., p. 268.

[17] The National Archives (TNA), SP 49/4, f. 57.

[18] *State Papers of Henry VIII*, Volume 5, 1534, p. 12.

[19] Ibid., p. 41.

[20] Ibid., p. 46.

[21] Henry VIII had instructed Carlisle Herald before a meeting with Queen Margaret in 1531 to 'remind her of her son's possibility of succession of the Crown of England'. Quoted in Linda Porter, *Crown of Thistles: The Fatal Inheritance of Mary Queen of Scots* (London, 2013), p. 234.

[22] See Weir, *The Lost Tudor Princess*, p. 42.

[23] Ibid., p. 53.

[24] M. A. E. Green (ed.), *Letters of Royal and Illustrious Ladies of Great Britain, from the Commencement of the Twelfth Century to the Close of the Reign of Queen Mary*, Volume 2 (London, 1846), p. 288.
[25] Quoted in Weir, *The Lost Tudor Princess*, p. 78.

Chapter 22

[1] See Linda Porter, *Crown of Thistles: The Fatal Inheritance of Mary Queen of Scots* (London, 2013), p. 278.
[2] Janet Hadley Williams (ed.), *Sir David Lyndsay: Collected Poems* (Glasgow, 2000), p. 108.
[3] Quoted in Porter, *Crown of Thistles*, p. 279.
[4] Not to be confused with the River Loire, its much larger namesake.
[5] Porter, *Crown of Thistles*, p. 263.
[6] Quoted in Rosalind Marshall, *Mary of Guise* (London, 1977), p. 87.
[7] J. Gairdner. and H. Brodie, eds., *Letters and Papers, Foreign and Domestic, of the Reign of Henry VIII*, Volume 16 (London, 1898), no. 829. For a fuller version of Hay's report, see *State Papers of Henry VIII*, Volume 4: CCCLXXX, 12 May 1541, pp. 193–4.
[8] Gairdner., *Letters and Papers*, no. 1307.
[9] T. Dickson and J. Paul (eds.), *Accounts of the Lord High Treasurer of Scotland (Treasurer's Accounts)*, Volume 8 (Edinburgh, 1908), p. 43. I am grateful to Michael W. Pearce for his expertise in tracking down these details.
[10] Gareth Russell, *Young and Damned and Fair: The Life and Tragedy of Catherine Howard at the Court of Henry VIII* (London, 2018), p. 297.

Epilogue

[1] It was claimed at the time, and has been suggested since, that the notarial instrument may have been forged by David Beaton.
[2] J. Gairdner (ed.), *Letters and Papers, Foreign and Domestic, of the Reign of Henry VIII*, Volume 17 (London, 1900), no. 1235.
[3] She was also well aware that her granddaughter, Arbella Stuart, the child of Charles Stuart and Elizabeth Cavendish, was also a claimant to both the Scottish and English thrones.

Bibliography

Manuscript Sources

Austrian National Library, Vienna
Cod. 1897, Gebetbuch Jakobs IV von Schottland

British Library
BL Add MS 19,401
BL MS Cotton Caligula BVI
BL MS Cotton Vespasian FXIII
BL MS Facs 581/85
BL Harley MS 2252

National Library of Scotland
Seaton Armorial, Acc 9309

National Records of Scotland
GD 220/6/254

Primary Sources

Acts of the Parliament of Scotland, Volume 2 (Edinburgh, 1814).
André, Bernard, *The Life of Henry VII* (New York, 2011).
Bergenroth, G (ed.), *Calendar of Letters, Despatches and State Papers Relating to the Negotiations between England and Spain* (London, 1862–1954).
Boffey, Julia (ed.), *Henry VII's London in The Great Chronicle* (Kalamazoo, 2019).
Brewer, J. S. (ed.), *Letters and Papers, Foreign and Domestic, of the Reign of Henry VIII*, 21 volumes (London, 1862–1932).

Brown, R. (ed.), *Calendar of State Papers relating to English Affairs in the archives of Venice (CSP Venetian)*, Volumes 1–3 (London, 1867).

Cavell, Emma (ed.), *The Heralds' Memoir, 1486–1490* (Donington, 2009).

Dickson, T. and J. Paul (eds.), *Accounts of the Lord High Treasurer of Scotland*, Volumes 1–7, 1473–1541 (Edinburgh, 1877–1905).

Drummond, William, *The History of the Lives and Reigns of the Five James's, Kings of Scotland, From the Year 1423, To the Year 1542* (Edinburgh, 1811).

Ellis, Henry, *Original Letters, Illustrative of English History*, third series, Volume 1 (London, 1846).

Gairdner, J. and Brodie, H. (eds.), *Letters and Papers, Foreign and Domestic, of the Reign of Henry VIII*, Volume 16–17 (London, 1898).

Hannay, R. K. (ed.), *Acts of the Lords of Council in Public Affairs, 1501–1544* (Edinburgh, 1932).

Hannay, R. K. and Hay, D. (eds.), *The Letters of James V* (Edinburgh, 1954).

Haslewood, Joseph (ed.), 'The Trewe Encountre or Batayle Lately Don Betwene Englande and Scotlande', *Proceedings of the Society of Antiquaries Scotland*, 7, March 1867, p. 146.

Holinshed, Ralph, *Holinshed's Chronicles of England, Scotland and Ireland*, Volume 3 (London, 1808).

Hume, David, *The History of the House and Race of Douglas and Angus. Written by Mr David Hume of Godscroft* (Edinburgh, 1748).

Hume Brown, P. (ed.), *Early Travellers in Scotland* (Edinburgh, 1891).

Kipling, G. (ed.), *The Receyt of the Ladie Kateryne* (Oxford, 1990).

Leland, John, *Collectanea*, ed. Thomas Hearne, Volume 4 (London, 1774).

Lesley, John, *The History of Scotland, From the Death of King James I in the Year 1436, To the Year 1561* (Edinburgh, 1830).

Lindsay, Robert of Pitscottie, *The History of Scotland; from 1436 to 1565* (Edinburgh, 1749).

Mackie, R. L. (ed.) *The Letters of James IV, 1505–1513* (Edinburgh, 1953).

Strathallan, William Drummond, 1st Viscount, *The Genealogy of the Most Noble and Ancient House of Drummond* (Edinburgh, 1681).

State Papers during the Reign of Henry VIII, 13 vols.

Teulet, Alexandre (ed.), *Relations Politique de la France et de L'Espagne avec L'Ecosse au XVIe siècle*, Volume 1 (Paris, 1862).

Williams, Janet Hadley (ed.), *Sir David Lyndsay: Selected Poems* (Glasgow, 2000).

Wood, Marguerite (ed.), *Flodden Papers, Diplomatic Correspondence between the Courts of France and Scotland, 1507–1517* (Edinburgh, 1933).

Secondary Works

Beer, Michelle L., *Queenship at the Renaissance Courts of Britain: Catherine of Aragon and Margaret Tudor, 1503–1533* (Woodbridge, 2018).

Blakeway, Amy, *The Regency in Sixteenth-Century Scotland* (London, 2016).

Brown, Michael, *The Black Douglases: War and Lordship in Medieval Scotland, 1300–1455* (New York, 1998).

Buchanan, Patricia, *Margaret Tudor, Queen of Scots* (Edinburgh, 1985).

Cameron, Jamie, *James V: The Personal Rule, 1528–1542* (East Linton, 1998).

Carlson, David R., 'Royal Tutors in the Reign of Henry VII', *Sixteenth Century Journal*, XXII, No. 2, 1991, pp. 253–279.

Carpenter, Sarah, '"TO THE XALTACYON OF NOBLESSE", A Herald's Account of the Marriage of Margaret Tudor to James IV', *Medieval English Theatre*, 29, 2007, pp. 104–20.

Coombs, Bryony, 'Albany and the Poets: John Stuart, Duke of Albany and the Transfer of Ideas between Scotland and the Continent, 1509–1536', in D. H. Steinforth and C. C. Rozier (ed.), *Britain and Its Neighbours: Cultural Contacts and Exchanges in Medieval and Early Modern Europe* (Abingdon, 2021).

Cunningham, Sean, *Prince Arthur, The Tudor King Who Never Was* (Stroud, 2017).

Douglas, Ian, *Clan Douglas, from Warriors to Dukes* (Galashiels, 2021).

Dunbar, J. G., *Scottish Royal Palaces* (East Linton, 1999).

Emond, Ken, *The Minority of James V: Scotland in Europe, 1513–1528* (Edinburgh, 2019).

Fradenburg, Louise, *City, Marriage, Tournament* (Madison, WI, 1991).

Goodwin, George, *Fatal Rivalry: Flodden 1513* (London, 2013).

Green, M. A. E. (ed.), *Letters of Royal and Illustrious Ladies of Great Britain, from the Commencement of the Twelfth Century to the Close of the Reign of Queen Mary*, Volume 2 (London, 1846).

Green, M. A. E., *Lives of the Princesses of England, From the Norman Conquest*, Volume 4 (London, 1852).

Guy, John, *Tudor England* (London, 1988), p. 81.

Hepburn, William, *The Household and Court of James IV of Scotland, 1483–1513* (Woodbridge, 2023).

Ives, Eric, *The Life and Death of Anne Boleyn* (London, 2004).

Laynesmith, J. L., *The Last Medieval Queens* (London, 2004).

Macdougall, Norman, *James IV* (Edinburgh, 1997).

Macdougall, Norman, *An Antidote to the English* (East Linton, 2001).

Macfarlane, Leslie, 'The Book of Hours of James IV and Margaret Tudor', *Innes Review*, 11–12, 1960, pp. 3–19.

Mackie, R. L., *King James IV of Scotland* (Edinburgh, 1958).

Marshall, Rosalind, *Mary of Guise* (London, 1977).

Newsome, Helen, 'Reconsidering the Provenance of the Henry VII and Margaret Tudor Book of Hours', *Notes and Queries*, LXIV, 2017, pp. 233–34.

Okerlund, Arlene N., *Elizabeth of York* (Basingstoke, 2009).

Oram, Richard (ed.), *The Kings and Queens of Scotland* (Cheltenham, 2021).

Perry, Maria, *Sisters to the King* (London, 1999).

Porter, Linda, *Crown of Thistles: The Fatal Inheritance of Mary Queen of Scots* (London, 2013).

Russell, Gareth, *Young and Damned and Fair: The Life and Tragedy of Catherine Howard at the Court of Henry VIII* (London, 2018).

Sadlack, Erin, *The French Queen's Letters: Mary Tudor Brandon and the Politics of Marriage in Sixteenth-Century Europe* (London, 2011).

Scott, Sir Walter, *Marmion: A Tale of Flodden Field* (London, 1868).

Streiberger, W. R., 'Henry VIII's Entertainment for the Queen of Scots, 1516: A New Revels Account and Cornish's Play', *Medieval and Renaissance Drama in England*, 1, 1984, pp. 29–35.

Strickland, Agnes, *Lives of the Queens of Scotland and English Princesses Connected with the Regal Succession of Great Britain* (London, 1851).

Stuart, Marie, *The Scot Who Was A Frenchman* (London, 1940).

Tallis, Nicola, *Uncrowned Queen: The Fateful Life of Margaret Beaufort, Tudor Matriarch* (London, 2020).

Thomas, Andrea, *Princelie Majestie: The Court of James V of Scotland, 1528–1542* (Edinburgh, 2005).

Weir, Alison, *Elizabeth of York: The First Tudor Queen* (London, 2014).

Weir, Alison, *The Lost Tudor Princess* (London, 2015).

Wormald, Jenny, *Scotland Revisited* (London, 1991).
Wormald, Jenny, 'Thorns in the Flesh: English Kings and Uncooperative Scottish Rulers, 1460–1549', in G. W. Bernard and S. J. Gunn (eds.), *Authority and Consent in Tudor England* (London, 2002), p. 70.

Dissertations

Hayes, Amy, 'The Late Scottish Medieval Queens, c.1371–c.1513', unpublished Ph.D. dissertation, University of Aberdeen (2016).
Kelley, Michael G., 'The Douglas Earls of Angus', unpublished Ph.D. thesis, University of Edinburgh (1973).
Newsome, Helen, '"Sche that schuld be medyatryce (mediatrice) in thyr (these) matars": Performances of Mediation in the Letters of Margaret Tudor, Queen of Scots (1489–1541)', unpublished Ph.D. thesis, University of Sheffield (2018).

Image Credits

1. Prisma Archivo / Alamy Stock Photo
2. incamerastock / Alamy Stock Photo
3. By permission of the Master and Fellows of St John's College, Cambridge
4. little_miss_sunnydale / Flickr
5. Lebrecht History / Bridgeman Images
6. France, Arras, Saint-Vaast Abbey Media Library – 266 (CGM 1136, inv. 1839) / ARCA
7. Iain Masterton / Alamy Stock Photo
8. The Royal College of Surgeons of Edinburgh
9. Photo: Antonia Reeve / Scottish National Portrait Gallery
10. Antiqua Print Gallery / Alamy Stock Photo
11. Bridgeman Images
12. ÖNB/Vienna, Cod. 1897, fol.24v-25r
13. © National Portrait Gallery, London
14. CBW / Alamy Stock Photo
15. Jean Williamson / Alamy Stock Photo
16. National Galleries Scotland
17. Scottish National Portrait Gallery
18. AB Historic / Alamy Stock Photo
19. ©National Trust Images / Derrick E. Witty
20. Scottish National Portrait Gallery
21. Keith Corrigan / Alamy Stock Photo

Author Note

I first became interested in Margaret Tudor more than a decade ago, while researching *Crown of Thistles*, my book which examined the rivalry between the Tudors and the Stuarts. Margaret was, of course, a part of this but I have always felt that a full biography that gives this redoubtable – and often overlooked – Tudor her due had yet to be written. Quite why she has been neglected is a mystery. Her life was one of high drama for much of her fifty-two years but she has been dismissed as an irrelevant whinger with a poor grasp of politics, driven by romantic fancies and a frivolous interest in her wardrobe. Sadly, female historians, led by those most censorious of Victorians, Elizabeth and Agnes Strickland, have often been among Margaret's most ill-informed critics. Yet, as recent research into Margaret's voluminous correspondence (more survives than that of any other Tudor monarch) has shown, Margaret was an important player on the diplomatic scene. Her underrated education and thorough training in queenship by her first husband, the charismatic James IV of Scotland, had given her an excellent grounding in the conventions of 16th century diplomacy in the British Isles and she was determined to use this as effectively as she could. Margaret's long-standing rivalry with her brother, Henry

VIII, is a key not just to understanding her, but also Anglo–Scottish relations in the first half of the sixteenth century, a fascinating field that is still not adequately appreciated by our continuing and very Anglo-centric obsession with the Tudors. For Margaret was, above all, a dynast, and her entire life after 1513 was committed to ensuring the survival of her little son, James V, as King of Scots, just seventeen months old when his father died at the battle of Flodden. It is a testament to her sheer, dogged determination, through innumerable setbacks, that he finally reigned in his own right, and with considerable success, between 1528 and his tragically early death in 1542, barely a year after Margaret herself had died. Of course, she was far from perfect and in writing about her it is easy to understand how she could irritate, nay, infuriate those who encountered her imperious spirit. She was a worthy sister to her brother in that respect but, unlike him, she harmed remarkably few people. I hope that I have done her justice.

Many people, as always, helped in the writing of this book. I am eternally indebted to Dr Nicola Tallis and Dr Steven Veerapen, who both read the first draft and provided numerous insightful comments at a time when they were extremely busy with their own projects. Both have recently published books, on young Elizabeth I and James VI and I, which I know will delight readers. Dr Marie Macpherson provided useful details on Haddington Priory and her usual encouragement. I am also grateful to the staff of the London Library, the British Library and to Dr Sean Cunningham at the National Archives in Kew for his continuing support and to Melita Thomas of Tudor Times for her interest. My agent, Andrew Lownie, who has fought a long and extremely important battle for access to royal records, has been a friend now for more than twenty years. I should also like to thank my editor, Iain MacGregor, my publicist, Kate Wands and the entire team at HOZ Books. Last, but most certainly not least, Dr Helen Newsome's ground-breaking doctoral thesis on Margaret Tudor's correspondence is a wonderful source for understanding the role a woman could play in 16th century diplomacy.

Linda Porter

Sevenoaks, January 2024

Index

A

Abernathy, Jean 273
Albany, Alexander Stewart, duke
    of 202–3
Albany, John Stewart, duke of 82, 178–9,
    182, 190, 191, 202–8, 244, 287, 289
    and Angus 227–8, 276, 278
    character 205
    and the earl of Arran 247
    family background 202–4
    and Margaret's divorce from
        Angus 300
    and Margaret's flight to
        England 213–16, 224, 225–7,
        236–7
    and Margaret's letters to
        England 209–12
    Margaret's relations with 258–60
    and Margaret's return to
        Scotland 238, 239, 242, 244–5
    regencies 212, 237, 245, 258–60, 261–3,
        268–74
    return to France 243, 245–6, 269–70,
        281–2
    return to Scotland 198, 199, 201–8,
        252, 253–4, 272–4
    war with England 269–70, 271, 272–4
Alcock, John 9
Alnwick Castle 71
André, Bernard 13

Angus, Archibald Douglas, 5th earl
    of 121–2, 151, 172, 184
Angus, Archibald Douglas, 6th earl
    of 180, 337
    and Albany 205, 268
    background 184–6
    and the earl of Arran 247
    in France 275–8
    Henry VIII's support of 193–5, 251–2,
        275–6, 278, 279, 280–4, 289, 290–1,
        292, 306, 324
    insurrection 288–9
    and James V 293–4, 299–306, 326
    death of 336
    regency council 290–3
    leaves Scotland 214–15, 216, 217,
        220, 259
    and Margaret's death 330
    and Margaret's return to
        Scotland 238–9, 242–3
    marriage to Margaret 179, 183–9,
        190–5, 212, 228–9, 234, 247–9,
        250–2, 259
    return to Scotland 227–9, 282–4
Angus, George Douglas, fourth earl
    of 185
Anna of Denmark 189
Anne of Brittany 127, 179, 196
Anne of Cleves 324
Argyll, earl of 79, 161, 164, 239, 251, 270

Arkinholm, Battle of (1455) 185
Arran, James Hamilton, earl of 177, 178,
    205, 228, 280–1, 287–8, 293
    rebellion against Albany 227
    as regent of Scotland 239, 246–7, 251,
        252, 269–70
Arthur, Prince (England) 3, 7, 20, 39,
    133, 144
    death 48–52
    education 12, 13
    investiture as Prince of Wales 10
    marriage to Katherine of Aragon 22,
        23–30, 31, 33, 37, 42, 66, 232, 235
Arthur, Prince (Scotland) 130
Arthur, Thomas 332
Arundel, earl of 9
Atholl, Lord 307, 337
Audley, Lord 19, 20
Avondale, Lord 285
Ayala, Pedro de 36, 39, 88, 91
Ayton, Truce of 34, 36, 90

B
Bacon, Francis 51–2
Bainbridge, Christopher, Archbishop
    of York 141, 155
Balcomie Castle 327
Balfour Paul, Sir James 120
Bannockburn, Battle of 83, 86, 152
Barlow, Elizabeth 115–16
Bastard Heron 162
Beaton, Cardinal David 335
Beaton, James, Archbishop of
    Glasgow 171, 190–1, 269, 287, 288, 293
Beaufort, Joan 174–5
Beaufort, Margaret 1, 8, 10, 15, 16–18, 53, 56
    character 17–18, 61–2, 118
    and Collyweston 59, 60–2
    and Margaret's betrothal to James IV
        of Scotland 36–7, 40, 125
    marriages 16–17
Beaulieu Abbey 20
Benestede, Edward 110
Bening, Alexander 96

Bening, Simon 96
Berkeley, Anne Fiennes, marchioness
    of 9
Berwick Herald (Henry Ray) 331, 332
Black Douglases 184–6
'Black Ellen' 129
Blackadder Castle 213, 214, 215, 216
Blackadder, Robert, Archbishop of
    Glasgow 32, 33, 39, 40–1, 72–3, 86,
        100, 101
Blackheath, Battle of 19–20
Blount, Elizabeth 315
Bluemantle (Rothesay Herald) 110
Boleyn, Anne 261, 308, 309, 313, 314,
    317, 318
    and Lady Margaret Douglas 315–16
Boleyn, Sir Thomas 308–9
Book of Hours (James IV and Margaret
    Tudor) 96–7, 330–1
Borders 19, 36, 77, 182
    families 73, 84, 85–6, 136–7
    the 'Rough Wooings' 336, 337
    wars and unrest 90, 272, 305, 314
Borthwick, Robert 151
Bosworth, Battle of (1485) 1, 8, 34, 35,
    65, 155
Bothwell, Patrick Hepburn, earl of 32–3,
    41, 43, 72–3, 186
Boyd, Marion 85, 123
Brandon, Charles, duke of Suffolk
    197–8, 234–5
Buckingham, duke of 17, 25, 39, 42

C
Cambuskenneth Abbey 84
Camner, John 110
Capello, Francisco 39
Carew, Nicholas 235
Carnavel, Mr 110
Carr, Robin 211
Catholic Church 117–19
    Easter and Royal Maundy 118–19
    and Lady Margaret Douglas 315, 338
Cecily of York, Princess 2, 3, 52–3, 111

Chadworth, Friar 251
Charles I, King 103
Charles V, Holy Roman Emperor 195,
    277, 289, 310–12
Charles VIII, king of France 140,
    201, 203
Christian, Prince of Denmark 36
Cistercian nuns 78, 216
Claude, Queen of France 198, 200
Cleg, Hamnet 110
Clement VII, Pope 286, 298
Cochleus, Johannes 309
Coldingham Priory 77
Coldstream Priory 216
Collyweston, Northamptonshire 59,
    60–2, 66, 67, 73, 98
Compton, Sir William 230, 231
Conyars, Lady 67
Cornish, William 235–6
Courtney, William 53
Cranmer, Thomas, Archbishop of
    Canterbury 333
Crawford, earl of 160, 161–2, 163
Crichton, Janet 79
Cromwell, Thomas 308, 320
Cumming of Inverlochy, Sir William
    (Lyon Herald) 148, 149, 150
Cyriac, St 97

D
Dacre, Elizabeth, Lady 219–20
Dacre family 136
Dacre, Lord 144, 164, 166, 179, 180, 182,
    193, 205, 206, 210, 275
    on Arran's regency in Scotland 247
    and Margaret's finances 250
    and Margaret's flight to
        England 212, 213, 215–16, 217,
        219–20, 226, 228, 229, 237
    and Margaret's return to
        Scotland 239–40
Dacre, Sir Thomas 154–5, 162–3
Dalkeith Castle 79–80, 92–3
Darcy, Lady 72

Darnley, Henry Stewart, Lord 337, 338
Daubeney, Giles 19
David I, King of Scots 78
Deane, Henry, Archbishop of
    Canterbury 33–4, 39
Dennet, Margaret 117
Denton, Elizabeth 45, 58, 100
Derby, earl of 8, 39
Dog, James 114
Dogge, Jammy 265
Dorset, marquis of 235
Douglas, Archibald, fifth earl of 174
Douglas family 86, 184–6, 193, 245, 280
    and James V 293–4, 299–304
Douglas, Gavin, bishop of
    Dunkeld 206, 226, 249, 259–60, 266
Douglas, George 206, 276, 301
Douglas, James, ninth earl of 185–6
Douglas, Janet, Lady Glamis 326
Douglas, Lady Margaret 220, 298,
    314–20, 330, 337–9
    birth 216–17, 225
    character 315
    childhood 258
    and the English succession 314–15,
        320, 339
    and her father (the earl of Angus)
        294, 305–6, 315, 337
    marriage 338–9
    religion 315, 338
    in the Tower of London 314, 317–20,
        321–2, 338
Douglas of Parkhead, James 301–2
Douglas, Sir George 335–6
Douglas, William, brother of the earl
    of Angus 275, 277
Douglas, William, eighth earl of 86, 185
Drummond, John, Lord 187, 206
Drummond, Margaret 85, 122, 123
Dudley, Edmund 134
Dumbarton Castle 89, 107–8
Dunbar Castle 77
Dunbar, Gavin, Archbishop 172, 287,
    288, 303

Dunbar, Isabel 173, 174
Dunbar, William 106, 113–14, 131, 188
   Ballad of a Right Noble 137–8
   on James IV 166
Dunfermline 124–5
Durham 71, 242
Duwes, Giles 12

E
Easter and Royal Maundy 118–19
Edinburgh 85, 232
   'Cleanse the Causeway' 247
   Holyroodhouse 94–6, 98, 124, 244
      Abbey of the Holy Cross 93–4,
        95, 329
      chapel 98, 100
      and the marriage of Margaret and
        James IV 93–103
Edinburgh Castle 83, 95, 123, 124, 227,
   244, 280
   and Angus's insurrection 288–9
Edmund, Prince 12
Edward IV, King of England 8, 11, 15, 18,
   22, 35, 60, 203, 206
Edward V *see* Princes in the Tower
Edward VI, King of England 336
Elizabeth I, Queen of England 14,
   63, 337
   and Lady Margaret Douglas 315,
      338, 339
Elizabeth, Princess 11, 12
Elizabeth of York, Queen of England
   appearance 80–1
   birth of Margaret 7–9
   coronation 1–3
   death of 55–6, 58
   and the death of Prince Arthur 48,
      52–3
   influence on Margaret 14–16
   and Margaret's betrothal to James IV
      of Scotland 36, 39, 40, 43–4,
      46–7, 125
   marriage to Henry VII 3, 8, 15, 43–4
   pregnancies and childbirth 11–12,
      51, 53–5

and Prince Arthur 24, 27–8, 49, 50–1
   death of 49, 50–1
   queenship 44–7
   sisters of 15–16
   and the Western Uprising 20–1
Elphinstone, Alexander 115–16
Elphinstone, William, Archbishop
   of St Andrews 33, 181
Elphinstone, William, bishop of
   Aberdeen 82, 151, 172
Eltham Palace 11, 13
Empson, Richard 134
England
   Albany and war with England
      269–70, 271, 272–4
   alliance with France 253–4
   Anglo-Imperial alliance 254
   Borders families 136–7
   Eltham Palace 11, 13
   James IV and Scottish policy
      towards 88–90
   Margaret in London 229–40
   Margaret's death and the English
      court 332–3
   Margaret's flight to 212–22, 223–9
   and the marriage of Prince Arthur
      and Katherine of Aragon 31
   Reformation 309–10
   representatives at the betrothal
      of James IV and Margaret
      Tudor 33–5
   Treaty of Perpetual Peace 38, 110,
      132, 136, 140, 158
   see also Henry VII, King; Henry VIII,
      King
English language 233
Erasmus of Rotterdam 13, 124
Eriksson, Gotschalk 310
Erroll, earl of 160, 161–2, 163
Erskine, Margaret 321
Essex, earl of 235

F
Falkland Palace 330, 332
Fast Castle 73, 77

Ferdinand of Aragon 18, 31, 33, 88, 133–4, 140, 141
Field of the Cloth of Gold 252, 253, 312
First World War 165
FitzRoy, Henry, duke of Richmond 314–15
Fleming, Lord 177, 178, 275
Flodden, Battle of 148–66, 269, 273, 316, 334
  assistance for widows of 172–3
  and France 177–9
  James IV's death at 164, 165–6, 169–70, 176–7, 183, 247, 261
  Scots casualties 165, 172, 184
'The Flowers of the Forest' 165
Ford Castle 152–3, 157
Forester, Sir Duncan 112
Forman, Andrew, bishop of Moray 32, 64, 94, 99
Fox, Richard, bishop of Winchester 34–5, 40
France
  alliance with England 253–4
  alliance with Scotland 88, 137–8, 140, 177–9, 247, 269
  and the death of James IV of Scotland 177–9
  earl of Angus in 275–8
  Guise family 326–7
  and Henry VIII 137, 138, 140–2, 144, 148–50, 231, 247
  and James V of Scotland 238
  Scots nobility in 137, 184
  Stewarts in 137–8
  see also Louis XII, King of France
Francis I, King of France 198, 199–201, 224–5, 238, 289–90
  and Albany 252–3, 254, 259, 268–9, 273, 281–2
  and the earl of Angus 276, 277–8
  and the Field of the Cloth of Gold 252, 253
  and James V of Scotland 322, 325, 327

G
Garneys, Sir Christopher 218–19, 219–20, 221–2
George, duke of Clarence 22, 60
Glasebury, Henry 64
Glencairn, Master of 288
Glenluce, abbot of 263
Gordon, Alexander 121
Gordon, Lady Katherine 19, 40, 89
The Great Chronicle of London 21, 27
Green, Maud 229
Greenwich Palace 49
Guillot, Sir John 70

H
Haddington 77–9
  St Mary's Priory 78
Hall, Edward
  Chronicle 235
Hamilton family 279–80
Hamilton of Finnart, Sir James 325
Hamilton, Sir Patrick 94
Hannay, Thomas 332
Hans, King of Denmark 36, 127–8
Harbottle Castle 216–17, 218
Hastings, Elizabeth 69
Hatfield Palace 11
Hawley, Thomas, Rouge Croix 157
Hay, Lord 275
Henrietta Maria, Queen 103
Henry V, King of England 134
Henry VI, King of England 16, 175
Henry VII, King of England
  Battle of Bosworth 1, 8, 18, 34, 35
  birth of 16–17
  character 87, 122, 133–4
  children of 12–13
  and the earl of Surrey 65–6
  education 13
  and Elizabeth of York
    coronation of 1, 2, 3
    death of 56
    marriage and relations with 3, 9, 15, 43–4, 51

failing health 22
and James IV of Scotland 81, 84, 89
and Margaret 10, 11, 12, 127, 144
　betrothal to James IV of
　　Scotland 34, 35–8, 45, 81
　birth of 8, 9
　journey to Scotland 56–7, 59, 62,
　　64, 67
　Margaret's letter after her
　　wedding 104–5
　marriage treaty 111
and peace with Scotland 32
Perkin Warbeck and the Western
　uprising 18–21, 90
and Prince Arthur
　death of 49–52
　marriage to Katherine of Aragon
　　24, 25, 26, 27, 29
and Scotland 230–1
and the Wars of the Roses 17
Henry VIII, King of England 63, 79,
　133–6
Act on royal marriages 317–18
and Albany 179, 201, 205, 259–60,
　262–3, 268–9, 282
appearance 231
birth 11
childhood 20, 21, 49
　death of mother 55–6
court painters 96
death 336–7
as duke of York 29–30, 66, 69
and the earl of Angus 193–5, 251–2,
　275–6, 278, 279, 280–4, 289, 290–1,
　292, 306, 324
and the English succession 314–15,
　329, 338
and the Field of the Cloth of Gold 252
and Flodden 153–4
and France 137, 138, 140–2, 144,
　148–50, 231, 247
and Francis I of France 224–5
and the Holy League 141
and James IV of Scotland 79, 136,
　140, 142–7, 148–50

and James V of Scotland 200, 312–13,
　336
and jousting 234–5
and Katherine of Aragon 133–6, 195,
　308, 310
　Prince Arthur's marriage to 25,
　　28, 29–30
and Katherine Howard 66
and Lady Margaret Douglas 315,
　316–20, 338
and Margaret 307–8
　betrothal to James IV of
　　Scotland 39, 42
　correspondence 144–5, 209–12,
　　223, 230, 252–8, 262–7, 281–2,
　　289, 313–14, 323, 329–30
　death of 332–3
　divorce from Angus 297–9
　financial support to 272
　flight to England 216, 217–18,
　　220–1, 223–5, 229, 237
　in London 230–2, 234–7
　as Queen of Scots 142–3, 144–5,
　　148–50
　as regent of Scotland 175–7, 181,
　　182, 284–7, 309–10
　return to Scotland 239–40,
　　241, 243
　sibling rivalry 13, 176, 230–1,
　　260–1, 266–7, 268, 324–5, 339
and Mary (sister) 198
Reformation 309–10
and Scotland 336–7
　the 'Rough Wooings' 336, 337
weddings 98–9
wives 66, 261, 308–9, 315–16, 318, 320,
　324–5, 332–3
Hepburn, Margaret 186
Hepburns 86, 136
Heron, Bastard 162
Heron, Lady Elizabeth 152–3, 162
Holt, John 13
Holy League 141
Home, Alexander 171–2
Home family 73, 85–6, 90, 136, 245–6, 302

Home, Lord 160, 161, 162, 163–4, 191,
206–7, 212, 213, 216, 219, 220–1, 227,
228
Home of Wedderburn, David 245, 246
Hone, William 13
Horenbout, Gerard 96
horsemanship 12
Howard, Catherine 66, 316, 332–3
Howard family in Norfolk 64–7
see also Surrey, Thomas Howard,
earl of
Howard, Lord Edmund 161, 162
Howard, Lord Thomas 316, 317–18,
320, 338
Howard, Lord William 312, 313, 317
Howard, Mary 315
Howard, Sir Edward 150
Howard, Thomas, admiral of the
fleet 157, 158, 161
humanism 13, 118, 123–4
Hume of Godscroft, David 247–8
Huntly, earl of 160, 161, 162, 163–4,
269–70
Huntly family 79, 89

I
infant mortality 130–1
Inglis, James 210
Ireland 85
Isabella of Castile, Queen of Spain 18,
23, 27, 31, 33, 88, 134, 155, 333
Italian wars 138, 140, 141, 201, 203, 277

J
James I, King of Scotland 109, 174
James II, King of Scotland 86, 174, 175,
185, 246
James III, King of Scotland 34, 81–4,
88–9, 97, 111, 175, 202–3
James IV, King of Scotland 81–91
accomplishments 91
appearance and dress 77, 79, 81, 91,
93, 100–1, 115, 160
character and rule 84–91, 97
childhood 82, 203

coronation 86
death 164, 165–6, 169–70, 176–7, 183,
247, 261, 333
and the earl of Angus 151
and the earl of Bothwell 32–3
and Flodden 151–3, 155–66, 247, 298
foreign policy and England 88–91
and Henry VII of England 81, 84, 89
and Henry VIII of England 79, 136,
140, 142–7, 148–50, 230–1
illegitimate children 84–5, 123–4
and Margaret
betrothal 30, 31–2, 35–8, 43
first meeting 79–81
marriage 62, 91, 92–103,
104–5, 339
New Year gifts 116–17
personal relationship 120–1,
124–5, 169–70
pregnancies 126–32, 151
regency granted to 150–1
royal progress 106–8, 122
and the Scottish court 106–19
mistreses 84–5, 112, 121–3, 125
and music 47, 92
navy 87, 138–40, 177, 246–7
pilgrimages 122, 128–9, 217
rebellion against his father 83–4
religion and public piety 119
and royal palaces 108–9
Seaton Armorial portrait of 114–15
support for Perkin Warbeck 19, 32,
36, 66, 89–90
and the Turks 140
James V, King of Scotland 147, 150, 199,
222, 274, 304–5
and Albany 178, 202, 207–8, 237, 274
birth 132
coming of age 284, 287, 301
coronation 170–1, 172
cruelty of 325–6
death 334–6
death of sons 329
and the Douglas family 293–4,
299–304, 326

and the English succession 310, 315
and France 238
French marriages 321–3
    Madeleine of France 311, 322–3, 325
    Mary of Guise 327–9
and Henry VIII of England 279
illegitimate children 321, 328
and Lady Margaret Douglas 294, 298, 315
and Margaret (mother)
    death of 330, 331–2
    flight to England 224, 238
    relations with 307
    second regency 279–80, 290–1
and marriage alliances 310–12
minority of 244–5, 250, 253–4, 258–9, 267, 268, 269–70, 272–3
and religion 309
and the rotating council
    regency 291–3
James VI and I, King 189, 339
Jones, Eleanor 58, 117
Joseph, Michael 19
jousting 234–5
Juana, Queen of Castile 140
Julius II, Pope 138, 140, 141

K

Katherine of Aragon 118, 122, 140, 147, 195, 218, 229
    appearance 23–4, 232
    and the death of Prince Arthur 49, 58
    and Flodden 150, 155–6, 157, 176–7, 308
    and James IV of Scotland 33
    and Margaret's return to London 232, 233
    marriage to Henry VIII
        annulment 29, 261, 279, 297, 308, 310
        pregnancies and childbirth 133–6, 231
    marriage to Prince Arthur 22, 23–30, 31, 33, 37, 42, 66, 232, 235

Katherine of York, Princess 53, 83
Keith, William, the earl Marischal 206, 208
Kelley, Michael G. 248
Kennedy, Janet 85, 121–3, 125
Kennedy, Lord 121
Kittcrosshill, Battle of 227
Kyme, Thomas 53

L

la Bastie, Antoine de 177, 243, 245–6
la Tour, Anne de 202
Lafayette, French ambassador 252
Langton Tower 245–6
Latimer, Lord and Lady 67
Lauder, Sir Robert 206
Leland, John 7
Lennox, Charles Stewart, 5th Earl of 339
Lennox, Matthew Stewart, 4th earl of 338–9
Leo X, Pope 181
Leopold, Holy Roman Emperor 330–1
Lesley, John
    History of Scotland 183
Lincoln, earl of 65
Lindsay of Piscottie, Robert 139
Linlithgow Palace 108–9, 146–7, 148, 150–1, 169–70, 214, 328, 334, 335
Lisle, Lord 335–6
Logy, Leonard 95
London 232–3
    Baynard's Castle 232
    Children of the Chapel Royal 235–6
    epidemics 10–11
    'Evil May-Day riots' 240
    Greenwich Palace 1, 11, 233–4
    and the marriage of Prince Arthur to Katherine of Aragon 26–9
    Palace of Westminster 2, 8, 10
    Scotland Yard 232
    Tower of London 1, 2, 3, 11, 20, 55, 65, 90
    Westminster Abbey 3
Longueville, duke of 326, 327

Louis XII, King of France 127, 135, 137,
138, 140, 142, 148, 149, 187, 198, 203
 alliance with Scotland 178–9, 247
 on James IV of Scotland 177–8
 marriage to Princess Mary
  Tudor 179, 193, 195–7, 200
Louise of Savoy 200, 273, 282–3, 289–90
Lovell, Sir Thomas 156
Luxembourg, the sieur de 8–9
Lyndsay of the Mount, Sir David 258,
 299–300, 325

M
McClellane, Patrick 173
Madeleine of France 311, 322–3, 325
Magnus, Thomas 213, 226, 286–7, 289,
 299, 305
Maid of Norway 335
makars 113–14
Mannering, Piers 110
Mar, John Stewart, earl of 125, 203
Margaret of Burgundy 18, 89–90
Margaret of Denmark, Queen of Scots
 77, 81, 82, 84, 203
Margaret of Savoy 135
Margaret (Scottish warship) 139
Margaret Tudor, Queen of Scots
 and Albany 179, 182, 190–1, 201–2,
  204–8, 212, 267, 270–2
 and Angus 282–3, 286–7, 330
  divorce from 251, 286, 297–9
  marriage to 179, 183–9, 190–5,
   212, 228–9, 234, 242–3, 247–9,
   250–2, 259
 appearance 63, 80–1, 97, 100, 114–15,
  231–2
 betrothal to James IV of Scotland
  30, 31–47
  betrothal ceremony 38–43, 72, 186
  gifts 47
  marriage treaty 37–8, 58, 111
  wedding journey to Scotland
   56–9, 60–73
 birth 7–9

 childhood 11–22, 45
  accomplishments 14
  christening 7, 9–10
  clothes 57, 100, 118–19, 120–1, 220,
   238, 323
  death 330–3
 and the death of James IV 169–70
 death of mother (Elizabeth of York)
  54–6
 and the earl of Surrey 66–7, 99, 100,
  102–3, 104, 107
 education 12–14
 financial affairs 248–50, 258, 306,
  313–14, 322–3, 331
 flight to England 212–22, 223–9, 236–7
 and Flodden 155, 166
 furnishings 57, 121, 238
 health 128, 131, 221–2, 242
 and Henry Stewart, Lord Methven,
  marriage to 285–6, 288, 292, 303,
  306–7
 and Henry VIII
  as Duke of York 69
  financial support 272
  letters to 144–5, 209–12, 223,
   230, 252–8, 262–7, 281–2, 289,
   313–14, 323, 329–30
  in London 230–2, 234–7
  Margaret as Queen of
   Scotland 142–3, 144–5, 148–50
  Margaret as regent of
   Scotland 175–6, 181, 182,
   284–7, 309–10
  Margaret's divorce from
   Angus 297–9
  Margaret's flight to England 216,
   217–18, 220–1, 223–5, 229, 237
  Margaret's return to
   Scotland 239–40, 241, 243
  sibling rivalry 13, 176, 230–1,
   260–1, 266–7, 268, 324–5, 339
 horses 57, 92, 93, 121
 households 58–9, 110–13
  funding 111–12

and hunting 71, 121, 302
and James V 258, 307, 322, 323, 330,
   331–2, 335
   minority of 224, 238, 279–80,
      290–1
jewellery 238
and Katherine of Aragon 176–7
and Lady Margaret Douglas 305–6,
   316–20
letter-writing 14, 104–5, 209–12, 236,
   271, 272
   holograph letters 262–3, 265
   memorial letters 264–7
   to Francis I of France 252–3
in London after fleeing
   Scotland 229–40
marriage to James IV of
   Scotland 62, 91, 92–105, 339
   coronation 101, 117–18
   entry into Edinburgh 93–6
   first meeting 79–81
   personal relationship 120–1, 124–5
   royal progress 106–8, 122
   wedding ceremony 95, 98–103
   wedding gift of Book of
      Hours 96–7, 330–1
and Mary of Guise 326, 328–9
and Mary (sister) 197, 330
and music 47
pilgrimages 129, 130–1
portraits of 47, 97
   Seaton Armorial 114–15
pregnancies and childbirth 125–32,
   134–5, 170, 173, 180, 208, 212, 214,
   216–17
and Prince Arthur
   death of 49, 52
   marriage to Katherine of
      Aragon 22, 23–4, 28, 29–30
as regent of Scotland 170–9, 180–3,
   189, 190–2, 274, 278–80, 284–5
religion and public piety 117–19, 309
return to Scotland 238–40, 241–7
and the Scottish court 106–19

Christmas and New Year
   gifts 116–17
English servants 110
marriages of ladies 115–16, 117
siblings 11–12
smallpox 271
Mary of Burgundy 96
Mary of Guelders 174, 175, 246
Mary of Guise, Queen of Scots 109,
   326, 328–9, 331, 332, 337
   and James V's death 334, 335
   and the minority of Mary, Queen of
      Scots 336
Mary, Queen of Scots 108, 189, 321,
   336, 337
   birth of 334
Mary Rose (English warship) 139
Mary Tudor, Princess (later Queen
   Mary I) 136, 141, 231, 261, 279, 310, 311
   and Lady Margaret Douglas 306,
      315
Mary Tudor, Princess (sister of Henry
   VIII) 147, 306, 330
   appearance 80–1
   birth 12
   childhood 20, 21, 23, 28, 40, 49
   death 309
   and Margaret's return to
      London 234
   marriage to Charles Brandon, duke
      of Suffolk 197–8, 234
   marriage to Louis XII of France 179,
      193, 195–7, 200
Massey, Alice 9
Maximilian, Emperor 53, 140, 141, 188
Maxton, Charles 115
Maxwell family 280
memorial letters 264–7
Methven Castle
   Margaret's death at 330
Methven, Lord see Stewart, Henry,
   Lord Methven
Milan, Francisco Sforza, duke of 188
Montrose, earl of 160, 162, 163

Moray, James Stewart, earl of
(illegitimate son of James IV) 123–4,
280, 293, 299, 302, 335
Moray, James Stewart, earl of
(illegitimate son of James V) 321
More, Thomas 13, 55, 224
Morpeth Castle 213, 216, 217–22, 225,
229, 230
Morton, George Douglas, earl of 243
Morton, John, Archbishop of
Canterbury 3, 10, 34–5
Morton, John Douglas, earl of 79
Mowbray, Anne 65
music 47, 64
Mytens, Daniel
portrait of Margaret as Queen of
Scots 47

N
Newark Castle 248
Newcastle 71
Newminster, abbot of 218
Norfolk, Duchess of 10
Norfolk, John Howard, first duke of
64, 65
see also Surrey, Thomas Howard,
earl of
Northumberland, earl of 68–70, 71, 72,
73, 242, 307–8

O
Ogilvy, James 236
Ogilvy, Sir Alexander 117
Ogle, Lord 218
Ormonde, Hugh Douglas, Earl of 185
Ormonde, marquess of 82–3
Oxford, earl of 8, 19–20

P
Paniter, Patrick 172, 173, 181
Papal States 141
Parr, Katherine 55, 318, 338
Parr, Sir Thomas 229–30

Pavia, Battle of 289
Perpetual Peace, Treaty of 38, 110, 132,
136, 140, 158
Perry, Maria 189
Perth
St John's Abbey 333
Philip of Burgundy 140
Philip, Mistress 235
Plains, Jean de 200–1, 211, 215, 236
Pole, Edmund de la, earl of Suffolk 22,
53, 141
Pole, Richard de la 138
Princes in the Tower 3, 17, 53, 65, 89, 90,
206, 224
Protestantism in Scotland 118
Puebla, Dr de 24, 39

R
Radcliff, Roger 286–7
Raglan Castle 54
Ratcliffe, Sir Edward 218
Rawlins, Dr 100
Ray, Henry (Berwick Herald) 331, 332
Receuil d'Arras 37, 47
The Recyt of the Ladie Kateryne 25–6,
27, 50
Red Douglases 184–6
Rede, John 13
Reformation 309–10
Richard, Duke of York *see* Princes in the
Tower
Richard III, King of England 15, 34, 35,
65, 67, 155, 203, 206, 224
Richmond Palace 22, 29, 35
Margaret's betrothal ceremony 38–43
Robert the Bruce 31, 83
Robert III, King of Scots 121
Ross, Alexander Stewart, duke of 180,
201, 208
death of 222, 223–4
Rouen, Treaty of (1517) 238, 269
Roxburgh Castle 175
Russell, Gareth 333

S

Sadler, Sir Ralph 322, 324–5, 326, 329
St Mary's Priory 78
Sauchieburn, battle of 83–4
Savage, Thomas, Archbishop of York 69,
  70, 71, 72, 99, 100, 101
Scandinavia 139
Scotland
  alliance with France 88, 137–8, 140,
    177–9, 247, 269
  Easter and Royal Maundy 118–19
  female regents in 174–5
  . Highlands 85
  Margaret's journey to 56–9, 60–73,
    77–9
  population 85
  representatives at Margaret's
    betrothal ceremony 32–3, 42–3
  Stewart dynasty 31–2
  Treaty of Perpetual Peace 38, 110,
    132, 136, 140, 158
  see also Borders
Scott of Buccleuch 288
Scott, Sir Walter
  'Marmion' 152–3
Scott, Sir William 236
Scrope, Lord 67
Seymour, Jane 320, 324
Shaw, James 82
Sheen manor 11–12
  fire and rebuilding of 21–2
Shelton, Mary 315
Shrewsbury, earl of 9, 10, 241, 242
Sinclair, Patrick 94, 265, 286
Skelton, John 13
Solway Moss, Battle of 334–5
Somerset Herald see Young, John,
  Somerset Herald
Spain
  and Henry VIII's foreign policy
    133–4
Spencer, Catherine 69
Spurs, Battle of the 142
Stafford, Henry 17
Stanley, Sir Edward 92–3, 162, 164

Stewart, Alexander, Archbishop of
  St Andrews 79, 99, 123–4, 124, 152,
  164, 171, 181
Stewart, Alexander (brother of James III)
  178
Stewart, Bérault 137
Stewart, Charles, 5th Earl of
  Lennox 339
Stewart dynasty 31–2
Stewart, Henry, Lord Methven 285–6,
  288, 292, 303, 306–7, 314, 329, 330, 337
Stewart, Henry, Lord Darnley 337, 338
Stewart, James (brother of James IV) 125
Stewart, Lady Janet 307, 337
Stewart, Lady Margaret (illegitimate
  daughter of James IV) 123, 124
Stewart, Lord Bernard 137–8
Stewart, Margaret, fourth countess of
  Angus 185
Stewart, Matthew, 4th earl of
  Lennox 338–9
Stewart, Princess Mary 246
Stewart, Sir James
  the Black Knight of Lorne 174
Stewart of Traquair, Lady Jane 186, 298
Stirling Castle 81, 83, 87, 108, 123, 187, 302
  the Black Dinner 86, 185
  and James V 258, 273, 279, 302, 303
  coronation 170–1
  Margaret's capitulation to
    Albany 205–6, 207–9, 226–7
  Queen's Chamber 108
Strangeways, Sir Thomas 305–6
Strickland, Agnes 188–9
Stuart, Marie 214
Suffolk, Charles Brandon, duke
  of 197–8, 234–5
Surrey, Thomas Howard, earl of, later
  2nd Duke of Norfolk 90, 110
  and Flodden 153–6, 156–9, 161–2,
    162–3, 164, 165
  and Margaret's wedding journey to
    Scotland 35, 65–7, 66, 72, 80, 316
  and Margaret's wedding to James IV
    99, 100, 102–3, 104, 107

Surrey, Thomas Howard, earl of, later 3rd Duke of Norfolk 270–1, 272, 316

T

Tallis, Nicola 61
Tantallon Castle 214–15, 227, 237, 289, 303, 305
Tennant, John 331
Tilney, Agnes 66, 316
Trevisano, Andrea 88
Tudor, Edmund, earl of Richmond 16–17
Tudor, Jasper 16, 17
Tyrell, James 53

V

van der Goes, Hugo 96–7
Verney, Lady Eleanor 58, 110
Verney, Sir Ralph 58, 110

W

Warbeck, Perkin 18–21, 22, 24, 32, 36, 40, 89–90, 115
Warham, William, Archbishop of Canterbury 135, 150

Wark, castle of 273
Wars of the Roses 17, 60, 65, 175
Warwick, Edward Plantagenet, earl of 22
Warwick, Richard Neville, earl of (the Kingmaker) 60
West, Dr Nicholas 144, 145–7, 148
Wewyck, Meynnart 47
Wolsey, Cardinal Thomas 141, 145, 155, 224–5, 236, 244, 254, 259, 260, 262, 266, 271, 275, 277, 283–4, 285, 289, 297, 299
women
    as queens 44–7
    as regents 173–5
Woodville, Elizabeth 8
Wright, Michael 95

Y

Yolande de Dreux 322
York 67–71, 117, 155–6, 242
Young, John, Somerset Herald 31, 63–4, 68, 70, 72, 80, 92, 94, 98
    on the wedding of James IV and Margaret Tudor 98, 99, 100, 101, 103